HERE FOR THE HEARING

**TRACKING POP**

SERIES EDITORS: JOCELYN NEAL, JOHN COVACH, ROBERT FINK, AND LOREN KAJIKAWA

RECENT TITLES IN THE SERIES:

Here for the Hearing: Analyzing the Music in Musical Theater
*by Michael Buchler and Gregory J. Decker, Editors*

Queer Voices in Hip Hop: Cultures, Communities, and Contemporary Performance
*by Lauron J. Kehrer*

Critical Excess: *Watch the Throne* and the New Gilded Age
*by J. Griffith Rollefson*

Soda Goes Pop: Pepsi-Cola Advertising and Popular Music
*by Joanna K. Love*

*The Beatles* through a Glass Onion: Reconsidering the White Album
*edited by Mark Osteen*

The Pop Palimpsest: Intertextuality in Recorded Popular Music
*edited by Lori Burns and Serge Lacasse*

Uncharted: Creativity and the Expert Drummer
*by Bill Bruford*

I Hear a Symphony: Motown and Crossover R&B
*by Andrew Flory*

Hearing Harmony: Toward a Tonal Theory for the Rock Era
*by Christopher Doll*

Good Vibrations: Brian Wilson and the Beach Boys in Critical Perspective
*edited by Philip Lambert*

Krautrock: German Music in the Seventies
*by Ulrich Adelt*

Sounds of the Underground: A Cultural, Political and Aesthetic Mapping of Underground and Fringe Music
*by Stephen Graham*

# HERE FOR THE HEARING

## Analyzing the Music in Musical Theater

Michael Buchler and Gregory J. Decker, Editors

University of Michigan Press
*Ann Arbor*

Published in the United States of America by the
University of Michigan Press
Manufactured in the United States of America
Printed on acid-free paper
First published May 2023

A CIP catalog record for this book is available from the British Library.

*Library of Congress Cataloging-in-Publication data has been applied for.*

ISBN: 978-0-472-13331-4 (hardcover : alk. paper)
ISBN: 978-0-472-03930-2 (paper : alk. paper)
ISBN: 978-0-472-90353-5 (open access ebook)

https://doi.org/10.3998/mpub.11969716

Sponsored in part by the Florida State University Libraries' Open Access Publishing Fund.

The University of Michigan Press's open access publishing program is made possible thanks to additional funding from the University of Michigan Office of the Provost and the generous support of contributing libraries.

# Contents

Digital materials related to this title can be found on the Fulcrum platform via the following citable URL https://doi.org/10.3998/mpub.11969716

# List of Examples

# List of Figures

# List of Tables

# Acknowledgments

Thank you to all of our authors, who brought tremendous breadth and musicality to our project, and who gamely and expertly created most of their own musical examples and charts. They were all delightful to work with, and unfailingly understanding when we encountered delays. When we started approaching people and collecting essays, and before that ideas for essays, we didn't know precisely what shape this project would take and what musical and intellectual paths would be traversed. But our authors' wonderful ideas, beautiful writing, and skillful analyses affected our own sense of what's possible in analyzing musicals. We have no doubt that their work will similarly inspire this book's readers to think more expansively about musical theater, just as they inspired us.

Sara Cohen, Anna Pohlod, and Marcia LaBrenz at the University of Michigan Press have been endlessly supportive in shepherding this book through the review process and helping us bring it to publication. The University of Michigan Press and Florida State University Libraries also provided funds to offset the cost of open-source publication. We are incredibly grateful that, through their support, this book will reach so many more people, including scholars who lack access to research libraries or the resources to purchase this volume.

Thank you, also, to Jeff Alcenius for creating the clean and lovely line art that you'll see in several chapters, where figures or musical examples required a level of skill that was beyond our authors' (and editors') expertise. Thank you to our colleagues at Florida State University and Bowling Green State University for your unfailing support of our work, and, most importantly, thank you to Nancy and Jeff for your endless love and support.

Michael Buchler (Tallahassee, FL)
Greg Decker (Bowling Green, OH)

# Introduction

MICHAEL BUCHLER AND GREGORY J. DECKER

Twenty years ago, very few music scholars examined Broadway musicals. If musicologists were a bit slow to approach the musical theater repertoire (and they were), theorists and analysts arrived—and are only now arriving—more than fashionably late to the party. We hope that this volume loudly announces that we are here.

Music theorists care about musical theater. We know this anecdotally, but convincingly so. Over the past several years, talks on musicals have become more commonplace at theory conferences in North America (especially those of the Society for Music Theory) and are often among the best-attended presentations; articles involving musical theater are also appearing with greater frequency, including in each of the SMT's journals: *Music Theory Spectrum*, *Music Theory Online*, and *SMT-V*. As the methodologies we employ and the repertoire we study have broadened, and as the entire field has, in turbulent times, become increasingly invested in expanding the scope of what we do, musical theater is one place we should be looking to do more work. While Broadway shows might not be as nimble as popular music at reacting to civil unrest and in reflecting our society's changing views, they nevertheless reflect our shifting musical tastes and common values.

Musicals (both entire shows and their constituent songs) offer a springboard for coupling notions of musical structure and style with the ways they derive and enhance meaning. Every essay in this collection examines the role musical structures play in conveying aspects of drama.

We are not trying to reinvent musical theater scholarship. Musicologists and theater historians have much to tell us about the genre's history and social contexts, and their critical readings of musicals form an important body of scholarship—one to which we eagerly contribute. Our collective goal is to enrich critical and historical research foci with deep musical engagement. This collection of essays introduces analytical techniques that ground our observations and also invite comparison between the structures of musical theater and those of other popular and common-practice repertoires. Because none of our essays requires a specialist's knowledge of analytical methodology, we hope this book will speak to musicologists, theater scholars, performers, musically astute aficionados, and of course our fellow music theorists.

## *PREVIEWING THIS COLLECTION*

Most scholarly collections on music group their constituent chapters into several large units that feature common threads, clustering essays by methodology or repertoire. We might well have done that here, but the intersection between chapters in this book is as complex as the web of relationships in *Into the Woods*. Sure, the baker's wife is married to the baker, but she also has a tryst with Cinderella's prince. And then there's Cinderella, who ostensibly is grouped with her prince, but who plays an important role in the storylines of the baker, his wife, Little Red Ridinghood, and of course the witch. Everyone is affected by the witch and also by the baker and certainly by Jack and his magical beans. In this tangled analogy, two common threads are braided like Rapunzel's hair from the top to the bottom of this book: the interactions of drama and musical structure.

Drafting a thumbnail sketch of this collection seems a bit like trying to write a pithy synopsis of *Into the Woods*. Like many contemporary books and journals on music analysis, we collectively examine both small- and large-scale readings of form: the form of music-theatrical phrases, of songs, and of entire shows; we also examine harmony and key relations; we study rhythm, meter, and, more broadly, temporality; and we engage with topic theory and the ways that musical style creates and enhances meaning beyond what one can readily read in scripts and lyrics. Like many books and journals on musicals, we collectively examine narrativity and drama, the ways in which love and its absence are expressed, social politics, racial and ethnic identity, and gender and sexuality, with a particular focus on queerness.

We wound up grouping the chapters according to whether or not they focused on a single show, but across these artificial boundaries you will, for example, find three chapters that explicitly offer **music-analytical readings of queerness**. Nicole Biamonte charts the various styles and overall key structure, offering a large-scale reading of *The Rocky Horror Show* and how gender dichotomies are established and challenged. Rachel Lumsden views the unusual structure of *Fun Home*, which cycles repeatedly through three different timelines, through the lens of "queer temporality," and she also closely examines musical structures in two songs, "Ring of Keys" and "Changing My Major," showing how they help to construct queer/lesbian identity. Those two songs contrast the central character with her father, delineating two pathways for Alison to understand and accept her own sexuality. Whereas Biamonte and Lumsden carefully contextualize their discussions of individual songs within the frame of their respective shows, J. Daniel Jenkins shows how an especially famous Broadway song, Sondheim's "Send in the Clowns," attains new meaning and produces sophisticated social commentary through parody and decontextualization. Jenkins convincingly demonstrates how The Kinsey Sicks' use of unconventional musical choices in their "Send in the Clones" enhances their critique of gentrifying and neoliberal trends in the gay community.

**Key structure** might have been another organizing principle. Like Biamonte, Michael Buchler examines how the relationship between song keys helps structure an entire musical, and he points to the differentiation of musical style in portraying two different groups. In his reading of *Guys and Dolls*, Buchler unpacks the different kinds of musical material sung by the gamblers and the missionaries and shows how their songs create an interwoven structure that gradually becomes less contrasting and more blended as the two groups better learn to communicate with one another. Buchler also demonstrates how duets between the four main characters inform the show's overall plot and formal structure.

Rachel Lumsden and Jonathan De Souza both focus on **unusual temporalities**. While Lumsden examines *Fun Home* through the lens of "queer temporality," De Souza analyzes *The Last Five Years*, a musical that portrays the burgeoning and disintegrating relationship of a heterosexual couple.

He draws on literary theory, philosophy, and music psychology, invoking the work of Gérard Genette and his description of discursive temporal reorderings as "anachronies," and on Paul Ricoeur's ideas of the double temporality of narrative. De Souza shows how musical repetition and musical style work together with a "bilinear presentation of the story" to open space for interpretation. He also makes more than passing reference to other shows that play these narrative games, including *Fun Home* and Sondheim's *Merrily We Roll Along.*

Greg Decker's chapter confronts the role that **style** and particularly **musical topic** play in establishing meaning and offering insight into the characters and their social place, issues also touched on in the chapters by De Souza, Biamonte, and Jenkins. Decker observes that some shows, including *Sweeney Todd*, primarily use topics to particularize their characters, telling us something specific about each of them; other shows, including *The Secret Garden*, lean more strongly toward topics as generalizing agents, identifying characters as members of either the upper or lower class. Its protagonist, Mary Lenox, uniquely transcends these groupings, occupying both musical and dramatic spaces. *The Fantasticks* blends both of these strategies: its musical topics group characters according to their generation, but the show's three waltzes frame the musical, inviting broader comparison of its contexts while simultaneously particularizing the singers in each of its iterations. Decker constructs a reading that explicitly compares the characters' different narrative and musical contexts. He also briefly explores how the waltz topic helps to differentiate women of different races in *Show Boat*. And Buchler similarly examines how an all-Black adaptation of *Guys and Dolls* from the 1970s signified racialized distinctions of morality by recasting some portions of Frank Loesser's duets as disco anthems.

In his chapter on *Hamilton*, Robert Komaniecki also examines stylistic differences and how those differences support characterization. Komaniecki demonstrates that two important aspects of flow in rap and hip-hop—**rhythm and rhyme**—reflect the personality traits, motivations, and character development of Alexander Hamilton, the Marquis de Lafayette, Thomas Jefferson, and others. These differentiated modes of delivery draw on particular styles of hip-hop, and the associations that surround those styles are brought to bear on listeners' interpretations.

Richard Plotkin provides a very different detailed examination of rhyme scheme, setting out ways in which rhyme, phrase structure, and formal function often interact in musical theater. He then lays out well-defined preference rules for rhyme expectation based on poetic and musical structure and applies these rules to diverse musical examples, showing how both domains work together to create (and sometimes thwart) listener expectations. This phenomenology of rhyme gives us tools to explain such things as why the landing of a particular word is funny or how collaborators can create songs that sound like the natural declamation of speech. Ultimately, Plotkin invites us to consider that lyrics and musical structure in musical theater are inseparable, and our analyses and interpretations do well to treat them as such.

Like Plotkin and Komaniecki, Rachel Short examines aspects of **song form**, with a particular eye (ear) toward bridges and the ways they diverge from the more familiar music that surrounds them. She limits her study to ballads, which often shed light on their characters' personal and emotional journeys. Her chapter explores a wide range of musical bridges, from shows as early as *Show Boat* to as recent as *Hamilton*. She views rhythmic elements of bridges from four distinct vantage points, examining "rhythmic density, phrase beginnings, rhythmic distribution, and syncopation." These musical attributes interact and overlap with one another and with other musical and textual elements.

Nathan Blustein examines a device that commonly occurs at the ends of bridges: the pump-up modulation, but Blustein's chapter looks at a relatively unusual situation where the composer pumps up to *return* to the song's original key. Like Short and Plotkin, Blustein draws on a wide range of musicals from different eras to form a compelling cross-stylistic corpus, shedding light on fascinating formal moves that might have eluded us. He considers these return modulations from several perspectives: whether they are perceptible as such, how and why they may have arisen during the compositional process, where they occur formally, and what meaning they might suggest within their dramatic contexts.

Many chapters, including Blustein, Decker, Plotkin, and Short, examine songs from **Stephen Sondheim's musicals**, but Drew Nobile takes on the impressive task of unpacking and demystifying Sondheim's idiosyncratic use of dissonant harmonies. He posits that bass notes, chords, and melody, while generally coinciding, are also somewhat independent of one another, allowing Broadway audiences to hear underlying tonal stability among dissonant and non-triadic harmonies. Nobile then considers how Sondheim's general musical strategies and their show-specific deployments create broad metanarratives at the level of the scene and show in *Sunday in the Park with George* and *Into the Woods*.

"Into the woods, it's always when you think at last you're through and then into the woods you go again to take another journey." After act 1's happily-ever-after ending, we learn in act 2 that we need to head back to the woods. There's more work to do. With this volume, we try to learn more about what the music is telling us about the stories and characters we love, and we do so in multiple, sometimes tangled ways. We hope you enjoy taking this journey with us, and we hope that the chapters that follow will inspire you to head into the woods yourself. The paths may not be well marked, but exploration is always rewarding.[1]

## NOTES

1. Unless you happen to be the Baker's Wife, who, tragically, doesn't survive act 2.

# PART 1

# Chapters That Engage Multiple Works

# 1

# "Was It Ever Real?"

## Tonic Return via Stepwise Modulation in Broadway Songs

*NATHAN BEARY BLUSTEIN*

For contemporary theater audiences, the ubiquity of tonal modulation has become a lyrical punchline.[1] In "The Song that Goes Like This," from *Spamalot* (2005),[2] adapted from the film *Monty Python and the Holy Grail*, Sir Galahad and the Lady of the Lake sing about the clichés of the Broadway love duet (rather than about their own affection for each other). As the orchestra swells into the third chorus, the pair labors chromatically upward at the end of the line: "And then we change the ke—e-e-ey!" At the arrival in the new tonic, a whole step higher than where the song began, they sing: "Now we're into E! / That's awfully high for me. / But as everyone can see / We should have stayed in D."[3]

These examples abound in Broadway parodies.[4] In "Show Off," from *The Drowsy Chaperone* (2006), which sends up the 1920s musical comedy, the diva Janet Van De Graaff announces her retirement from show business and the public eye with a showstopper that belies her message. In a performance of the song from the 2006 Tony Awards, Sutton Foster builds up to the final chorus with flashy choreography and costume changes, all while she declares: "You'll never see this! Never see that! Never see these again! . . ." The final syllable of the line moves up by half step and becomes the leading tone of the upcoming new key; the chorus marks the new key's arrival with the lyrics: "I don't wanna change keys no more."

More recently, in "The Farmer Refuted," from *Hamilton* (2015), the title character mocks a loyalist who reads from the same script over and over again.[5] The musical as a whole is not a parody, but this number imitates eighteenth-century European dance music—clashing against the amalgam of Broadway and hip-hop that permeates the rest of the score. Between the loyalist's second and third reading of his script, he sings at the top of his range as the key moves up, from C major to D♭ major. Hamilton castigates the Farmer for this gesture: "Don't modulate the key and not debate with me."

All of these characters—the courtly lovers, Janet, Alexander Hamilton—use generalized terms: "We change the key"; "I don't wanna change keys no more"; "Don't modulate the key." But each of these lines is set specifically to a direct modulation *up by a half or whole step*. In musical theater, as in popular music, these pump-up modulations[6] engage with a network of musical, emotional, and dramatic conventions. They typically occur with the return of a refrain or chorus and signal an intensification of mood or overall drama. Instrumental textures become richer and more virtuosic, or the singer jumps up to a new register. And of course, in the aftermath of this particular kind of key change, a song will conventionally end in the new (higher) key.

In this chapter, I explore songs that use stepwise modulation in an unusual and apparently paradoxical way. The modulation occurs at the end of a *series* of key changes, bringing the song back to the key in which it began—that is, although we associate the device with tonic departure, in these cases, it brings about tonic return.

This alignment seems highly uncommon, and this chapter covers virtually every example I know of—fifteen in all. Dai Griffiths (2015, 28–31) refers to stepwise tonic return briefly in separate pop/rock examples without attaching any interpretive significance: for him, they are examples of "Elevating modulation" (an upward *or* downward direct change of key)[7] without "Elevating form" (a song that begins and ends in different keys). And in Brian Hoffman's (2013) discussion of intensifying chromatic third modulations, he notes that "America" from *West Side Story* (1957) uses an intensifying gesture associated with stepwise modulation to complete an entire *major-third* cycle.

Michael Buchler (2008) illustrates this effect with analytical notation, which he applies to several of Frank Loesser's Broadway songs. For passages with an immediate and direct modulation, Buchler uses an upward arrow (↑) to indicate a new, higher version of the *same* scale degree on a *higher* pitch, in an otherwise identical musical context; and he uses a plus sign (+) to indicate a more gradual upward shift. For the songs in this chapter, these notations can accurately describe the immediate sensation of the final key change, but an ascent by ↑ or + ultimately leads to the original, *unaltered* pitches.

Buchler's notation invites nuance in exploring the expressive power of tonal relationships within musical theater songs even if "tonal consistency might not be necessary to produce a sense of tonal unity" (46). Indeed, some of this chapter's songs seem to actively play with this expectation of stepwise modulation—that is, the expected *absence* of tonal unity. As Scott Hanenberg notes in his wide-ranging discussion of modulation in rock music (2016), a singular emotional interpretation of a tonal relationship may be difficult to confirm, but deviations from *expected* relationships open up questions for narrative analysis.

Like many musical theater analysts, I follow in the footsteps of popular music studies more broadly. But I also offer this study of key changes in musicals to unsettle the hierarchical conception of Broadway's music as within (and beneath) the pop umbrella, as Jocelyn Neal (2007) and Braxton Shelley (2019) have done in country and gospel contexts, respectively. As Masi Asare and Oliver Wang note, musicals are generically laden with "sentimentality" and "affective excess," while pop songs carry less universal baggage (2019, 47). The pop pump-up, on the other hand, is generically a *sentimental* trope reliant on *affective excess* to smooth over the absence of new melodies or lyrics. In this exploration of key changes concentrated on musical theater songs, event and genre align.

In the vignettes below I show how the specific departure-return paradox of ascending *back to* tonic expands a song's rhetorical potential. In part I, I examine three songs that use a direct stepwise modulation in the final chorus to return to the opening key. I discuss the musical elements that support *and* obscure hearing stepwise modulation as large-scale tonic return, and I connect this musical event with each song's dramatic context. In parts II–IV, I examine various confounds that problematize this connection: *who* writes or performs the modulation, plus *how* it happens and *when*.

## *I. DIRECT MODULATIONS TO TONIC IN FINAL CHORUSES*

My first example is "What a Game," from Stephen Flaherty and Lynn Ahrens's *Ragtime* (1998), a musical about the racial, social, and political tensions of early 1900s New York. The number offers comic relief in the highly charged second act of this musical. Father—so named in the show—introduces his son Edgar to baseball. As the game progresses, Father realizes that low-class rowdiness and ethnic diversity have "corrupted" his all-American pastime. Like *West Side Story*'s "Gee, Officer Krupke!," "What a Game" is full of slapstick and sarcasm and has a catchy tune, but its humor stems from the societal tensions that color the show.

This number is an abbreviated rag, complete with a contrasting trio section (a large-scale **AA'BA"**, where **B** is the trio). The rag form is also dramatized: in a classic rag, the trio can serve as the ending itself; a return to the primary theme is entirely optional. But in "What a Game," the turnaround to the final **A** is climactic.

Before the rag proper, Father outlines his expectations of high-society collegiality. The first **A** section, in a jaunty C major, dashes his hopes once the crowd begins jeering and heckling the players; during **A'**, in D♭, Father despairs about the changes to the game while the crowd mocks him. The crowd narrates a single at-bat in the B♭ major trio, and at the end Edgar catches a home-run ball in the stands. Finally, at **A"**—where thematic return collides with the return of C major—an all-out fight erupts among the spectators.

Example 1.1 sketches the tonal transitions between each section, with a quarter note representing each measure. All three employ direct modulations: an authentic cadence in one key immediately progresses to a dominant chord in the new key. In the parlance of Hoffman (2014) and Ricci (2017, 98), this progression is labeled by the functions of the two chords that bridge the key change: a "I [in the old key]–V [in the new key] type." Griffiths (2015, 39–40) is more precise, describing the sensation of the modulation up by step that we see in example 1.1a: a tonic-to-dominant "transformation," in which $\hat{1}$ in the old key *transforms* into a leading tone in the new key.[8]

The first transition, between **A** and **A'**, ascends by half step—but against convention, it *decreases* in intensity: an imperfect authentic cadence is followed by a measure of silence while the spectators hock and spit, and a dominant sting gives way to a thinned-out orchestration of soft solo

**Example 1.1.** "What a Game" transitions. Each quarter note in the example is equivalent to one $\frac{4}{4}$ measure in the score.

**Example 1.1a.** From **A** to **A′** (mm. 37–41).

**Example 1.1b.** From **A′** to trio (mm. 77–81).

**Example 1.1c.** From trio to **A″** (mm. 102–105; m. 105 as written in score).

instruments. But the calm dissipates: during the instrumental interlude, a heckler shouts to one of the players: "Take your head out of your ass!"—which Edgar tries to imitate, until an alarmed Father puts his hand over his son's mouth at the last second.

The trio (Example 1.1b) further thins out, but the transition between the trio and **A″** (Example 1.1c) is the climactic passage: after the ensemble has reached a satisfying cadence in B♭ major, the outer voices climb upward on a tonic voice exchange, followed by the same gesture on the "transformed" dominant. The harmonic sequence might make us wonder whether *thematic* return has rhetorical weight equal or similar to that of *tonic* return. And although these types of return coincide, the instrumental and vocal crescendos at the end of the trio raise the intensity of this passage, which adheres to the generic characteristics of a stepwise modulation. The shouting is more frantic in **A″** than in earlier choruses, and orchestrated performances of the song, like in the original Broadway cast recording, include loud, high, sustained violin notes and a fast banjo rhythm, both of which indicate an instrumental intensification that lasts throughout all of **A″**.

Yet there are elements that support hearing tonic return. The chorus is singing in the same register in both C-major sections, *with the same vocal forces*. And formally, **A″** occurs right when we *might* hear a double-return of theme and key in a classic rag. Our expectations have been set up, and **A″** meets them—with the twist of achieving tonic return through a modulation associated with musical theater, and *not* one associated with ragtime. This song strikes a balance between the two styles.

Ragtime in this show symbolizes novelty, literal and figurative—for societal progress and its attendant surprises. But in this song the sense of "progress" is ironic. Given the segregated nature of early modern baseball, this number is one of the only ones in the show without Black characters—the origin of ragtime in Black musical spaces is removed. Robinson (2009) describes the entanglement of assimilation and minstrel show–like appropriation that ragtime dancing signified in immigrant communities through the early twentieth century; in this scene, there is no dancing, and yet the rag form and style sharpen the ethnic and class divides in the stands. In the number's final chorus, the use of a device associated with musical theater to satisfy the formal conventions of a rag reflects the song's meaning for Father: even his dependable diversions face change.

In my second example, "The Wizard and I" from Stephen Schwartz and Winnie Holzman's *Wicked* (2003), the modulation back to tonic is not at a dramatized formal juncture. Instead, it is in the song's thrilling final measures. At its surface, this is a textbook "I Want" song. Elphaba, the future Wicked Witch of the West, expresses her desire to meet the Wizard, whom she expects will not only ask her to work with him, but will also "degreenify" her. Elphaba's anticipation boils over, and I will compare three passages in the song that reflect this.

First is Elphaba's moment of epiphany: "Unlimited, my future is unlimited." This passage is a striking "detour," as Brian Jarvis and John Peterson describe it (2020), in G♭ major—a tritone away from the starting key of C. Elphaba stops herself from completing the eponymous refrain, which we have already heard close an earlier chorus with a plagal cadence. As outlined in Example 1.2, there is no pivot chord; instead, the cutoff ends on IV in C major, immediately followed by what we eventually register as a $I^7$ chord (with a major seventh) in the new key above a subdominant pedal—for which F, a tritone above the new bass and the seventh of the new tonic harmony, is the only common tone. When Elphaba resumes singing, Schwartz uses an oblique quotation: *Wicked* devotees know well that the first seven notes of the "Unlimited" melody come from "(Somewhere) Over the Rainbow."

This key change corresponds with Elphaba's prediction of her personal and moral triumph, and it initiates a much more gradual instrumental and vocal buildup—the preparation of *some* new key, in bright neon lights. The specific key, though, is a surprise. Twice in a row, Schwartz sets up a resolution only to defy it. The last line of the interlude ("that's all to do with me") first modulates to E♭ major, reaching a half cadence on the final word. Elphaba's B♭ is then reharmonized: first by a $Gm^7$ chord, then by $C^7$—creating a *new* half cadence in F. The C in the bass descends to B♮, and

**Example 1.2.** "The Wizard and I": "Unlimited" interlude into thematic return in B major.

Elphaba's sustained B♭ becomes the leading tone to the new tonic on the line: "And I'll stand there with the Wizard . . ."

This arrival in B major is the point of *thematic* return. And dramatically, this is the climax of the song, when all of Elphaba's intentions are summed up: she is describing her awaited triumph as she imagines that she and the Wizard will work together to do good throughout Oz. What could top this dramatic summation?

The last key change is a relatively simple "I–I juxtaposition": B major up to C, via tonic chords in each key. Earlier, at the epiphany, we heard a radical modulation by tritone; the subsequent interlude blossomed into the B-major climax. By contrast, this *stepwise* modulation happens across two of three rhyming lines right before the song ends. We hear the start of the refrain on the lyrics "Held in such high esteem," but do not yet hear the title line. Instead, the modulation repeats this refrain a half-step higher on new, rhyming lyrics. Elphaba holds fast to this key as she rhymes yet again, finally reaching the song's title on this third attempt.

Nearly every solo song in Stephen Schwartz's best-known shows, including *Godspell* (1970) and *Pippin* (1972), begins and ends on the same key. In the world of musical theater—especially within the past fifty years—this is far from a given. But "The Wizard and I" is only one of two examples in Schwartz's output that modulates up by step to return to tonic; the other example, briefly discussed below, is in the same musical. The expansiveness of "The Wizard and I" does make it difficult to hear the half-step modulation as a tonic return, and it is unlikely that this modulation *solely* satisfies a compositional pattern. Were that the case, we could reimagine this song with a simpler key structure: modulating up by tritone and then, at the climax, modulating right back.

There are two consequences of the last-second tonic return as written, in addition to hearing it as a moment of intensification. The first is vocal: this modulation allows the singer to hold off on the top of her belt range until the last possible moment. In the B-major section, Elphaba sings D♯, $\hat{3}$, three times; once the song modulates up again to C major, she only sings the corresponding high E once. For a soprano at the top of her belt range, this half-step difference is significant, and "The Wizard and I" shows how sensitive Schwartz is to this fact.[9]

There is also a dramatic consequence, which relates to Elphaba's lyric, "Unlimited." The modulation from C major to G♭ major occurs right at Elphaba's epiphany, but both the number of steps and the amount of time it takes to convincingly return to the original key demonstrate just how remote this first key change was.[10] I interpret this departure and return as mirroring Elphaba's determination to overcome her obstacles and solve her problems—or more accurately, to find the person who will solve them for her. And this tonal overcoming, the rhyme with "esteem," happens on the line with the heaviest foreshadowing in the song: "When people see me," Elphaba correctly predicts, "they will scream."

As with "Game" and "Wizard," "So Much Better," the act 1 finale of Laurence O'Keefe and Nell Benjamin's *Legally Blonde* (2006), returns to tonic through stepwise modulation—but in this song, the stepwise modulations keep going, ending in a higher key than where the first chorus began. The musical's plot hews to the movie on which it is based: after surprising everyone in her life by getting into Harvard Law, Elle Woods learns—to her *own* surprise—that she has won a coveted internship only earned by a select group of students in her class. "So Much Better" is all about Elle's excitement, which is reflected through the frequency of stepwise modulations throughout this song—each chorus alone has at least one.[11]

The pop-rock form of the song, and the distant tonal relationships between verse (G major) and chorus (E major), are not out of the ordinary. Indeed, they provide a major-mode example of what Doll (2011) calls the "Breakout Chorus": a convention of rock in which a more contemplative verse blossoms into an emotionally bright chorus, punctuated by an "expressive" modulation. The "pump-up" modulation happens *during* the chorus, from E to F major, as Elle answers her own rhetorical questions in the first phrase (the first chorus begins: "Is that my name up on that list? Does someone know that I exist?"; in the next phrase she answers: "That is my name in black and white! Looks like I'm doing something right."). This seemingly cheesy modulation, though, does not cadence in F at the end of the phrase. Instead, on Elle's closing hook ("I am so much better *than before*"), O'Keefe writes what Frank Lehman describes as a "cadential switch" (2013, 5.2). First, Elle's final three notes hint at a cadence on the relative *minor*, landing on $\hat{6}$ in F. Next, the orchestra pivots to D *major* through a fanfare-like ♭VI–♭VII–I.[12] After this switch, Elle's next verse begins where she left off—now reinterpreting D as $\hat{5}$ of G major, the same key as the opening.

As with "Wizard," the transition out of the bridge—returning to the main theme—is again the song's first major highlight. Elle leaps up to a high E♭ at the start of the chorus, a small change that makes the line much more demanding to sing. The first chorus opens with a leap up to B on $\hat{5}$, appropriately matching the lyric "Is that my name *up* on that list"; this is four half steps lower than the E♭ at the top of "I'm too busy lovin' my name *up* on that list" at the start of the post-bridge chorus. By comparison, when Elle modulates up to E major (returning us to the key that opens the first chorus), "Look at my *name*" lands inconspicuously on $\hat{5}$, now back to B.

But this chorus is cut short. The E-major hook cuts off at "I am so much better—" and immediately pumps up to F—now with a stepwise modulation *across two different* choruses. And since this line is the start of another chorus, yet another stepwise modulation is inevitable; the song ends a whole step higher than where the first chorus began.

Unlike Elphaba, Elle has already overcome a major obstacle in "So Much Better." Toward the end of her song, Elle's mind is racing from one task to the next ("Oo, wait, where's my cell? . . . I'll be there on Monday nine o'clock . . . No, no, I can't wait, I will be there at eight . . ."), and so going *just* too far past that tonic return, when the song could have ended earlier in the home key, reflects her unbounded excitement.[13] Stepwise modulation is considerably more common throughout the songs in *Legally Blonde* than in *Wicked*. While many other pump-up modulations in the show are conventional, the tonic return in "So Much Better" turns this device on its head. In a song where Elle's transformation finally yields the results that propel the plot of act 2, the pump-up modulation plays a fundamental role.

## *II. THE ARRANGER'S ROLE: UNDERSCORE, DANCE BREAKS, AND LONGER NUMBERS*

All of the examples above are sung-through, without extended breaks of any kind. Therefore, a majority of the melodic, harmonic, and tonal material most likely originated with the composers. But songs with intensifying direct modulations provide an opportunity for interpretive elements that often lie beyond the purview of composers—such as instrumentation and specific accompanimental textures. For instance, in creating *Wicked*, Schwartz collaborated with orchestrator William Brohn and arrangers Alex Lacamoire and Stephen Oremus. An orchestrator's job is often clear, but an *arranger's* function is more ambiguous. In personal correspondence,

Lacamoire discussed how the choice of keys in the sung-through numbers belonged to Schwartz—it was "part of the composition." Lacamoire and Oremus set the "groove," essentially defining the musical material that would go to each member of the orchestra's rhythm section.[14] Listening through "Wizard" illustrates the potency of this collaboration. At the "Unlimited" passage, the instrumentation changes radically—including the groove-generating rhythm section, which drops out. By contrast, at the B-major arrival, the drums shift from heavy tom fills and cymbal crashes to a steady pop-rock groove that *continues* past the stepwise modulation, right up to the final refrains in C. The only instrumental intensification at the final key change—a sixteenth-note scalar run in the violins—is left out of the published piano-vocal score.

Through the lens of the collaboration between composers, orchestrators, and arrangers, we can see Brohn, Lacamoire, and Oremus reflecting and amplifying Schwartz's compositional and lyrical material. In musical theater, "who did what?" is inevitably a blurry question.[15]

Orchestrators, arrangers, and choreographers all influence the music that we play, or see on the page, or hear in a performance or on a recording. In the following examples, I will discuss passages where these collaborators probably had a significant role in melodic, harmonic, and formal decisions.

"'Til Him," from Mel Brooks's *The Producers* (2001), provides such an example where alterations between versions of a number can affect our hearing of key relationships. The first and final choruses are both in F major; the middle, in E. The modulation back *up* after the middle chorus is a "V–V handover"—the orchestra swells to prepare a grand finale—before the nervous and aloof Max Bialystock cuts them off and begins the singing with unexpected tenderness. The first modulation is more drawn out, as shown in Example 1.3. Max's partner, Leo Bloom, ends his chorus on a deceptive cadence, and the underscoring continues in D♭ major. Even before Max begins singing the second chorus, the orchestra modulates to E, anticipating his entrance by six measures. In the soundtrack to the film musical, not shown in the example, the passage that includes both instrumental interludes is left out entirely—and so the track can be heard as resolving directly down and back up again.

Returning to "Show Off," Janet's not-quite-retirement number from *The Drowsy Chaperone*, we see a conspicuous case of stepwise return to tonic at the end of the dance break, well before the final key change. Following

**Example 1.3.** "'Til Him": modulations across choruses, via underscoring in D♭ major.

an extravagant authentic cadence in G♭ major, with the entire ensemble singing, a common-tone pivot strongly implies a dominant (cadential) $^6_4$ in A major. The next four measures build excitement to the expected resolution with a rallentando and crescendo—but the harmony resolves to the dominant seventh chord a half step *higher*. At the intervening fermata, Janet cartwheels from one corner of the stage to another before she finally resumes singing ("Please! No more attention . . ."). Janet is resuming the bridge, which begins on IV before resolving to tonic; as a result, while Janet's arrival is on E♭ major, this is as a large-scale modulation to B♭—a step above the grand buildup at the end of the dance break, and also the return of the starting key. With all of this before Janet's final chorus, her line "I don't wanna change keys no more" resonates with the entire number, rather than the singular moment she is lampooning.

The opening number to *Legally Blonde*, "Omigod You Guys," contains another stepwise return to tonic in the middle of the song. Elle's sorority sisters open the show celebrating her expected engagement to her boyfriend. The number includes a break in the musical action, when the sisters realize they cannot find Elle at their house; a change of setting, from the sorority house to the mall; and a musical interlude, when Elle outmaneuvers a subpar sales clerk to find her dream dress. Most of this nearly six-minute number utilizes a single verse-chorus module. The first two verses are in E major; the first two choruses, in C. While the verses stay in E major throughout, each C-major chorus suddenly modulates up to E♭ major at the cadence, before veering in yet another direction. When we are finally introduced to Elle at the mall, she sings a solo verse-chorus pair that maintains the opening tonal relationship. She begins a half step lower, in

E♭ major; and her chorus begins in B. The second phrase of the chorus, though, modulates up to C—a tonic return following contrasting sections in distant keys as the sisters set out to find her.

This tonic return, though, is far from the end of the song. The last verse-chorus pair continues and expands on the internal modulation in Elle's chorus. The verse shifts up from E♭ to E major after only four measures; the chorus, starting in C major, lifts up by minor third—so that the entire final chorus is in E♭ major, the same key that the first two choruses *attempted* at their cadences but failed to maintain.

For this number, stepwise modulations come in gradually, after another key relationship is thwarted in early choruses. But eventually, pump-up modulations saturate the song, helping to reach the triumphant final key change. Similarly to "So Much Better," "Omigod You Guys" *does* rise by step to reach the starting key, and once again, that is not entirely the point. In the act 1 finale, tonic return occurs close to the end of the song; in the musical's opening number, a larger process is just getting started.

## *III. NOT-SO-DIRECT: DESCENDING AND ASCENDING BY STEP*

Almost every Broadway song I know of that uses this device as simply as possible—down by step, then right back up—modulates strangely. The one song I know of that uses direct modulations exclusively is "Colored Lights," the opening of John Kander and Fred Ebb's *The Rink* (1984). The verses, primarily in A major, use V–I and I–V juxtapositions into and out of (respectively) choruses in G major. These modulations are subtle, contrasting a key change across the final two choruses, in which an instrumental reverie uses the same pair of progressions to descend briefly by another half step.[16] It is the last time we hear the protagonist Anna list the colors that have entranced her. In previous choruses, the list ends conventionally with $\hat{2}$–$\hat{1}$; here, the final color in the list ascends, but only by half step to ♭$\hat{3}$ (". . . and pink, and yellow, and *green*"). The entire song waxes nostalgic, but Anna is ambivalent and forgetful. This visceral key change is over almost as soon as it starts—just two phrases in a fast-paced waltz—and so the earlier, smoother shifts immediately become a distant memory.

By contrast, "Maybe," from Charles Strouse and Martin Charnin's *Annie* (1977), uses an array of chromatic techniques across a classic **AABA** form. It begins in A major, descends to A♭ major for the bridge, and ascends back to A at the return of the main tune. This formal/tonal outline seems simple, reflecting the innocence of what the orphan Annie imagines her parents might be like.

In **A′**, Strouse disrupts a descending-fifths sequence to modulate downward. First, a briefly tonicized vi (F♯ minor) progresses to V/V (B major)—the start of the sequence. But instead of progressing to V, as Strouse does in **A**, he reinterprets the root, B♮, as a common tone with G major ("She's sitting playing pi-*a*-no, / *He's* sitting paying . . ."). He then reiterates this process: G major descends by fifth to C major, and then C becomes the common tone to A♭ (". . . [a] *bill*. / *Bet*cha they're young . . ."). At first, G major functions as an applied dominant to a chromatic harmony; in retrospect, it's the upward steppingstone between a fleeting local tonic and reinterpreting ♭$\hat{3}$ in a new key.

In **B**, Strouse again starts the modulating passage with vi, and ends with a reinterpretation of ♭$\hat{3}$—only now, of course, a half step lower. The bridge ends with Annie repeating $\hat{1}$ (A♭) as the third above F minor ("*Their one* mis*take* . . ."). Strouse eventually reinterprets this pitch as the leading tone (G♯) back to the original key, but only in retrospect: first, Annie moves to A♭: ♭$\hat{3}$ above iv$^7$ (". . . was giving up *me*"); then this harmony serves as a pivot chord, reinterpreted as iii$^7$ in A, which progresses to the dominant and arrives back on tonic for **A″**.

This song is split between refrains of "Maybe" in each **A** and "Betcha" in each **B**. The more definitive lyric lives in a key right below the more uncertain one's, and Annie only needs a single altered scale degree to switch between them—but the accompaniment complicates the relationship these two worlds, placing them at odds with each other in spite of their proximity.

In each version of the score to "Maybe" I have seen, the key signature never changes in the bridge; instead, it is replete with accidentals.[17] The same is true of "A Little Bit in Love," from *Wonderful Town* (1953), which descends from F major to E major in the bridge and returns to F at the arrival of **A″**. In this song, Leonard Bernstein uses each modulation to show that the protagonist, Eileen, is just beginning to acknowledge her feelings of affection for Frank, the manager whose store she has visited daily since moving from Ohio.

Eileen's melody in the opening **A** section ends with a descent from C to B♭, landing on $\hat{4}$ at a half cadence. In the next phrase, Eileen's melody moves *up* from F to B♮, tracing the three whole steps of the spanning tritone. This B♮ is the root of a dominant seventh chord, which resolves to E major at the start of **B**. A direct descent from C to B♮ in **A'** would highlight the downward shift from F to E major, and B♮ would be immediately recognizable as a lowered $\hat{5}$. Instead, Eileen's ♯$\hat{4}$ grates against the dominant seventh underneath.

The return to **A** flips this melodic/harmonic clash: Eileen's melody directly confirms the shift from one key to another. She ascends from $\hat{3}$ to $\hat{5}$ in E major, and then reaches a half step further to $\hat{5}^{+}$ (following Buchler) in F major. As expected, the top note of this melody is supported by a $C^7$ harmony. Yet the three sonorities before it are surprising: rather than, for instance, $IV^7$–$ii^7$–$V^7$ beneath the diatonic ascent in E major, Bernstein planes chromatic seventh chords that cloud the tonal certainty offered by Eileen's melody.

Throughout the entire song, Eileen muses over her confusion—not concerned or worried, but intrigued. Her first lyric sets up her amusement, humming at first and then singing, "Mm, I'm a little bit in love."[18] In **B**, she repeats a steady chromatic cluster that reflects her newfound attraction: "[everything's hazy] and all out of focus . . . a strange hocus pocus." The modulations between phrases heighten this sensation. At the end of **A'** Eileen sings about feeling "perhaps a *little bit more*," and her melody emphasizes the scale degree just a "little bit" past where she had ended the first half of the section. At the end of **B** she gives up on trying to articulate her feelings: "I don't know / But I know / If it's love / Then it's lovely." The last line provides certainty, aligned with a $C^7$ harmony that resolves at the start of **A''** to F major. These modulations almost encourage Eileen's ambivalence: on the one hand, the complex interactions of melody and harmony reflect the anxieties of being in love; on the other, the ultimately simple structure reflects her untroubled whimsy.

"Unworthy of Your Love," from Stephen Sondheim's *Assassins* (1991/2004), follows the same general path as "A Little Bit in Love"—down by step, and back up again—but it occurs over the scope of the entire number, rather than within a single chorus (Example 1.4). "Unworthy" is a love duet in which neither singer addresses the other. It alternates between two would-be assassins, singing to the (absent) people with whom they are (were) obsessed. John Hinckley, who attempted to assassinate Ronald Reagan, sings to Jodie Foster; Lynette "Squeaky" Fromme, who attempted to assassinate Gerald Ford, sings to Charles Manson. The duet is set in a

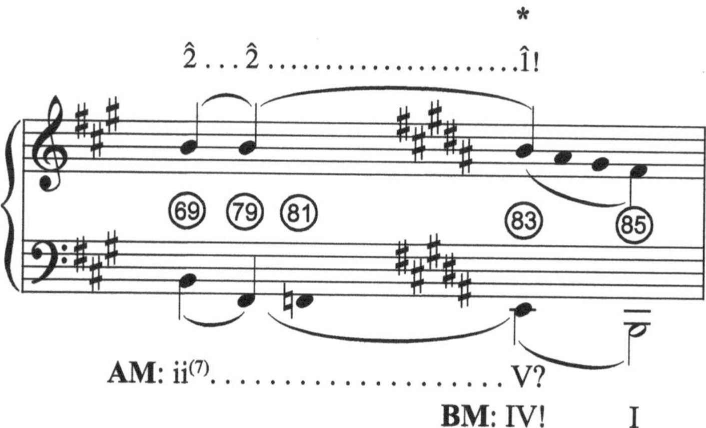


**Example 1.4.** "Unworthy of Your Love": modulation up by whole step, from the end of the bridge to the duet chorus (home key marked with asterisks).

folk-rock style, which provides a darkly humorous backdrop to Hinckley and Fromme's lyrics. Even the form is conventional: Hinckley sings a verse-chorus pair, followed by Fromme, and they sing together for the bridge and final chorus.

Sondheim sets up a strictly utilitarian tonal relationship between verse-chorus pairs, with Hinckley singing B major and Fromme singing in A. Such key changes account most commonly for singers' ranges, free of dramatic subtext. In this case, though, the *lack* of intensification in this passage heightens the duet's irony. This song is preceded by a scene between the two characters: Fromme mocks Hinckley for stalking Jodie Foster and leaves the stage, calling Hinckley a "fruit." Hinckley, alone, writes yet another letter to his "dearest Jodie" before picking up his guitar and beginning the song. Until Fromme sings, the song sounds like Hinckley's intimate solo. And although the modulation is utilitarian, the descent of *key* by whole step allows Fromme's verse to pick up on the same pitch where Hinckley left off: C♯ as $\hat{2}$ on a half cadence becomes $\hat{3}$ on tonic in the new key. The smoothness of this segue, combined with its unexpectedness, forges a connection that the pair seems to resist in the preceding scene. Fromme's verse even begins with the same words as Hinckley's, but she twists his somewhat kind opening line: "I am / Nothing / You are / Wind and water and sky" becomes ". . . Wind and Devil and God."

As with "A Little Bit in Love," the return to tonic in "Unworthy" is circuitous. The bridge cuts off Fromme's chorus before she reaches the expected half cadence. Instead, Hinckley begins a call-and-response on ii in A major. In the final measures of the bridge, shown in Example 1.4, Hinckley and Fromme are singing a high B while the bass descends from F♯ to F♮; the vocal B holds over as the bass descends one more half step, arriving on an E-major harmony.

This may seem to be the arrival of the dominant harmony that was missing from the end of Fromme's solo in A major, but instead, it begins a brand-new chorus as IV in B. Whereas the transition from Hinckley to Fromme proceeds through a "V–I juxtaposition," the transition from the bridge to the duet chorus denies the arrival of the expected dominant harmony at all.[19]

The modulations in this duet—the utilitarian transition from Hinckley's solo to Fromme's, and the dramatic upward shift for the final chorus—are fairly typical musical devices in the style that Sondheim evokes for "Unworthy." The melodic smoothness at each seam, though, is rare. The two assassins in this scene view their individual emotions as more important than anything else in the world, and the alternation between their lyrics shows them in a kind of competition with each other. But the unexpected musical connections through the song show that as they reject their commonalities, in doing so, they are lying to themselves.

## *IV. STEPWISE MODULATION TO TONIC AT OTHER FORMAL JUNCTURES*

In all the above examples, the stepwise return to tonic coincides with the arrival of a chorus or **A** section (in the case of songs that don't have distinct verse-chorus pairs)—or it occurs *within* this section, such as in "The Wizard and I," "So Much Better," and "Omigod You Guys." But other songs use this highly charged modulation at unexpected formal junctures. "Defying Gravity," the end to act 1 of *Wicked*, provides a straightforward example into a *verse*: Elphaba's final solo in the number ("So if you care to find me . . .") confirms a modulation from B major to D♭, the opening key; unlike "The Wizard and I," where the showstopping key change precedes the tonic return, these events coincide in the first-act finale. The remaining examples similarly consider stepwise modulations back to tonic *during* and *into* formally distinct verses, as well as *across* longer formal sections that have internal key changes.

"I Can Cook, Too," from Bernstein's *On the Town* (1944), is structured similarly to "A Little Bit in Love": two refrains bookend a contrasting section one step lower. But in "Cook," the modulation back to tonic happens *during* the verse. Each key change in the song reflects a lyrical shift from boastful to modest—and back again. "I Can Cook, Too" is Hildy (the New York cabbie)'s song of seduction, which she sings to Chip (the visiting sailor) in her apartment. Amid a twenty-four-hour shore leave in the city, Chip begins the scene distracted: he is trying to help his fellow sailor, Gabey, find "Miss Turnstiles," a pageant winner whose poster they spotted earlier on the subway. In "I Can Cook, Too," Hildy convinces Chip to turn his attention to her.

At the start of the verse—the downward shift in key—the song's fast-swinging texture relaxes amid a conventional "V–V transformation." Hildy introspectively—at first—compares herself to "some girls," who "make magazine covers" and "keep house on a dime." The second half of the verse, though, is the punchline: *She's* one of those girls. Meanwhile, the song shifts back up to the starting key, and a long crescendo builds to the return of the refrain eight measures later.

Example 1.5 shows the surprisingly gradual modulation that accompanies this setup-punchline frame. The melody begins identically in each phrase, differentiated only by the stepwise relationship and new lyrics. The melodic repetition suggests a full return to G major, but the first harmony is the *subdominant*, not *tonic*. This passage is closely related to a standard "V–I" ascending modulation: when the two keys are a whole step apart, the pivoting V chord is reinterpreted in hindsight as IV in the new key. But Bernstein delays the arrival of the expected V in F major: rather than appearing at the end of the first phrase, it *begins* the second, when Hildy has *already* arrived melodically at the next key. Bernstein finally confirms the supporting tonic two measures later, when Hildy sings her *second* affirmation ("I do keep house on a dime"). Hildy is connecting the dots for Chip: he may be preoccupied by a mythically perfect woman he has yet to meet, but he is already in the same room as a woman who is the complete package.

In "Intermission Song," the opening number of Michael R. Jackson's Pulitzer Prize and Tony winning musical *A Strange Loop* (Off Broadway 2019, Broadway 2022), these tonal relationships are less subtle; they also have intertextual connections beyond the show. *A Strange Loop* is about a Black queer playwright named Usher, who hates his day job *as* an usher;

**Example 1.5.** "I Can Cook, Too," verse: beginning (left); modulation up by whole step in second phrase (right).

he is trying to write a musical about a Black queer playwright who hates his day job—hence, its name. The musical opens with Usher's "Thoughts," personified by six additional Black queer performers, pelting him with questions about his project during an intermission of *The Lion King*. Usher's goal aligns with Jackson's: to create a "Big, Black, and queer-ass American Broadway show."

Jackson has frequently noted the structural and stylistic references of his musical to Sondheim's *Company* (1970), which cemented Sondheim's and producer-director Hal Prince's reputations as Broadway mavericks. Instead of Usher and his Thoughts, the perennially single Robert celebrates his thirty-fifth birthday in nonlinear scenes with his friends—five married (or soon-to-be-married) couples. His friends are calling him through the opening number, with affectionate nicknames: "Bobby, Bobby baby, Bobby bubby, Robert darling, Rob-o . . ." This contrasts with the Thoughts folding over Usher's name in repetitious counterpoint—hearkening back to Jackson's own experience as an usher, when he was summoned by his job title by older, white theatergoers feigning respectability.

Figure 1.1 does not show the key change back to tonic; instead, it notes the similarities in tonal relationships between the first sections of "Company" and "Intermission Song." Both songs' verses are a half-step *higher* than their respective choruses, which are in turn prepared by similar elevations: In "Company," from Verse **B** to the pre-chorus, Sondheim ascends by three whole steps on extended tertian sonorities to the dominant of the

**Figure 1.1.** Comparisons between form and key through the first halves of "Company" (chorus leads to a verse in a new key) and of "A Strange Loop" (chorus leads to a verse without modulation); note that these charts do not show modulations back to the home keys.

| Verse A | Verse B | Verse A | Verse B' | Pre-chorus | Chorus | Verse A |
|---|---|---|---|---|---|---|
| V/D♭M | ~... | V/D♭M | ~... | V/CM [HC] | CM~... | V/E♭M[!] |
| *Bobby, Bobby... ...we've been trying to call you.* | *Bobby... ...how have you been?* | *Bobby, there's a concert on Tuesday...* | *Bob, we're having people in Saturday night.* | *Bobby, come on over for dinner...*<br>*We looooove you!* | *Phone rings, Door chimes, In comes company...*<br>*...really about!* | *Bobby, Bobby... Angel, will you do me a favor?* |

**Figure 1.1a.** Chart for "Company."

| Intro | Verse A/B | Verse A/B | Pre-chorus | Chorus/Break | Verse A |
|---|---|---|---|---|---|
| AM | AM [HC] | AM [HC] | AM→[...]DM→ | A♭M[!] | A♭M |
| *Usher! Usher! Usher! Usher!* | *How many minutes 'til the end of intermission?*<br>*He has to show what it's like...* | *How many minutes 'til the end of intermission?*<br>*He has to fight for his right...* | *Blackness, queerness, fighting back to fill this cishet all-white space...*<br>*That are casting spells to conjure up a...* | *Big, Black, and queer-ass American Broadway...*<br>*show!* | *How many minutes 'til the end of intermission?* |

**Figure 1.1b.** Chart for "A Strange Loop."

new key; in "Intermission Song," from the pre-chorus to the chorus, Jackson runs through a series of pump-up modulations until suddenly dropping down to the new tonic by tritone.[20]

But the last column in each diagram is where the songs diverge. Sondheim modulates at the end of the chorus by minor third, and so the second verse begins a whole step higher than the first; Jackson *does not* change keys, and stays a half step down. Eventually, "Company" follows the same tonal path it did in the first half of the song—with similarly rich counterpoint through the entire second verse—ultimately closing a half step higher than where it began. By contrast, "Intermission Song" has an abbreviated second verse, returning to the introductory calls, and—with the Thoughts singing in unison, *not* counterpoint—shifts back up to the opening key.

The thematic return heralded by tonal return is emotionally wrought.

Each attempt at a verse is interrupted by a snippet of the chorus trying to break through, and it finally does only when Usher's Thoughts are at their most toxic: "Lacking both in craft and rigor / Cause you're just a fucking—/ Big, Black, and queer-ass American Broadway . . ."

*A Strange Loop* confronts Broadway's structural whiteness. In "Intermission Song" Jackson does not use "Company" as a mold as much as a springboard. By the end of the song we finally hear "Usher, Usher" in lyric counterpoint—a cappella, as the protagonist, wavering between writer's block and identity crisis, repeats "Oh my God, oh my God."

A duet from Sondheim's *Follies* (1971) takes these blurred modulations further. "Too Many Mornings" is between two would-be lovers, Ben and Sally, both of whom married the other's best friend. The couples are attending the thirty-year reunion of the fictionalized "Weisman Follies," during which nearly everyone on stage is haunted by their younger self (played by a corresponding younger actor). Ben and Sally confess their feelings for each other in the duet—but the romance is imbalanced, as Ben sings first to *Young* Sally before her present-day counterpart says, "If you don't kiss me, Ben, I'm going to die." By the end of the duet Ben and Sally are embracing and singing together—but this harmonious ending precipitates a collective emotional collapse.

Each of the three verses—Ben's and Sally's, and their duet—ends a tritone away from where it began. Ben's verse starts in B♭ major and promises a cadence in E major, but ends on a deceptive cadence, landing on ♭VI. This cadence elides with the start of the next verse, now in C major, a step above where Ben's verse began.

Sally's verse does reach an authentic cadence, in the now-expected F♯ major, through a new closing melody. The duet rises by step twice more, eventually reaching the starting key again. First, Ben repeats Sally's closing melody an enharmonic step higher, in A♭ major; he answers her question "Was it ever real?" with "*It was always* real." Next, the interlude before the final verse—during which the lovers sing together—rises to B♭ major; unlike Ben's opening solo, the duet reaches an authentic cadence, and concludes in E major.

Based strictly on this overview, the return to the starting key is fairly direct. The modulations themselves are far from dramatic "intensifications," though—indeed, as shown in Example 1.6, the orchestral texture is sparse throughout. The exact moment marking each key change is also unclear. In m. 71, right at the cadence in F♯ major, the harp begins playing

**Example 1.6.** "Too Many Mornings": Stepwise modulations from Sally's solo (F♯ major) to duet (B♭ major).

C♮; when Ben's melody comes in on the same pitch, it sounds at first like a chromatic lower neighbor of $\hat{5}$ and is only retroactively confirmed as $\hat{3}$ in A♭ major. During the instrumental interlude, the harp oscillates on the same pitches above a bass line that simply shifts up from A♭ to B♭, confounding the arrival of B♭ major until the lovers finally sing $\hat{3}$ together.

The three stepwise modulations in this song are not equivalent in form. The first, which precedes Example 1.6, is from Ben's solo to Sally's (B♭ to C), a larger-scale connection between verses; the second is an immediate repetition of a phrase (F♯ to A♭); the third links the end of a verse to the start of another. The last of these, direct as it is at the surface, is in fact the most questionable. If the repeated closing melody reaches a cadence in A♭ major, and the corresponding passage in the duet verse reaches a cadence in *E major*, is it accurate to call the transition a "stepwise ascent"? This large-scale *descending major-third* relationship lurks beneath the surface-level *stepwise* modulation. Like Ben loving Sally for who she was, or Sally expecting a kiss to fulfill what she's missed, the stepwise ascent is illusory, masking the fall to where the song began.

## CONCLUSION

A corpus study would probably reveal more examples of this paradoxical tonal relationship, at least in the arrangements and orchestrations of extended numbers such as the opening of *Legally Blonde* or "Show Off" in *The Drowsy Chaperone*—where the composer is not the only person writing the notes of a song or number, and it is up to a collaborator to decide how to bridge a gap between two different parts of a single song. This is a tricky avenue to pursue: cast recordings are almost always abridged, and when mounting revivals, part of the production process often includes writing new orchestrations and arrangements, which often feature modulations to different keys. Despite these obstacles, such an undertaking might not only yield more examples; it may also open further avenues to understand how specific key relationships can relate to dramatic circumstances, shedding new light on the sentimentality and affective excess of a musical phenomenon that has swept up so many of us.

## NOTES

1. This chapter furthers the research of a paper I presented at the 2015 Society for Music Theory Annual Meeting in St. Louis, MO. My thanks to William Marvin, Bret McCandles, and Patrick McLaughlin, who introduced me to "A Little Bit in Love," "'Til Him," and "Colored Lights," respectively; and to Judah Cohen, under whose mentorship I began this project.

2. Unless otherwise noted, dates of musicals correspond to their Broadway openings.

3. The duet has actually modulated to G major, but a musically accurate lyric would force a clumsy neologism ("but as everyone can gueff . . .").

4. Though they abounded in film long before: as submitted on the wiki AllTheTropes, two examples include "Everybody Wants to be a Cat," from *The Aristocats* (1970)—"Let's take it to another key / Modulate, and wait for me"; and the title song from *High Anxiety* (1977)—"Key change!" shouted by Mel Brooks, before the final chorus, which is recalled in "Haben Sie gehört das deutsche Band" from Brooks's *The Producers* (2001). Stephen Farrow, via the Facebook group CAST RECORDINGS, notes an example from *The Hunting of the Snark* (1987); other group members, including Kenneth Brock, note the word painting in the Credo of Bernstein's *Mass* (1971).

5. See also Robert Komaniecki's analysis of the number in this volume.

6. Ricci's (2017) overview of pop-rock pump-up modulations includes a table of ten different names given this compositional device by songwriters, critics, musicologists, and music theorists, including Josefs's "Arranger's Modulation" and McCreless's "Barry Manilow Tonality." In this paper I use a number of the (less loaded) terms rather interchangeably to indicate ascending stepwise modulation, including "shift," "direct stepwise modulation," and "pump-up," unless otherwise noted.

7. Griffiths chooses the term "elevating" for its functionality: "recall that the elevator . . . goes down as well as up" (28).

8. The four "types" that each author discusses support the *directness* of the

direct stepwise modulation. The Roman numeral on the left of each en dash is in the original key; the Roman numeral on the right, in the new key. In addition to I–V described in text, there is also I–I, V–V, and V–I (which Griffiths refers to respectively as "juxtaposition," "handover," and again "juxtaposition").

9. In a 2006 concert at the Kennedy Center billed "An Evening with Stephen Schwartz," the composer/lyricist described this delay of the highest note in "The Wizard and I" in light of the performance capabilities of Idina Menzel, who originated the role of Elphaba on Broadway: "Here's what we know about Idina Menzel: we know that she's going to come out and belt, 'cause that's what Idina does. So what if . . . I make them wait a really, really long time for her to belt?"

10. I am indebted to Sue Swaney for this dramatic interpretation of key structure in "The Wizard and I."

11. YouTuber Hilmi Jaidin has juxtaposed *all* of the song's key changes in the original Broadway cast recording (OBCR)—including from verse to chorus—into one thirteen-second clip. https://youtu.be/m7GtS8QFZ28 (accessed March 28, 2022).

12. In this paragraph, Lehman notes a similarly kaleidoscopic progression at the end of the film *Key Largo*, for which Max Steiner's score concludes with a fanfare that switches from E♭ major to C via a "Picardy-aeolian cadence (♭VI–♭VII–I)."

13. In a video recording of a 2010 event that offered a preview of Seattle's 5th Avenue Theatre production, with O'Keefe at the piano and Annaleigh Ashford singing, the ascent between the last two choruses is omitted—and so the final chorus begins in E major, key at the start of Chorus 1, yet still shifts up to F major at the *internal* modulation; as a result, the song in this performance ends a half step higher, rather than a whole step. https://www.youtube.com/watch?v=fKqmylM4R-Q (accessed March 28, 2022).

14. Alex Lacamoire, email message to author, October 23, 2015.

15. Suskin (2009) describes anecdotal examples in golden-age musical theater songs where an arranger or orchestrator's work has a significant melodic or harmonic effect on the number as most commonly performed; McHugh (2015) investigates composers such as Rodgers, Loesser, and Porter and their working relationships with their musical collaborators.

16. In the original production, the penultimate chorus starts a dance break in F major, a whole step lower than the first two choruses; this is where the song ultimately ends. In the Kander and Ebb revue *And the World Goes Round* (Off Broadway 1991), every chorus except the reverie is in the same key.

17. The harmony occasionally changes, too: in the vocal selections, "was *giving up me*" is all supported by V of the original key, without the intermediary pivot chord.

18. In the Leonard Bernstein Collection at the Library of Congress, an early sketch of this song is in fact called "MM."

19. It is also viable to interpret the chord at the end of the bridge as an applied

dominant of the subsequent E major chord, rewritten as a tritone substitution. The arrival of IV in B major, then, functions as a resolution—though one without an applied leading tone, which would introduce D♯ before the modulation at the beginning of Chorus 3.

20. In the earliest version of "Intermission Song," available on Jackson's YouTube channel, the sequence from A to D major was originally set to a series of names beginning with the letters A, B, C, and D during each respective key: parents calling for their children to behave or be patient at the theater. https://www.youtube.com/watch?v=ItA7w8aA6o4 (accessed March 28, 2022).

## WORKS CITED

All The Tropes Wiki. "Truck Driver's Gear Change." Last modified September 21, 2018. https://allthetropes.org/wiki/Truck_Driver%27s_Gear_Change

Asare, Masi, and Oliver Wang. 2019. "Shame." In Jake Johnson et al., "Divided by a Common Language: Musical Theater and Popular Music Studies," *Journal of Popular Music Studies* 31 (4): 32–50.

Buchler, Michael. 2008. "Modulation as a Dramatic Agent in Frank Loesser's Broadway Songs." *Music Theory Spectrum* 30 (1): 35–60.

CAST RECORDINGS. "(Cross-posting with Professional Music Directors)." July 26, 2020. https://www.facebook.com/groups/castrecordings/posts/3307379685948912/

Doll, Christopher. 2011. "Rockin' Out: Expressive Modulation in Verse-Chorus Form." *Music Theory Online* 17 (3).

Griffiths, Dai. 2015. "Elevating Form and Elevating Modulation." *Popular Music* 34 (1): 22–44.

Hanenberg, Scott J. 2016. "Rock Modulation and Narrative." *Music Theory Online* 22 (2).

Hoffman, Brian. 2013. "'I'll Never Know What Made It So Exciting': Dramatic Intensification in Musical Theater's Chromatic Third Modulations." Paper presented at the Society for Music Theory Annual Meeting, Charlotte, NC, October 31.

Hoffman, Brian. 2014. "Mapping the Modulation Zone: A Formal and Stylistic Study of Stepwise Modulation in Pop-Rock." Paper presented at Music Theory Midwest, Appleton, WI, April 25.

Jackson, Michael R. "'Intermission Song'—by Michael R. Jackson." Michael R. Jackson, May 25, 2012, YouTube video, 4:56. https://www.youtube.com/watch?v=ItA7w8aA6o4

Jaidin, Hilmi. "Ruining Musicals, ep. 1: Laurence O'Keefe with no key changes." Hilmi Jaidin, June 23, 2019, YouTube video, 5:22. https://www.youtube.com/watch?v=m7GtS8QFZ28

Jarvis, Brian Edward, and John Peterson. 2020. "Detour or Bridge? Contrasting Sections and Storytelling in Musical Theater." *SMT-V* 6 (2).

Lehman, Frank. 2013. "Hollywood Cadences: Music and the Structure of Cinematic Expectation." *Music Theory Online* 19 (4).

McHugh, Dominic. 2015. "'I'll Never Know Exactly Who Did What': Broadway Composers as Musical Collaborators." *Journal of the American Musicological Society* 68 (3): 605–52.

Neal, Jocelyn R. 2007. "Narrative Paradigms, Musical Signifiers, and Form as Function in Country Music." *Music Theory Spectrum* 29 (1): 41–72.

Ricci, Adam. 2017. "The Pump-Up in Pop Music of the 1970s and 1980s." *Music Analysis* 36 (1): 94–115.

Robinson, Danielle. 2009. "Performing American: Ragtime Dancing as Participatory Minstrelsy." *Dance Chronicle* 32 (1): 89–126.

Shelley, Braxton D. 2019. "Analyzing Gospel." *Journal of the American Musicological Society* 72 (1): 181–243.

Suskin, Stephen. 2009. *The Sound of Broadway Music*. New York: Oxford University Press.

# 2 Sondheim's Dissonant Tonality

*DREW NOBILE*

## *INTRODUCTION: SONDHEIM AS COMPOSER*

In October 2017, *T Magazine* ran a feature on Stephen Sondheim with the headline "Stephen Sondheim, Theater's Greatest Lyricist" (Miranda 2017). Though that headline was certainly meant as a sign of deference—after all, many might bestow that title on the article's author, Lin-Manuel Miranda—the compliment could be seen as a bit backhanded. Sondheim, of course, is not merely a lyricist, but a *composer*-lyricist; as Stephen Banfield has noted, the effusive praise of Sondheim's skills as a wordsmith often implies reservations about his musical contributions (Banfield 1993, 1). Though Sondheim is far from unappreciated in that regard, the bulk of the criticism lodged against him targets his music. Sondheim got so tired of others claiming he couldn't compose a memorable melody that he worked that criticism into his 1981 show *Merrily We Roll Along*: the main characters' big-talking producer complains that "there's not a tune you can hum," followed by a not-so-subtle reference to *South Pacific*'s "Some Enchanted Evening" ("Opening Doors," No. 16, mm. 122–170).[1] If the composer felt pressure to write more like Richard Rodgers, it is probably because many viewed Sondheim as the only one capable of carrying on Broadway's golden-age legacy through the second half of the twentieth century (see Sternfeld and Wollman 2011, 122). Indeed, Rodgers and Sondheim are often paired as the composers responsible for Broadway's two sweeping style shifts in the twentieth century: first, Rodgers and Hammerstein's 1943 *Oklahoma!* ushered in the "integrated" musical—where songs reflect and reinforce the dramatic narrative instead of serving as plot-adjacent song-and-dance numbers—and next, Sondheim's 1970 *Company* pivoted theater toward the "concept" musical, where all elements of the show—book, lyrics, music, scenery, staging, etc.—act in service of some central dramatic *idea* (see, e.g., Block 2011).

Sondheim's association with the concept musical has led critics and analysts to concentrate largely on his ability to coordinate words and music in service of the drama. The small number of Sondheim studies that can be considered music-analytical in nature—foremost among them Stephen Banfield's 1993 monograph *Sondheim's Broadway Musicals*, plus a handful of more recent dissertations (Purin 2011; Hudlow 2013; Blustein 2020)—focus especially on his strategic use of Wagnerian leitmotifs and stylistic pastiche.[2] Both are central aspects of Sondheim's compositional style; his manuscript sketches show elaborately conceived motivic schemes (see, e.g., Horowitz 2010, 82–83), and Sondheim's own comments reveal that he consciously emulates specific composers and styles, referring to this or that moment as the "Chopin thing" or "Stravinsky motif" (Horowitz 2010, 21, 128).[3] But what is also clear, and what I would like to focus on in this essay, is that Sondheim considers harmony to be the most important aspect of musical composition. "Harmony is what makes music," he says; "Rhythm and melody? That's secondary. Harmony is what it's about, as far as I'm concerned" (Swayne 1999, 345; see also Horowitz 2010, 198). Sondheim's harmonic language grows out of a unique approach to tonality, one rooted in tradition but adapted to fit both the postmodern aesthetic of the late twentieth century and the demands of commercialized musical theater.

In this essay, I offer some preliminary steps toward a theory of Sondheimian tonality. While each of Sondheim's shows establishes its own harmonic sound world, I aim to demonstrate that in Sondheim's mature output—defined as his Broadway shows from 1970 onward—those show-specific idioms are all built on a consistent tonal foundation basic to his idiosyncratic style.[4] In particular, Sondheim's compositional framework allows striking dissonance to pervade the harmonic layer without obscuring listeners' sense of key; as the composer himself puts it, "they don't feel Schoenberged into anything" (Horowitz 2010, 159). My discussion of Sondheim's tonality further aims to put his music in dialogue with trends in twentieth-century tonal music outside the Broadway sphere. Steve

Swayne has cataloged Sondheim's extensive classical (small c) influences, and so it seems natural to consider him alongside not only Lloyd Webber and Schwartz but also Britten, Vaughan Williams, and Hindemith (Swayne 2005). To this end, I will make use of concepts from Daniel Harrison's theoretical investigation of the contemporary tonal repertoire in his recent book *Pieces of Tradition* (2016). Harrison does not mention Sondheim in his book, and Broadway examples make only occasional appearances, but his target repertoire of "backwards-compatible" music that inherited and supplemented common-practice tonality perfectly describes Sondheim, who lists his classical roots as "Brahms through 1930s Stravinsky" (see Swayne 2005, 44). Through applying Harrison's theory to Sondheim, I suggest that his relationship to classical tonality is not only one of influence, but rather mirrors the stylistic developments across twentieth-century art music.

I first lay some theoretical groundwork aimed toward an understanding of Sondheim's basic harmonic vocabulary. I show that Sondheim's dissonant sonorities derive from a small number of fundamental chords that are "colored" (as Harrison puts it) with additional, often chromatic tones. Following the theoretical portion, I turn to two larger analyses showing how Sondheim deploys his tonal system for dramatic effect. I begin with *Sunday in the Park with George*, whose cacophonous cluster dissonances eventually give way to serene diatonicism as the painter distills chaos into an artistic magnum opus. I conclude with *Into the Woods*, which refuses to resolve $\hat{4}$ to $\hat{3}$ until the characters abandon their selfish pursuits for the greater good. These two analyses demonstrate that Sondheim's musicalization of drama is not only a matter of explicit signifiers such as leitmotifs and strategic pastiche, but also infuses the deepest levels of his compositional idiom. Sondheim's tonal system forms a distinctive blend of functional tonality and modernist techniques devised to maximize the potential for dramatic expression while remaining accessible (and marketable) to musical-theater audiences and critics.[5]

## *NOTE ON EXAMPLES AND EDITIONS*

As is the case with most Broadway composers, Sondheim does not orchestrate his own shows, so the final document he prepares himself is a piano-vocal score. The subsequently orchestrated version results in a piano-conductor score used in performance; rarely does a full orchestral score exist. For many of Sondheim's shows, the first published vocal score was a reduction of this piano-conductor score rather than Sondheim's own piano-vocal score. In 2010–2012, Rilting Music, in consultation with Sondheim, published revised editions of most of Sondheim's shows prepared instead from the composer's original scores. (Those that were not revised for this set—*Into the Woods*, *Sunday in the Park with George*, *Company*, and *Follies*—had previously been published based on Sondheim's scores.) All musical examples in this essay, including song and measure numbers, refer to the revised editions. Full publication information for the editions used appears in the bibliography. For clarity (and to comply with copyright restrictions), this essay's examples are presented in reduced form, rhythmically simplified and often using "octave-dropped" treble and bass clefs to avoid excessive ledger lines. Readers are encouraged to consult the published scores whenever possible, especially in regard to the longer analyses in the final section.

## *ZONES*

It will prove helpful to think of Sondheim's music in terms of three compositional zones: the bass zone, the chordal zone, and the melodic zone. The first two together constitute the accompaniment—the piano part in Sondheim's vocal scores—and the third resides in the voice parts. Bass and chordal zones differentiate themselves by occupying distinct registers, which correspond to Daniel Harrison's "root space" (below C3, which is an octave below middle C) and "chord space" (C3 through C6) (Harrison 2016, 104–5). Sondheim typically fills his bass zone with slow-moving lines, which may be doubled at the octave (as in example 2.13) or fifth (as in example 2.1), or expanded through Broadway's favorite "oom-pah" figure (as in example 2.14). The chordal zone generally consists of what we think of as "chords"—vertical sonorities of three or more notes, often texturized through repetition (example 2.2) or arpeggiation (example 2.8)—but sometimes contains inner melodies in counterpoint with the melodic zone (example 2.3c). The melodic zone is, of course, the vocal melody, which sometimes involves sophisticated polyphony (*Sweeney Todd*'s "God, That's Good," for example) and/or multivoice harmonies forming a chordal profile of their own. The melodic zone tends to be diatonic and anchored to the bass line in counterpoint, though it does not always follow the bass's implied harmonies. The three zones operate with various levels of coordination, sometimes working in sync but at other times seeming entirely independent, often clashing in harsh dissonance.

In this essay, I focus mainly on the bass and chordal zones, the latter being the primary agent of dramatic dissonance. I consider the two accompaniment zones individually, showing how the bass projects harmonic function and the chordal zone colors the basic chord functions in various ways depending on the dramatic situation.

## BASS ZONE

"Musical harmony, as you know, moves by bass line. That is the motive that changes things." So says Sondheim (quoted in Horowitz 2010, 17), and despite his reputation for dissonance and hard-to-hum melodies, his bass lines are firmly grounded in standard tonal practice, generally centering on $\hat{1}$, $\hat{4}$, and $\hat{5}$ with various levels of embellishment. In fact, the simplicity of the bass is what allows him to incorporate so much dissonance. Sondheim's above statement continues with "And it doesn't matter how you screw around with the notes on top; if the bass remains solidly consistent, it's going to sound that way throughout." In other words, harmonic function is essentially determined by the bass alone. Sondheim's bass notes act as what Daniel Harrison (following Hindemith) calls "root representatives": bass notes that are sufficiently emphasized to act as functional chord roots even in the absence of a third or fifth above them (Harrison 2016, 111–12).

Thus, $\hat{1}$ planted firmly in the bass zone will project tonic function no matter what other notes sound on top. Similarly, $\hat{4}$ projects subdominant function and $\hat{5}$ projects dominant. Other bass notes will likewise act as roots: $\hat{6}$ will usually indicate VI and $\hat{2}$ will usually indicate II (or, in certain contexts, V/V).[6] A few examples are in order. Example 2.1 gives a reduced version of the accompaniment to "Being Alive" from *Company*. Despite chord structures combining tertian and quartal stacks with the occasional chromatic embellishment, the bass settles into a clear and standard I–VI–IV–II–V progression. Example 2.2 shows the middle section of the "Johanna" sequence from act 2 of *Sweeney Todd*. Here, the bass persists on a tonic pedal (embellished through an oom-pah texture) while the chordal zone becomes increasingly dissonant, its highest voice following the mel-

**Example 2.1.** "Being Alive" (*Company*): chordal reduction of first vocal phrase (mm. 3–11).

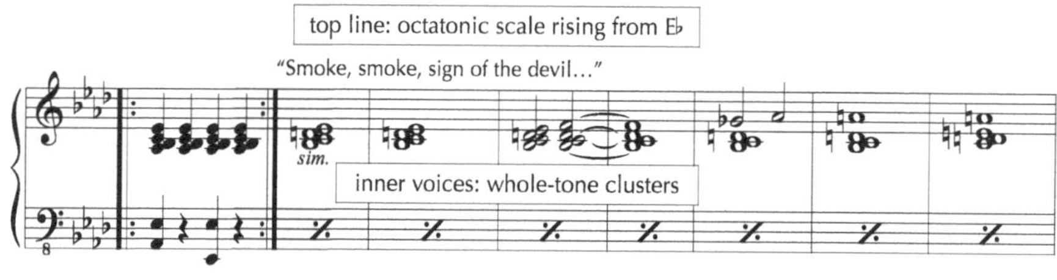


**Example 2.2.** "Johanna (Todd)" (*Sweeney Todd*, No. 20): chordal reduction of "City on Fire" section, mm. 57–86.

ody through an octatonic scale over whole-tone-flavored clusters in its lower three notes. The disconnect between chords and bass reflects the disconnect between Sweeney's peace with his new purpose (killing everyone) and the chaos it sows in the outside world. Despite the dissonance, we never lose the sense of tonic function.

Tonic pedals such as this are common in Sondheim's songs. Sondheim has talked a lot about his use of pedal tones, the gist being that he sees them as a way to free up the chordal zone without losing the tonal grounding (for the sake of both the composer and the audience).[7] In addition, pedal tones generate a significant amount of anticipation of the moment the pedal will break. Sondheim refers to the "wonderful tension that occurs . . . in pedal points—the waiting for the release" (Horowitz 2010,

158). Sondheim's tonic pedals tend to break by moving to IV, often accompanying a melodic apex, a formal shift, and/or an important lyric (Sondheim: "you change chords . . . when you're changing thoughts" [Horowitz 2010, 199]). Typical examples include *Into the Woods*'s "Agony" (as the prince cries "Agony!"), *Sunday in the Park with George*'s "We Do Not Belong Together" (on the title line), *Merrily We Roll Along*'s "Old Friends" (on "are we or *are* we unique?"), *Sweeney Todd*'s "Wait" (on "I've been thinking *flowers*"), *Pacific Overtures*'s "The Advantages of Floating in the Middle of the Sea" (on "*kings* are burning"), *Assassins*' "Another National Anthem" (on "it says *listen*"), and many others.

## CHORDAL ZONE

With the bass zone providing the tonal grounding and the melodic zone reflecting the expression of the characters' agency, the chordal zone becomes the primary carrier of dramatic significance. Sondheim's chords comment on the drama by inserting sharp dissonances into otherwise diatonic frameworks, as we saw in example 2.2. But not all dissonance has dramatic meaning. Sondheim's basic harmonic palette does not consist of the pure triads and seventh chords of classical-era tonality, nor is it the extended tertian stacks characteristic of Tin Pan Alley and jazz. Instead, Sondheim builds from fundamental, dissonant chord types involving certain combinations of stacked fifths and thirds, which differ based on the harmonic function involved. The autonomy and power of the bass allows these dissonant chords to sound stable, reflecting what Harrison calls "relativized" consonance (2016, 97).

Sondheim's fundamental tonic sonority is what many would call an "added-ninth" chord, combining $\hat{1}$, $\hat{2}$, $\hat{3}$, and $\hat{5}$. But the added ninth is not really "added," in the sense that Sondheim does not treat this chord as a triad with an extra note. I find it more appropriate to consider it a combination of two fifths and two thirds stacked above the tonic. We have already seen this chord in action in the first and last measures of example 2.2, and it will appear again in examples 2.9, 2.12, 2.16, and 2.17. The first chord in example 2.1 enlarges this basic tonic chord by adding another note to the fifth stack, resulting in the sonority $\hat{1}$–$\hat{2}$–$\hat{3}$–$\hat{5}$–$\hat{6}$. (This five-note tonic seems to be the default in *Company*, also appearing in "Company," "The Ladies Who Lunch," and "Sorry-Grateful," among others.) Example 2.1

further demonstrates one of Sondheim's hallmark accompaniment patterns: an expansion of tonic through an alternation of a chord with $\hat{3}$ and a chord with $\hat{4}$. The former acts as a state of repose and the latter acts as a state of quiet tension, the oscillation creating a sense of motion over the static bass pedal. The chord with $\hat{4}$ is still a tonic chord even if it begins to resemble IV or $V^7$ in its pitch collection; the oscillation is a voice-leading phenomenon, and with the bass firmly planted on tonic it is less a chord progression than motion within a single chord.

Sondheim uses oscillations between $\hat{3}$ and $\hat{4}$ over a tonic pedal throughout his output. It seems to be his way of indicating the launch of a *song*. With Sondheim's stylistic blurring of the book/number boundary through sung dialogue and instrumental underscore, the tonic $\hat{3}$–$\hat{4}$ oscillation acts as a signal that we are entering "lyric time," stepping out of the plot-advancing "book time" for a reflective number (see McMillin 2006, chapter 2). Example 2.3 shows some representative examples, with accompaniments presented in reduction to better show the chordal structure. *Follies*'s "In Buddy's Eyes," Sally's not-so-convincing description of her perfect life with Buddy (example 2.3a), contains what we can consider the basic form of the oscillation: a tonic added-ninth chord exchanging its $\hat{3}$ for $\hat{4}$, resulting in the four-note sonority $\hat{1}$–$\hat{2}$–$\hat{4}$–$\hat{5}$ in the second measure. (This same progression underlies the main portion of *Sweeney Todd*'s "Johanna" sequence [No. 20, mm. 25ff.], which precedes the dissonances we saw in example 2.2; here the lyric time of Sweeney's inner reflection is set to a montage of him slitting Londoners' throats.) The basic chord forms often acquire additional tones: in example 2.3b, the first chord becomes a pentachord through the addition of *Company*'s characteristic $\hat{6}$, and in example 2.3c, a melodic line sways between $\hat{7}$ and $\hat{6}$ over the basic chords. Conversely, the chords are sometimes reduced to trichords: in example 2.3d, the first chord is a simple tonic triad, and we will later see the second chord reduced to just $\hat{1}$–$\hat{4}$–$\hat{5}$ in example 2.12 and example 2.16. Example 2.3e lists one additional example of a prominent $\hat{3}$–$\hat{4}$ oscillation from each of Sondheim's Broadway shows from *Company* (1970) through *Passion* (1994).

Like tonic chords, dominant chords rarely appear in pure triadic form outside of Sondheim's pastiche numbers. Sondheim does not rely on cadential closure as regularly as some of his classical forebears, but unlike the pop and rock music of his day, his music is still based on a fundamental polarity between tonic and dominant (see Nobile 2020). That said, Sondheim's dominant chords very frequently avoid what others consider the fundamental expression of dominant function: the leading tone.[8] Steve Swayne traces Sondheim's use of the "suspended dominant" to the composer's interest in twentieth-century tonal composers, especially Paul Hindemith and Maurice Ravel (Swayne 2005, 31–32). Suspended dominants are often some variant of a "7sus4" sonority containing $\hat{5}$–$\hat{1}$–$\hat{2}$–$\hat{4}$, as in the C–F–G–B♭ chord sustained from measures 13–66 of *Pacific Overtures*' "Someone in a Tree" (No. 8, at "I was younger then . . ."). The V chord we saw in example 2.1 added a ninth to this suspended dominant, allowing Sondheim to voice it as an open fifth in the left hand with a major triad in the right hand, a type of chord Sondheim has referred to as his "favorite."[9]

## *COLORED CHORDS AND THE (0148) SET*

According to Daniel Harrison, a characteristic of twentieth-century tonal music is the "colored triad": a consonant triad combined with one or more extra notes that act as appendages, adding "color" without affecting the chord's basic consonant structure (Harrison 2016, 107–9). The use of colored triads in Harrison's examples from Ravel and Prokofiev—two composers Swayne identifies as major influences on Sondheim—can be compared with Sondheim's own use of chromatically dissonant sonorities. The chords that Sondheim colors are not necessarily triads but often one of the fundamental harmonies described above, namely the tonic added-ninth chord or the dominant 7sus4. What Harrison calls the "hue" and "intensity" of a coloring agent depends on both the harshness of the intervals it forms (e.g., semitones are harsher than whole tones) and its degree of chromaticism. Many of Sondheim's dissonant sonorities can be understood as diatonic structures with one or more coloring agents. Here, I focus on two related sonorities that Sondheim returns to throughout his work to portray unsettled tension: a major triad with appended minor sixth (e.g., C–E–G–A♭) and a minor triad with appended major seventh (e.g., C–E♭-G–B♮). Unlike Sondheim's fundamental dissonant chords, these colored chords are non-diatonic, the coloring agent injecting harsh chromaticism into a pure triad. Readers familiar with musical set theory will notice that these two chords are pitch-class inversions of one another, and more specifically that they are both members of set-class (0148)—notice, for instance, that both contain an augmented triad plus a fourth note a semitone away from a member of that augmented triad. I will use the (0148)

**Example 2.3.** Instances of $\hat{3}$–$\hat{4}$ oscillation over a tonic pedal.

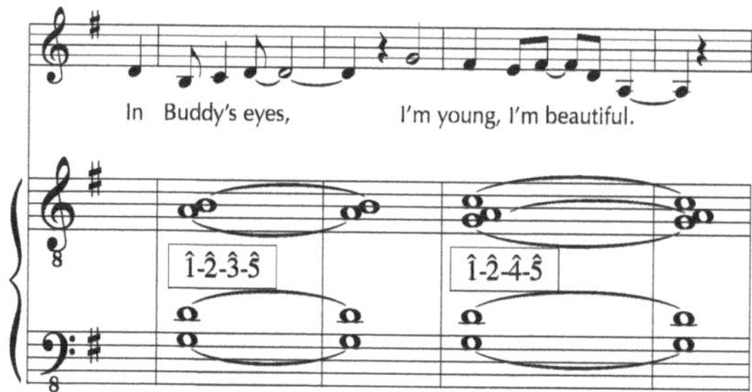


a) "In Buddy's Eyes" (*Follies*), mm. 45–48.

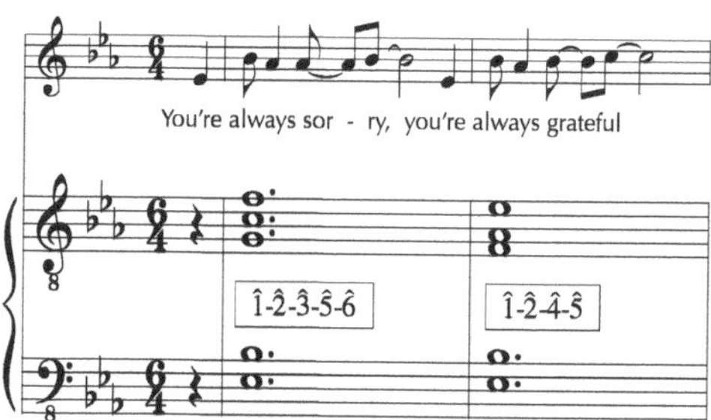


b) "Sorry-Grateful" (*Company*), mm. 3–4.

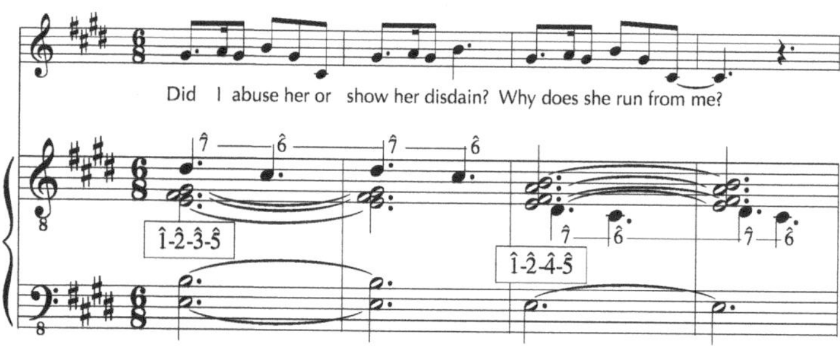


c) "Agony" (*Into the Woods*, No. 10), mm. 2–5.

nomenclature to highlight this relationship (see also Harrison 1994, 108–9, for a discussion of [0148] in tonal contexts).

Sondheim's most famous use of the (0148) sonority is in *Sweeney Todd*. Sondheim himself has referred to its instantiation as a third-inversion minor-major seventh chord as the "Sweeney" chord (Horowitz 2010, 127–28), though it does not seem to relate exclusively to Sweeney (the

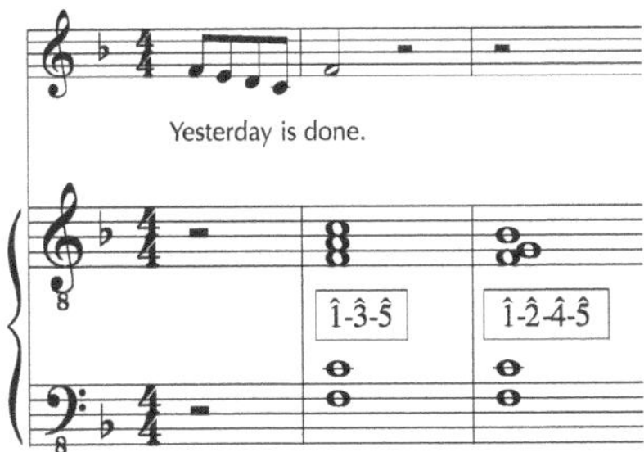


d) "Merrily We Roll Along" (*Merrily We Roll Along*, No. 2), mm. 6–7.

*Company*: "Company" ("Phone rings...")
*Follies*: "Too Many Mornings"
*A Little Night Music*: "Soon"
*Pacific Overtures*: "Next"
*Sweeney Todd*: "Not While I'm Around"; "Wait" ("Easy now...")
*Merrily We Roll Along*: "Merrily We Roll Along"
*Sunday in the Park with George*: "Gossip Sequence"
*Into the Woods*: "Your Fault"
*Assassins*: "Another National Anthem" ("There's another...")
*Passion*: "Happiness" ("All this happiness..."); begins w/$\hat{4}$

e) Some other examples of $\hat{3}$–$\hat{4}$ oscillation from *Company* (1970) to *Passion* (1994).

clearest example is in the Judge's confessional [No. 11, mm. 1–2]). Craig McGill traces the use of (0148) throughout the *Sweeney* score, arguing that it underscores moments of "unease" (McGill 2012).[10] This sonority's association with unease extends beyond this show, however. In the opening sequence of *Into the Woods*, the eerie entrance of the witch involves a subtle switch from the suspended dominant that has so far dominated the score to an (0148) sonority (example 2.4a); later, the characters' chaotic quarreling in "Your Fault" receives an inverted form of the set (example 2.4b). The central gang of criminal misfits in *Assassins* laments their marginalized social status in "Another National Anthem," whose $\hat{3}$–$\hat{4}$ oscillation begins with an (0148) sonority—a tonic E-major chord colored with a C♮, reminding us that the rosy stories we tell about the American dream are stained with the dissonant realities of social exclusion and oppression (example 2.5).

*Passion* exhibits many (0148) sonorities across the through-composed score. The opening sequence begins with the (0148) set G♭–B♭–D–F fur-

**Example 2.4.** (0148) in *Into the Woods.*

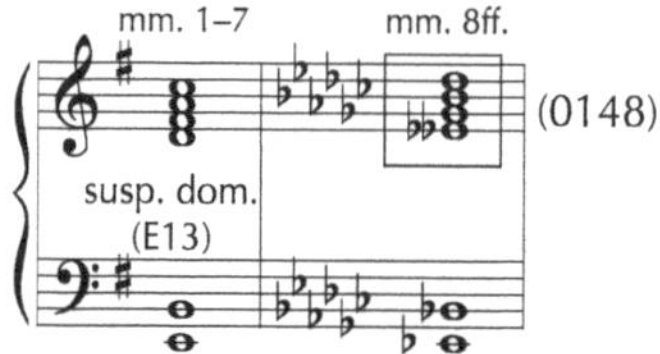


a) "Opening (Part III)" (*Into the Woods*, No. 1C).

b) "Your Fault" (*Into the Woods*, No. 22), opening vamp.

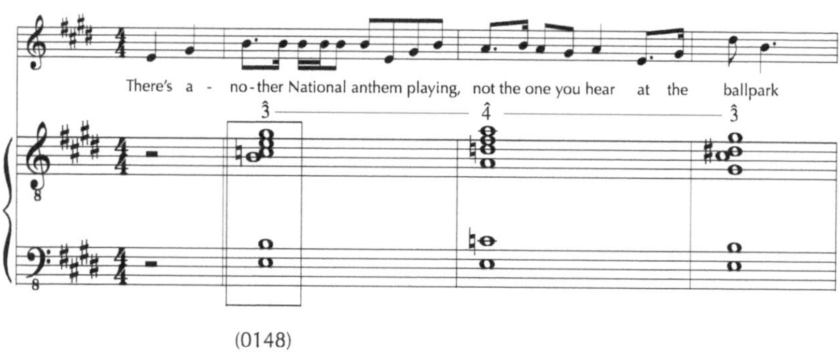


**Example 2.5.** (0148) at the beginning of "Another National Anthem" (*Assassins*, No. 8, mm. 83–85).

ther colored by an A♭, making an (02458) pentachord (example 2.6). As the music settles on a vamp (m. 11), the chord acquires a D♭ as the tonality coalesces around G♭ major. The resulting hexachord G♭–A♭–B♭–D♭–D♮–F can be thought of as a tonic added-ninth chord colored by both D♮ and F. However, the way Sondheim distributes the voices suggests hearing this sonority as the combination of a G♭ added-ninth chord and a B♭-major triad—i.e., a *polychord.* (There is also a D♭-major triad subset, though Sondheim hides it within the texture; one could ascribe some significance to this chord's construction as major triads built from each note of the tonic triad—G♭, B♭, and D♭. Note as well that the polychord has two (0148) subsets: G♭–B♭–D♭–D♮ and B♭–D♮–F–G♭.) During the vamped polychord, the scene opens up to a postcoital moment in which the characters Giorgio and Clara declare their utmost "Happiness" with one another. The unease that accompanied Sondheim's other uses of (0148) does not seem present in this case. However, perhaps the accompaniment knows something the characters do not: that Giorgio and Clara are not destined to end up together. The harmonic combination of two tonally incompatible chords might reflect the two characters' ultimate incompatibility. Looking forward to the show's conclusion, we see that (0148) underscores most of the "Farewell Letter" ending Giorgio's and Clara's relationship (example 2.7), but as Giorgio realizes that he reciprocates Fosca's love for him ("No One Has Ever Loved Me"), the music settles on a diatonic version of the opening vamp (example 2.8). The large-scale resolution of dissonance to consonance over the course of *Passion* parallels Giorgio's break from Clara and union with Fosca; in Gary Konas's reading, Fosca's spirit is transferred to Giorgio upon her death ("your love will live in me," etc.), reflecting the fusion of the two triads into a single diatonic structure (Konas 1997).

## *ANALYSES*

The combination of functionally grounded bass, diatonic melody, and colored chords forms the basic frame of Sondheimian tonality. In many ways, this tonal system is merely the foundation on which Sondheim erects his musical-dramatic structure. But a show's specific implementation of the tonal foundation can itself carry dramatic significance. We saw a bit of this in the above examples. In the remainder of my essay, I take a broader look at Sondheim's deployment of his dissonant tonality across two shows: *Sunday in the Park with George* and *Into the Woods*. Both shows are frequent targets of motivic analyses, as they each build on an intricate web of Wagnerian leitmotifs. My analyses will show that their motivic features sit on the surface of a deeper interweaving of music and drama.

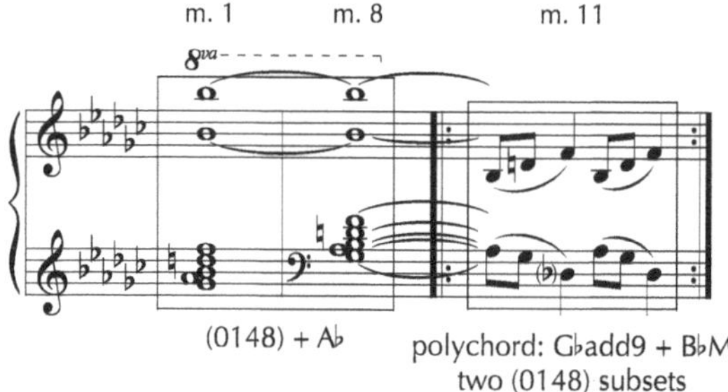


**Example 2.6.** Opening of "Happiness (Part I)" (*Passion*, No. 1).

**Example 2.7.** "Farewell Letter" (*Passion*, No. 16, titled "Scene 13" in the vocal score): (0148) and polychord at beginning and end.

**Example 2.8.** End of "No One Has Ever Loved Me" (*Passion*, No. 17, mm. 39–43, titled "Scene 14" in the vocal score).

## SUNDAY IN THE PARK WITH GEORGE

The first act of *Sunday in the Park with George* follows George Seurat's struggle to distill the chaos of bourgeois life into an ordered work of art. The show's first few minutes portray the fundamental conflict between George and the outside world. Later on, George will describe this divide as a "window" filtering his perception of reality in "Finishing the Hat." In his mind, he controls everything, from the placement of every tree to the number of boats on the water; as Joanne Gordon puts it, "Anything is possible. Worlds can materialize and vanish" (Gordon 1990, 268). In noisy reality, his mistress Dot is uncomfortable in the heat, snooty critics deride his work, and societal demands interfere with his obsessive pursuit of order.

The show opens with a brief soliloquy as George lays out his vision of "bring[ing] order to the whole." Under George's speech, we hear a series of flourishes opening into an arrival on E-flat major. The silhouette of a melody emerges—on the French horn in Michael Starobin's original orchestration, though Sondheim imagined it on trumpet (Horowitz 2010, 102)—one that will ultimately achieve full realization as the "Sunday" theme in the finales of both acts. A scene coalesces into the titular park, where Dot poses—reluctantly—as George sketches her.

The musical shift from George's soliloquy to Dot's inner thoughts (example 2.9) is abrupt and introduces a tonal juxtaposition that underpins much of the first act. The flourishes that accompany George's manipulations of the canvas, as well as the inchoate "Sunday" theme, are entirely diatonic, in E-flat major in Nos. 1–2 and then briefly in F-sharp major opening No. 3. The final flourish gives us the same chord (in the same key, spelled enharmonically) that later accompanies George's description of the "window" (see the second half of m. 2 in example 2.9 and m. 41 in "Finishing the Hat" [No. 15]). After the last flourish, the music snaps to the other side of the window (example 2.9, m. 3). Over the bass's F♯, the chordal zone gives us E♯–F♯–A, which we can understand as an F♯-minor triad colored with an E♯. (The missing C♯ is not difficult to interpolate as an overtonal fifth above the bass note; indeed, the repeat of this passage in m. 9, now a semitone higher and with a different bass note, includes the full triad.) This chord is Sondheim's signature (0148) sonority. Diatonicism has given way to chromatic dissonance, as George's vision of order collides with the noisiness of real life.

**Example 2.9.** Transition from opening flourishes into "Sunday in the Park with George" (*Sunday in the Park with George*, No. 3, mm. 1–3).

The ensuing number—Dot's "Sunday in the Park with George"—expands on example 2.9's chromatically colored triad. Example 2.10 gives a harmonic reduction of the number's first section, showing an overall outline of II–V–I in E major followed by V–I in F major. Over these tonal progressions, projected largely by the bass line, the chordal zone engages in various chromatically colored triads. In the example, the triads are given in open noteheads with the coloring elements in solid noteheads. Over the F♯ bass note, the first three chords are F♯-minor, G♯-major, and A-major triads colored with E♯, E♮, and D♯ respectively. (Notice the contrary motion of rising triads and descending coloring notes.) Next, we get a polychord completing the B bass note with both E-major and B-major triads (I and V). The resolution to tonic gives us D- and E-major triads, hinting at a suspension-resolution relationship supporting the melody's A–G♯ (a nod to a $\hat{4}$–$\hat{3}$ oscillation and an important pitch motive in this number). The addition of C♮, however, turns the resolution chord into another dissonant (0148) set (further colored by an F♯, suggesting a basis in an added-ninth chord), negating a satisfying tonic arrival.

The whole passage then repeats a semitone higher, this time skipping the first bass note so that V underlies the first four chords and adding more coloristic elements so that most chords contain five notes. A developmental section ensues, outlining the three bass notes A, F♯, and B. Each bass note gives rise to a dominant-functioning chord, based largely on the "7sus4" sonorities A–D–E–G, F♯–B–E, and B–E–A. The first of these, spanning mm. 18–23, includes heavy figuration, but one can reduce this passage to a static A–E–G with an alternation of D and C♯, again recalling Sondheim's $\hat{4}$–$\hat{3}$ oscillation but in a dominant rather than tonic context. The F♯ and B sonorities act as V/V and V respectively, sending us back to the original key of E major and the return of the opening material in m. 36.

**Example 2.10.** Reduction of "Sunday in the Park with George."

If, as Stephen Banfield suggests, the show's first act traces the resolution of pervasive chromaticism into "radiant diatonicism" (1993, 335–36), then we might interpret the (0148) colored triads to reflect the cacophonous reality that George ultimately filters into his artwork. Instances of (0148) recur throughout the first act, especially in "The Day Off" (example 2.11), in which, as in "Sunday in the Park with George," George sketches a scene in the park. Act 1 also has several moments of pure diatonicism, as in the opening flourishes discussed above as well as most of "Finishing the Hat." These passages tend to associate with George's inner thoughts, as he contemplates the artist's work and life.

**Example 2.11.** (0148) sets in "The Day Off" (*Sunday in the Park with George*, No. 12, mm. 55–56).

Since the act concludes with the completion of the artwork, a natural musical correlate might be for the finale to remove all hints of chromaticism and sink into the calmest of diatonic frameworks. This, for the most part, occurs: the flourishes that opened the show return, with the ensuing "Sunday" theme now fully worked out, as shown in example 2.12. As Joanne Gordon puts it, George "takes the chaos of sound, motion, and emotion and recomposes it into a balanced composition" (1990, 285). The theme is set to an unadorned expression of Sondheim's fundamental harmonies: a $\hat{3}$–$\hat{4}$ oscillation complete with a tonic added-ninth chord. But the finale is not devoid of chromaticism; a C♯ creeps in in m. 29, followed by an E♭ in m. 32 and an F♮ in m. 38. As the number approaches a climax, the E♭ returns in both bass and melody, now combining with the chordal zone's G-major triad to form an (0148) sonority, which we thought we were done with (example 2.13). As the characters sing "forever" from their eternal resting places within George's painting, the E♭ resolves to D in the outer voices, climactically absorbing the act's signature chromaticism into a diatonic context. In the end, George hasn't erased the dissonance of real life, but rather captured it within his ordered work of art.

## INTO THE WOODS

As a fairy-tale parody, *Into the Woods* naturally has an overabundance of morals. The plot revolves around a baker and his wife who, in their desire to conceive a child, must "go in and screw up everybody else's fairy story," as Sondheim describes it. The fairy-tale characters—Little Red Ridinghood, Jack (of beanstalk fame), and Cinderella—have wishes of their own, and

**Example 2.12.** Flourishes leading into "Sunday" (*Sunday in the Park with George*, No. 24, mm. 9–26).

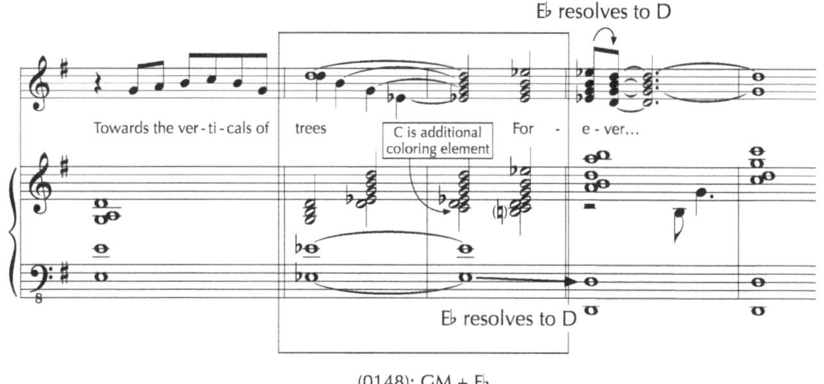


**Example 2.13.** The return and resolution of (0148) in "Sunday" (mm. 41–45).

the first act tracks all of them as they chase their desires into the woods. By the end of the act, every wish is fulfilled, and in typical fairy-tale fashion, each character has learned something through the process. But the show is not over. The second act shows that the characters' selfish pursuits of their personal wishes have consequences. As Sondheim explains, "in order to get what they wanted, they each had to cheat a little, or lie a little, or huckster a little," and the second act becomes a story of "how the characters have to band together and make amends for what they did." The individual lessons learned in the first act give way to a broader moral of "community responsibility."[11]

The harmonic content of the first act—especially the "lesson" songs—contains a subtle hint that not all is right. Specifically, tonic chords tend to omit their chordal third. The thirdless tonic first arrives with significant emphasis in the "into the woods" theme (example 2.14). This passage evokes Sondheim's classic $\hat{3}$–$\hat{4}$ alternation, but here $\hat{4}$ (A♭) stubbornly persists in the chordal zone's highest voice. This accompaniment recurs as a sort of "promenade" throughout the first act, where at each stroke of midnight the characters step out of the plot to recite various clichéd morals relevant to their respective situations ("no knot unties itself," "slotted spoons don't hold much soup," etc.).[12] The only harmonic activity is a "thumb line" (the lowest voice of the piano's right hand) rising stepwise from $\hat{5}$ to $\hat{7}$; the basic harmonic structure of the accompaniment figure involves a static $\hat{1}$–$\hat{2}$–$\hat{4}$ and tonic pedal framing this moving tenor line.[13]

The association of the thirdless tonic with moralizing continues with the three fairy-tale characters' solo numbers describing the lessons they learned while pursuing their goals. Three numbers—"I Know Things Now" (Little Red Ridinghood, No. 6), "Giants in the Sky" (Jack, No. 9),

**Example 2.14.** Tonic with persistent $\hat{4}$ in the "Into the Woods" theme (*Into the Woods*, No. 1A, mm. 1–2).

**Example 2.15.** Accompaniments to the three "lesson" songs from *Into the Woods*.

a) "I Know Things Now" (No. 6, mm. 9–10).

b) "Giants in the Sky" (No. 9, mm. 7–8).

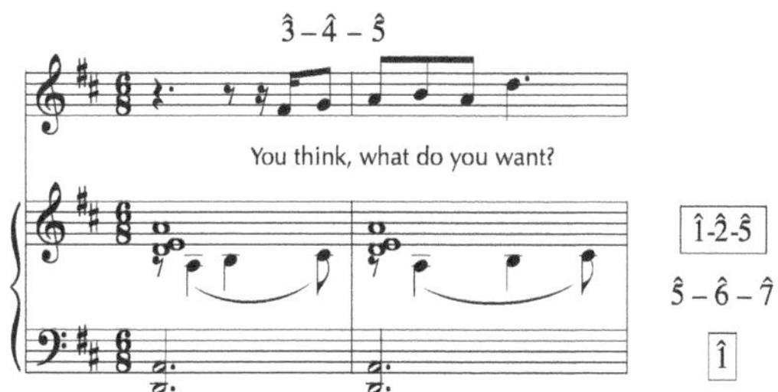


c) "On the Steps of the Palace" (No. 13, mm. 23A–25).

and "On the Steps of the Palace" (Cinderella, No. 13)—are built on the same accompaniment structure and all begin with $\hat{3}$–$\hat{4}$–$\hat{5}$ in the melody, as shown in example 2.15. (The accompaniment returns in act 2's "Moments in the Woods," sung by the baker's wife, though it takes on a different form as that song has a somewhat different dramatic purpose; see Stoddart 2000, 216–17, for more on this song's role.) Linking the three songs in this way not only brings out their similar roles but also musically intertwines the characters' largely separate plotlines; as Stephen Banfield puts it, "here Sondheim's main purpose is not just to exhibit structural replication but to move toward an understanding of the characters' moral interdependence" (1993, 385). These songs' accompanimental vamps derive from the "into the woods" theme seen above but without $\hat{4}$ so that the basic tonic chord is simply $\hat{1}$-$\hat{2}$-$\hat{5}$ along with the thumb line. That the accompaniment decidedly omits $\hat{3}$ while the melody makes regular use of it suggests a disconnect between the characters' perception and reality; the characters declare themselves enlightened ("I know things now") but the omniscient accompaniment knows they have more to learn.[14]

Tonics without thirds might just be a motivic feature of the score, a characteristic of the show's "sound world" with no inherent significance. In the context of Sondheim's harmonic language, these chords are not especially dissonant, so it is not necessarily the case that we will perceive them as needing eventual resolution. However, the dramatic way in which Sondheim brings thirds back into tonic chords suggests a deeper significance. Sondheim lays out his stated theme of community responsibility at the end of the show in three moral-of-the-story numbers: "No More," in which the baker realizes that abandoning his baby son is the same thing his father did to him as a child; "No One Is Alone," in which the survivors band together to rebuild their community; and "Children Will Listen," in which the characters understand that their actions affect other people. In "No More," the previously stubborn $\hat{4}$ is domesticated into a $\hat{3}$–$\hat{4}$ oscillation (example 2.16), with the same fundamental chords seen in "Sunday" above. "No One Is Alone" expands the oscillation to an alternation of I and IV chords, both of which prominently display $\hat{3}$ in the highest voice of the chordal zone. Especially notable is the gesture on the title lyric, which leads to an arrival on $\hat{4}$ rather than the expected $\hat{3}$, highlighting the word "alone," followed by an emphatic $\hat{3}$ beginning the next phrase (example 2.17). We are now getting the idea that these moralizing songs are settling a central musical question. "Children Will Listen" extends the family meta-

$\hat{3}$ — $\hat{4}$

Running away, let's do it.

$\hat{1}$-$\hat{2}$-$\hat{3}$-$\hat{5}$

$\hat{1}$-$\hat{4}$-$\hat{5}$

**Example 2.16.** "No More" (*Into the Woods*, No. 23, mm. 69–70): appearance of $\hat{3}$ within a tonic $\hat{3}$–$\hat{4}$ oscillation.

**Example 2.17.** "No One Is Alone" (*Into the Woods*, No. 25, mm. 1–12): prominent $\hat{3}$.

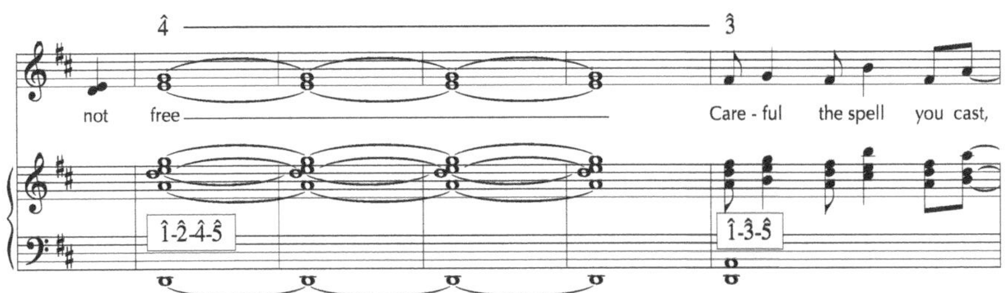


**Example 2.18.** "Children Will Listen" (*Into the Woods*, No. 26B, mm. 80–84, titled "Finale (Part III)" in the vocal score): resolution of $\hat{1}$–$\hat{2}$–$\hat{4}$–$\hat{5}$ to $\hat{1}$–$\hat{2}$–$\hat{3}$–$\hat{5}$ in final section.

phor to the characters' actions ("wishes are children"), succinctly summing up the show's main message in the line "wishes come true, not free." The final word of this phrase extends for four measures, holding the $\hat{1}$–$\hat{2}$–$\hat{4}$–$\hat{5}$ chord from the "into the woods" theme but this time following it up with a prominent $\hat{3}$ to kick off the final section of the number (example 2.18).

Of course, the show does not end there; we proceed with a reprise of the "into the woods" theme, along with its persistent $\hat{4}$, and the show ends with a last "I wish" from Cinderella as the curtain descends. We realize here that wishing is "a perennial human state," as Ben Francis argues: "somebody has only to have their wish granted for them to want something else" (Francis 2014, 352). At the opening, we might have expected the typical fairy-tale narrative of characters pursuing goals and learning something from the process. But in the end, the message is that fulfillment does not come from getting your wish but in mediating your personal wishes within a concern for the communal good.

## *CONCLUSION*

Sondheim is a musical-theater category of his own. Combining deep knowledge of nineteenth-century classical tonality, golden-age Broadway, and twentieth-century art music, he forged a new compositional language embracing avant-garde trends while remaining in dialogue with his tonal roots (see Swayne 2005). Sondheim has already been lauded for his leitmotivic prowess, intertwining recurrent musical themes in coordination with each show's narrative themes. More generally, Sondheim himself has explained how he seeks to create a new sound world in each show, one specifically tailored to that show's dramatic content. Indeed, it would be hard for an experienced Sondheim listener to mistake, say, a *Sweeney Todd* excerpt for something from *Into the Woods*, even if the listener did not immediately recognize that specific material. That said, there is also something that ties all of Sondheim's (non-pastiche) output as recognizably *Sondheimian*, despite his inter-show distinction. This personal style, I have argued, arises largely from an idiosyncratic tonal framework built on dissonant diatonicism, chromatic coloration in the chordal zone, and firmly grounded bass lines. The musical elements I have discussed in this essay merely scratch the surface, though, and I believe a more comprehensive theoretical investigation of Sondheim's compositional practice would be both rewarding and important in giving musical theater a more central position in academic music theory. But what is already clear is that Stephen Sondheim's tonal contributions place him as a groundbreaking historical figure not only in musical theater but in twentieth-century music writ large.

## NOTES

1. On the criticisms and Sondheim's response, see Swain 2002, 349–50, and Zadan 1986, 155–56.

2. On Sondheim's use of pastiche, see Smith 1998 and Knapp 2005, 162–78. See also Gordon 1990 and Swayne 2005.

3. Sondheim's breadth of musical influence is remarkable; few others are as conversant in the languages of nineteenth-century art music (Chopin, Wagner, Strauss), twentieth-century tonal music (Ravel, Rachmaninov, Hindemith, Satie), golden-age Broadway (Kern, Berlin, Rodgers, Arlen), and classic film scores (Herrmann, Steiner, Waxman), while also claiming personal mentorship from a Broadway legend (Oscar Hammerstein II) and a modernist icon (Milton Babbitt) as well as a collaboration with a top American composer and conductor (Leonard Bernstein). Steve Swayne has expertly excavated Sondheim's musical influences in his book *How Sondheim Found His Sound* (2005), showing that Sondheim not only was acquainted with the aforementioned composers' styles, but wove together elements of all of them throughout his own compositions.

4. The shows considered in this essay include, in chronological order, *Company* (1970), *Follies* (1971), *A Little Night Music* (1973), *Pacific Overtures* (1974), *The Frogs* (1974; revised for Broadway in 2004), *Sweeney Todd* (1979), *Merrily We Roll Along* (1981), *Sunday in the Park with George* (1984), *Into the Woods* (1987), *Assassins* (1991), and *Passion* (1994). I do not include *Road Show* (2008, a revision of *Bounce* [2003]) because, besides the show's never having appeared on Broadway, no published score exists.

5. In identifying Sondheim's idiosyncratic style, I should specify that I am excluding the large portion of Sondheim's output that falls under the category of pastiche. In most shows, Sondheim includes one or more numbers written in a specific, non-Sondheimian style, often that of the Tin Pan Alley songbook. See Smith 1998; Knapp 2005, 162–78; Swayne 2005, chapter 2; and Banfield 1993, esp. 196–201.

6. Because Sondheim's sonorities often have an ambiguous modal character, I will use exclusively capital Roman numerals. These should not be taken to imply major chords.

7. Two quotes from Horowitz 2010: "That's fear that it's going to fall apart unless I keep a pedal tone going. . . . Quite often I will put a pedal tone underneath

so that I still get the coloristic changes but I don't run the risk of its going off the rails as far as the audience is concerned" (199); "A pedal tone is like an anchor—you're always there, tethered, like a goat tethered to a pole. The goat can wander around, but always, in the center, is this immovable tonic chord. . . . You can get away with a lot of murder when you're over a pedal tone. You can put in a lot of dissonance because the audience's ear—the listener's ear—is firmly anchored in that basic first step of the scale, so they don't feel lost" (159).

8. Ratner 1962 calls dominant function "7" in reference to the leading tone; Harrison 1994 considers $\hat{7}$ the "agent" of dominant function.

9. See Horowitz 2010, 29–30. Mark Spicer has referred to this type of V chord as the "soul dominant" (Spicer 2017). Harrison 1994 also discusses this and similar chords in reference to late-nineteenth-century music (esp. 41–42 and 48–49).

10. McGill, going off of Sondheim's own statements, calls (0148) the "Herrmann" chord after film composer Bernard Herrmann, who scored (among others) Alfred Hitchcock's *Psycho*.

11. The Sondheim quotes in this paragraph are from Zadan 1986, 355–56.

12. Sondheim had previously mulled over a promenade idea in *Sunday in the Park with George* but largely abandoned it in the final version. See Banfield 1993, 358–64. A similar idea—with another $\hat{3}$–$\hat{4}$ oscillation—arises in the "Transition" numbers from *Merrily We Roll Along*.

13. Sondheim has famously used the phrase "thumb line" in reference to his contribution to "Something's Coming" from *West Side Story*—namely the syncopated and chromatic cello line heard in the number's opening measures. See Secrest 1998, 119, and Swayne 2005, 91–92.

14. Sondheim at one point had the idea of naming all four songs "I Know Things Now," and a variant of that phrase occurs in each ("you know things now" in "Giants in the Sky," "and you've learned something too" in "On the Steps of the Palace," and "now I understand" in "Moments in the Woods"). See Banfield 1993, 385.

## WORKS CITED

Banfield, Stephen. 1993. *Sondheim's Broadway Musicals*. Ann Arbor: University of Michigan Press.

Block, Geoffrey. 2011. "Integration." In *The Oxford Handbook of the American Musical*, edited by Raymond Knapp, Mitchell Morris, and Stacy Wolf, 97–110. New York: Oxford University Press.

Blustein, Nathan Beary. 2020. "Through Arrangements of Shadows: Experiences of Reprise in Stephen Sondheim's Leitmotivic Musicals." PhD diss., Indiana University.

Francis, Ben. 2014. "'Careful the Spell You Cast': *Into the Woods* and the Uses of Disenchantment." In *The Oxford Handbook of Sondheim Studies*, edited by Robert Gordon, 350–64. New York: Oxford University Press.

Gordon, Joanne. 1990. *Art Isn't Easy: The Achievement of Stephen Sondheim*. Carbondale: Southern Illinois University Press.
Harrison, Daniel. 1994. *Harmonic Function in Chromatic Music*. Chicago: University of Chicago Press.
Harrison, Daniel. 2016. *Pieces of Tradition: An Analysis of Contemporary Tonal Music*. New York: Oxford University Press.
Horowitz, Mark Eden. 2010. *Sondheim on Music: Minor Details and Major Decisions*, 2nd ed. Lanham, MD: Scarecrow Press.
Hudlow, Adam. 2013. "Harmony, Voice Leading, and Drama in Three Sondheim Musicals." PhD diss., Louisiana State University.
Knapp, Raymond. 2005. *The American Musical and the Formation of National Identity*. Princeton: Princeton University Press.
Konas, Gary. 1997. "*Passion*: Not Just Another Simple Love Story." In *Stephen Sondheim: A Casebook*, edited by Joanne Gordon, 203–22. New York: Garland.
McGill, Craig. 2012. "Sondheim's Use of the 'Herrmann Chord' in *Sweeney Todd*." *Studies in Musical Theater* 6 (3): 291–312.
McMillin, Scott. 2006. *The Musical as Drama*. Princeton: Princeton University Press.
Miranda, Lin-Manuel. 2017. "Stephen Sondheim, Theater's Greatest Lyricist." *T Magazine*, October 16, 2017. https://www.nytimes.com/2017/10/16/t-magazine/lin-manuel-miranda-stephen-sondheim.html
Nobile, Drew. 2020. *Form as Harmony in Rock Music*. New York: Oxford University Press.
Purin, Peter. 2011. "'I've a Voice, I've a Voice': Determining Stephen Sondheim's Compositional Style through a Music-Theoretic Analysis of His Theater Works." PhD diss., University of Kansas.
Ratner, Leonard. 1962. *Harmony: Structure and Style*. New York: McGraw-Hill.
Secrest, Meryle. 1998. *Stephen Sondheim: A Life*. New York: Alfred A. Knopf.
Smith, Helen. 1998. "The Art of Glorification: A History of Pastiche, and Its Use within Sondheim's *Follies*." *British Postgraduate Musicology* 2: 24–31.
Sondheim, Stephen. 1983. *The Complete Company Collection*. Author's edition. Milwaukee: Hal Leonard.
Sondheim, Stephen. 1987. *Sunday in the Park with George*. Vocal score. New York: Rilting Music.
Sondheim, Stephen. 1989. *Into the Woods*. Vocal score. New York: Rilting Music.
Sondheim, Stephen. 2006. *The Complete Follies Collection*. Author's edition. Milwaukee: Hal Leonard.
Sondheim, Stephen. 2010a. *A Little Night Music*. Vocal score. Revised edition. New York: Rilting Music.
Sondheim, Stephen. 2010b. *Merrily We Roll Along*. Vocal score. Revised edition. New York: Rilting Music.
Sondheim, Stephen. 2010c. *Sweeney Todd*. Vocal score. Revised edition. New York: Rilting Music.

Sondheim, Stephen. 2011a. *Assassins*. Vocal score. Revised edition. New York: Rilting Music.

Sondheim, Stephen. 2011b. *Passion*. Vocal score. Revised edition. New York: Rilting Music.

Sondheim, Stephen. 2011c. *The Frogs*. Vocal score. New York: Rilting Music.

Sondheim, Stephen. 2012. *Pacific Overtures*. Vocal score. Revised edition. New York: Rilting Music.

Spicer, Mark. 2017. "Fragile, Emergent, and Absent Tonics in Pop and Rock Music." *Music Theory Online* 23 (2).

Sternfeld, Jessica, and Elizabeth L. Wollman. 2011. "After the 'Golden Age.'" In *The Oxford Handbook of the American Musical*, edited by Raymond Knapp, Mitchell Morris, and Stacy Wolf, 111–26. New York: Oxford University Press.

Stoddart, Scott F. 2000. "'Happily . . . Ever . . .' NEVER: The Antithetical Romance of *Into the Woods*." In *Reading Stephen Sondheim: A Collection of Critical Essays*, edited by Sandor Goodhart, 209–20. New York: Garland.

Swain, Joseph. 2002. *The Broadway Musical: A Critical and Musical Survey*, 2nded. Lanham, MD: Scarecrow Press.

Swayne, Steve. 1999. "Hearing Sondheim's Voices." PhD diss., University of California, Berkeley.

Swayne, Steve. 2005. *How Sondheim Found His Sound*. Ann Arbor: University of Michigan Press.

Zadan, Craig. 1986. *Sondheim & Co.*, 2nd ed. New York: Harper & Row.

# 3 *Topical Interpretive Strategies in American Musical Theater*

## Three Brief Case Studies

*GREGORY J. DECKER*

Can musical topics be at work in a Broadway show?[1] This question might seem strange at first: why invoke a principal semiotic strategy of eighteenth-century music in interpreting American musical theater? But there are parallels between the semiotic systems at work in both repertoires. Danuta Mirka explains that the hermeneutic potential of eighteenth-century music—from operas to symphonies to string quartets—was frequently predicated on the use of referential and disparate musical styles, genres, and gestures that were "taken out of their proper context and used in another one" (2014, 2). Mirka demonstrates that topical signification in these works is a two-step process—topics are first an iconic sign for other styles and genres through similar configurations of musical characteristics. The identified style or genre then signifies sociocultural associations and affects indexically (2014, 31; see figure 3.1).[2]

Similarly, although the Broadway musical is commonly identified with a generalized "sound," it has often been a site for mixing musical styles and genres, many of which originate outside the Broadway theater (Laird

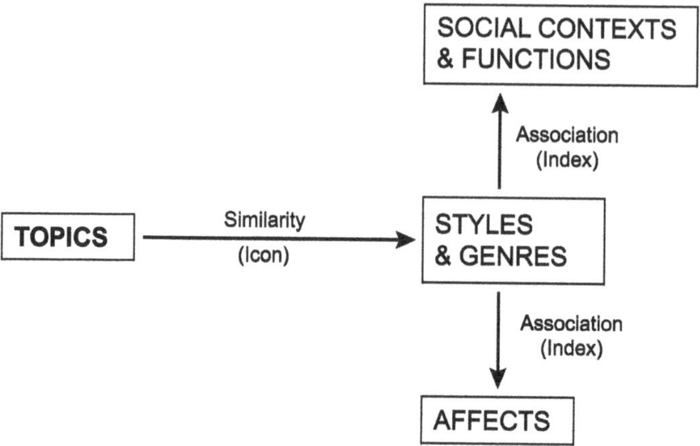


**Figure 3.1.** Mirka's semiotics of topical signification (modified).

2011, 33).[3] The use of different musical styles within one work is indeed at the heart of the musical's semiotics. For example, Todd Decker (2013) has shown that the differences between stereotypically "Black music" and "white music" are markers for race, privilege, class, and especially voice in Kern and Hammerstein's *Show Boat* (1927). And Bernstein and Sondheim's *West Side Story* (1957) mixes Afro-Caribbean styles with midcentury jazz and lyrical, operatic writing (Laird 2011, 36–38). If these different styles and genres used in a show have brought external social, functional, or affective associations to bear on our interpretations, then they might fairly be thought of as topics. They would signify in ways similar to topics in eighteenth-century music.

But while signification occurs along the same semiotic path in eighteenth-century music and the Broadway musical, interpretive results are not always similar. Topics in the eighteenth century are often understood as suggesting specific dramatic interpretation, either through musical combination (e.g., troping, see Hatten 1994) or when considered in combination with other domains, such as the libretto and plot of an opera. Wye Jamison Allanbrook's analyses of *Le nozze di Figaro* and *Don Giovanni* (1983) are well-known examples of this latter type of interpretation: in "Se vuol ballare," for instance, Allanbrook sees Figaro's use of the polite minuet as an ironic cloaking of his anger toward the Count. Associations with the minuet in general combine with lyric and plot to suggest both how Figaro is feeling and what he is thinking. A topic used this way might be said to *particularize*, providing subtext to a character's words or context for surrounding music.[4] In these kinds of analyses, meaningful oppositions are usually found within one number or otherwise in close proximity: the differences among characters' explicit statements, their dramatic situation, and associations with immediate musical topics help a listener create subtext, draw conclusions about motivations, and ultimately build an understanding of a character. The use of topics in Broadway shows often differs from classical music. Topical oppositions in Broadway, where they exist, are frequently only musical. That is, the affective or sociocultural associations with a given number's musical topic may not have much friction with the lyrics, dramatic situation, or character singing, but the accrued use of topics throughout the work may create musical oppositions on a larger scale. Instead of particularizing, then, in many cases topics in musicals imbue the work with atmosphere, providing *generalizations* about time, place, and characterization. Thus, these stylistic references, while similar in semiotic structure to eighteenth-century topics, are not always analogous in hermeneutic spirit.

A brief example will help illustrate generalization in a musical and will serve as a reference point for a topic that appears frequently in this chapter—the waltz (see figure 3.2).[5] The song "You Are Love" from *Show Boat* is a love duet between the two principal characters, Magnolia and Ravenal. The fact that the number is also a waltz is appropriate to these characters and the plot: they sing "You Are Love" toward the end of the first act, just after they have gotten engaged to be married (see Laird 2011, 33; Puccio and Stoddart 2000, 124–26). The waltz has no sociocultural or affective dissonance with this situation. It supports the drama via its physical associations: it is an intimate, close-position couple's dance in which a dizzying spiral floor pattern focuses the dancers' gazes on one another, blurring their vision of the rest of the room (McKee 2012, 91–92). Magnolia and Ravenal's words echo the dancing position with conventional references to being close ("in my arms") and never separating again.

That these two characters are white and privileged makes the choice of the waltz especially appropriate. Prior to this scene, secondary characters Julie and Steve undergo an embarrassing public spectacle in which Steve narrowly escapes arrest for miscegenation (he is white, but Julie is mixed race). They are subsequently fired from the show boat's production and must leave. Magnolia and Ravenal have no such prohibition to their engagement, which the waltz's air of social acceptability communicates

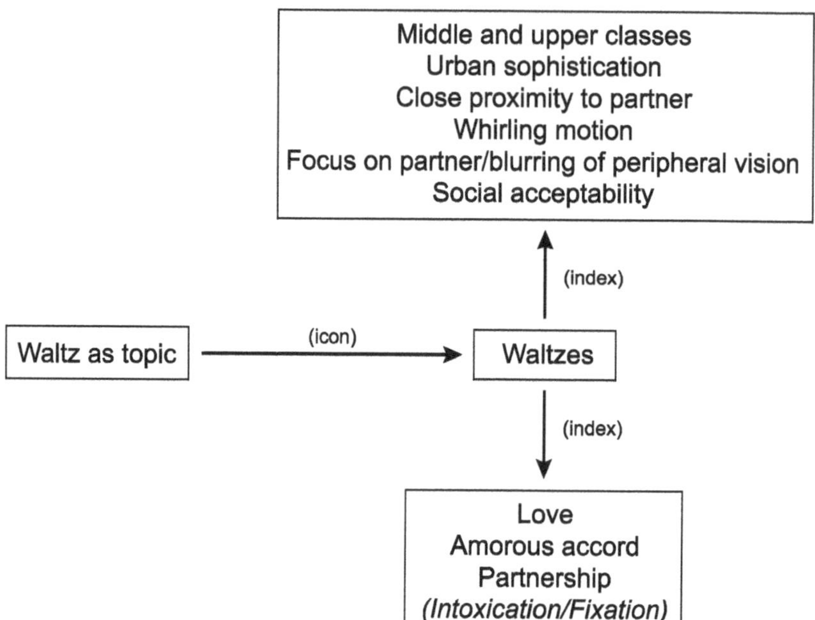


**Figure 3.2.** Common associations with the waltz.

clearly (see Giordano 2007; McKee 2012). Black characters in the show do not have access to this kind of "white music." They generally sing in a more popular idiom influenced by blues and gospel music. Likewise, white characters in the show do not have ready access to Black music. Musical oppositions separate characters into broad groups across the work, and topics support these generalizations.[6]

In the remainder of this chapter, I advance topical readings of three musicals to demonstrate how the strategies of generalization and particularization contribute to broader readings of the works. Two of the shows engage almost exclusively in one or the other of these topical interpretive strategies, and the third presents a situation in which these two strategies are used in combination. In Lucy Simon and Marsha Norman's *The Secret Garden* (1991), oppositional sets of musical topics generalize about the principal characters, and in doing so help to support a kind of metanarrative surrounding the story's metaphor. By contrast, topics in Stephen Sondheim's *Sweeney Todd* (1979) support characters' motivations and dramatic subtexts on individual bases, and so they particularize. The primary topical strategy in Harvey Schmidt and Tom Jones's *The Fantasticks* (1960) is generalization, but the waltz topic interacts with text and plot to create some particularizing interpretations. Admittedly, these are three very different shows. But because their uses of topics are so distinctive, I find it useful to view them as a set to foreground and explore these different strategies.

## SOCIAL CLASS, METAPHOR, AND GENERALIZATION IN THE SECRET GARDEN

In *The Secret Garden*, topics and other referential musical devices are used to generalize about characters, primarily their social class. The show follows the plot of Frances Hodgson Burnett's 1911 novel fairly closely; however, there is additional focus on the adults in the story, and their relationships are altered to heighten the drama. Dickon's age is advanced so that he, too, is an adult. The additional lower-class adult character helps to underscore the difference in social class between him, his sister Martha (Mary Lennox's chambermaid), and Mary's family (Archibald, Lily, and Neville Craven). Overall, the work has a cohesive, lyrical, contemporary-Broadway sound that by itself might not be heard as conveying strong topical associations, but it becomes the indicator of Mary's and her uncles' high social standing along with reinforcement from some elevated topics. Music for these upper-class characters is juxtaposed with folk and children's songs, folk-rock, contredanse, and modally inflected pitch-class collections. These topics and sounds belong to the world of servants Martha and Dickon. Topics in the show generalize about characters' social standing through the musical oppositions present across the work. Relevant numbers from the show, their characters, and their topics/styles are summarized in figure 3.3.

What supporting interpretations do the topics in use suggest? The strongest associations come from topics used by lower-class characters. Modern audiences are likely to group folk songs, children's songs, and contredanses together, primarily because many children's songs and traditional tunes still sung today are contredanses that began as popular songs in the eighteenth and early nineteenth centuries (see Tawa 1980; Scott 2001; Giordano 2007; and especially Gregory 2010). Good examples of this kind of song still popular today are "Yankee Doodle" (c. 1852?

| | | Upper-Class Music | | Lower-Class Music | | |
|---|---|---|---|---|---|---|
| Song | Characters | Lyrical/ Conventional | Waltz/ Elevated Topic | Folk/Children's Song/Contradanse | Folk Rock/Pop | Modal Inflection |
| "Opening" | Lily, Mary | | | X | | X |
| "I Heard Someone Crying" | Lily, Mary, Archie | X | X | | | |
| "If I Had a Fine White Horse" | Martha | | | X | | |
| "A Girl in the Valley" | Archie, Lily | X | X | | | |
| "It's a Maze" | Mary, Dickon, (Ben) | | | X | | X |
| "Winter's on the Wing" | Dickon | | | | X | X |
| "Show Me the Key" | Dickon, Mary | | | X | | X |
| "A Bit of Earth" | Archie | X | | | | |
| "The Girl I Mean to Be" | Mary | X | | | | |
| "Quartet" | Archie, Lily, Neville, (Rose) | X | | | | |
| "Race You to the Top of the Morning" | Archie | X | | X | | |
| "Wick" | Dickon, Mary | | | | X | |
| "Come to My Garden" | Lily | X | | X | | |
| "Come Spirit, Come Charm" | Mary, Dickon, Martha, Lily | | | X | | X |
| "Disappear" | Neville | X | | | | |
| "Hold On" | Martha | | | | X | |
| "Letter Song" | Mary | | | X | | |
| "Where In the World" | Archie | X | X | | | |
| "How Could I Ever Know" | Lily, Archie | X | | | | |

**Figure 3.3.** Summary of numbers, characters, musical characteristics, and social-class divisions.

[1755?]) and "Billy Boy" (c. 1776?).[7] These tunes demonstrate typical contredanse characteristics—smooth, constant rhythm with a light duple feel, often similar to a march or bourrée (see Allanbrook 1983, 55–60; Burford and Daye, *Grove Music Online*, s.v. "Contredanse"). By the mid to late nineteenth century, these contredanses and other folk tunes were out of fashion with the urban middle and upper classes but remained popular in rural areas into the first decades of the twentieth century (see Burford and Daye, *Grove Music Online*, s.v. "Contredanse"; Giordano 2007, 267–86; McKee 2012, 91). Thus, they have lower-class, country associations and might also call up feelings of nostalgia for simpler times. Modally tinged folk tunes are associated in the United States with Appalachian Mountain culture and an almost mythical understanding of country life in the British Isles. The use of these topics for servants in *The Secret Garden* is not

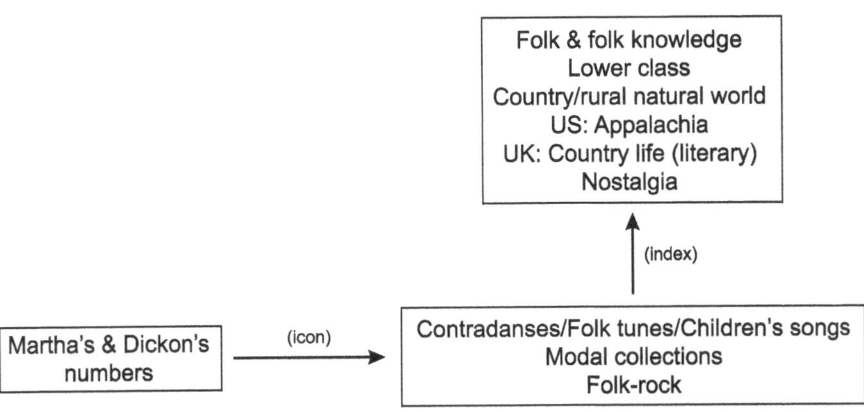


**Figure 3.4.** Semiotic representations of folk associations in *The Secret Garden.*

surprising. They characterize most of Martha's and Dickon's music. The semiotic path of signification is represented in figure 3.4.

For instance, Martha's first number in the show, "A Fine White Horse," is a clear contredanse in melody and rhythmic character, though two bars of the usual $\frac{2}{4}$ time have been grouped together into $\frac{4}{4}$[8] Further, the melody is fairly simple and repetitive, immediately repeating the implied opening scale-degree sequence $\hat{1}$–$\hat{2}$–$\hat{7}$–$\hat{1}$ ("had a fine white horse") up a third to $\hat{3}$–$\hat{4}$–$\hat{2}$–$\hat{3}$ ("take you for a ride today"). The harmonization is straightforward and uses only the I, IV, and $V^{(7)}$ chords. I highlight the contredanse character of the number in example 3.1 by re-barring the music in $\frac{2}{4}$ time.

Dickon's two solo numbers take modal elements of folk music and spritely rhythms of fiddle music and transfer them into contemporary folk-rock. In the opening of "Winter's on the Wing" (example 3.2), note the A Dorian melody with special emphasis on $\hat{7}$ and $\hat{6}$ and the open perfect consonances in the accompaniment, often associated with folk harmony and fiddle playing.[9]

These topics mark Martha and Dickon as local country people, and along with lyrics that reference the natural world and fantastic situations, they further suggest that the pair have some knowledge hidden from upper-class society—a common trope of urban/rural dichotomies. But this music does not offer oppositions to plot or motivations that provide specific subtextual insight into these characters. In terms of characterization, their music serves to generalize about them, group them together, and

**Example 3.1.** Melody of "A Fine White Horse," mm. 1–4, re-barred.
*The Secret Garden*. Lyrics by Marsha Norman. Music by Lucy Simon. © 1991, 1992 ABCDE Publishing Ltd. and Calougie Music. All rights administered by WC Music Corp. All rights reserved. Used by permission of Alfred Music.

**Example 3.2.** Melodic reduction of "Winter's on the Wing," mm. 5–6.

separate them from the "upstairs" characters. The topics in use coordinate with these characters.

The upper-class characters, especially brothers Archie and Neville Craven, mostly sing in what might be called a contemporary lyrical Broadway style—there's no pervasive modal inflection, and most tonal and rhythmic structures are conventional by the standards of twentieth-century mainstream popular music, with occasional mode mixture. These upper-class characters are instead identified through large-scale musical oppositions with lowered topics and styles. The link between their overarching, generalized musical style is thus primarily indirect, since there is little in this musical language alone that would suggest a high social station. There are, however, a few elevated topics that help foster associations with the upper classes, the urban, and related social-physical spaces (see figure 3.5).

Two numbers in the show are connected to opera, noble characters,

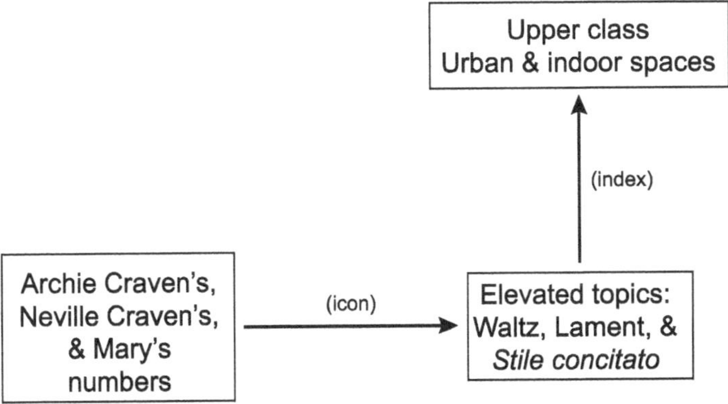


**Figure 3.5.** Elevated topics assist musical class oppositions.

and classical music in general through the use of topics stemming directly from the seventeenth century.[10] In "I Heard Someone Crying," sung by Archie Craven, the ghost of his deceased wife Lily, and Mary Lennox, a modified lament bass is repeated throughout and forms the harmonic and hypermetric basis of the number (in D minor: i–VII–ii$^{ø4}_{3}$–V). The topic makes clear reference to the crying the characters hear and to their respective emotional states, but it also carries implications of the high-style register. Archie's final solo number, "Where in the World," makes reference to the *stile concitato* through fiery repetition.

Additionally, the waltz topic makes an appearance in Archie and Lily's duet "A Girl in the Valley." The waltz certainly refers to the couple's love for one another through its physical gesture—an intimate, whirling couple's dance in close position—and through its use as a love duet topic in operetta and earlier musical theater works. But it also calls forth associations of mid- and late-nineteenth-century urban high society; it was *the* preferred social dance of its era (along with the polka), overtaking and relegating to rural areas the contredanse and its successors by midcentury (Burford and Daye, *Grove Music Online*, s.v. "Contredanse"). As the action of the show is supposed to take place in the first years of the twentieth century, we can imagine that Archie and Lily would have danced the waltz together. These elevated topics support reading upper-class characters' entire musical language in opposition to that of lower-class characters.

Topics and other musical structures suggest a separation of characters into groups by social class, but this hermeneutic generalization also pen-

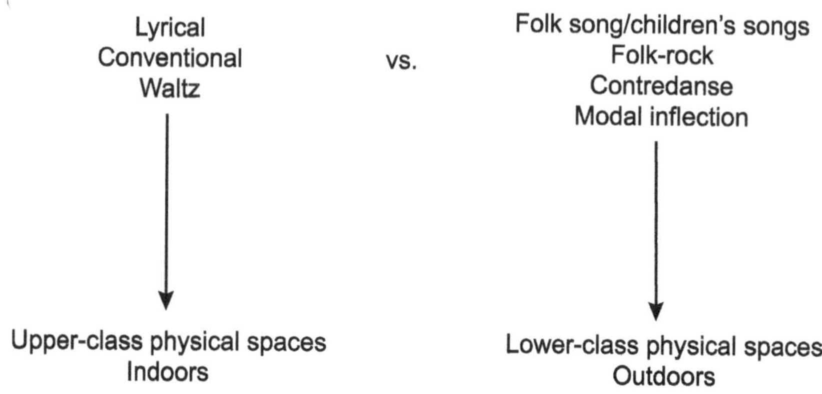


**Figure 3.6.** Musical associations with physical space in *The Secret Garden.*

etrates the work a bit more deeply. Central to the show (and the novel) is the symbol of the secret garden itself; its rediscovery and revitalization are metaphors for the Craven family. Characters who are able to physically enter and tend to the secret garden are marked as emotionally open, as desiring change, growth, and love; characters who have built emotional walls either do not know about or refuse to enter the garden and are not seen outdoors in general. The characters' emotional states directly correspond to the social-class dichotomy—Martha and Dickon know about and enter the garden, whereas Neville, Archie, and his son Collin cannot or will not enter. Therefore musical topics associated with these two groups divide them by emotional status as well.

Musical generalization draws together these disparate character attributes and gives them concrete connection through topical associations with class and, by extension, the assumed physical spaces of those classes (that is, indoor and urban versus outdoor and rural—see figure 3.6).

Topics connect these assumed physical spaces of their sociocultural contexts to the secret garden itself. These interactions between musical generalization and plot forge an overarching commentary or a kind of a metanarrative that suggests being both physically and emotionally closed off is stifling, but openness to love and to the natural world is freeing and healing. This metanarrative is further supported by the fact that Mary and Lily are revealed to have access to both of these spaces and, accordingly, to both sets of musical topics (refer again to figure 3.3). Mary's songs "I Heard Someone Crying," "The Girl I Mean to Be," and "The Letter Song" fit comfortably in the lyrical, conventional Broadway style of Archie and Neville, but the rest of her music is more similar to that of Martha and Dickon. She sings a children's song in "It's a Maze," and uses folk tunes and folk rock in "Show Me the Key," "Wick," and "Come Spirit, Come Charm." Lily also accesses both sets of topics and physical spaces—the secret garden was hers to tend before she died, and while she joins in the waltz topic with Archie, she also bookends the show with a children's song about the garden. Together, Lily and Mary serve as musical models for Archie and Collin, eventually leading them into marked healing musical, physical, and emotional spaces. Mary's music is especially revealing in this regard—it discloses to us that she has the power and capacity to mend the broken Craven family even before she realizes this herself.[11]

## *WALTZES, SUBTEXTS, AND PARTICULARIZATION IN* SWEENEY TODD

One might argue that my analysis of musical topics in *The Secret Garden* particularizes the characters, but this end result is a product of topical generalization and the metanarrative it underpins, as opposed to the product of cross-domain oppositions in a particular number. This number-specific strategy is the usual situation in which a topic particularizes, and is the case for most of the music in *Sweeney Todd*. In contrast to *The Secret Garden*, *Sweeney Todd* uses musical topics in strategic ways for individual situations and characters. True, many of the topics used locate the show within the world of the nineteenth century—there are polkas, waltzes, songs from the music hall and the parlor—but these topical elements do not combine to generalize about a group of characters. Instead, their associations contribute to interpretation of specific characters' thoughts and motivations.

Much of Mrs. Lovett's music, for instance, seems to particularize her instead of generalizing about her. When she uses the waltz in "The Worst Pies in London," the topic does not identify her class or immediate surroundings. Mrs. Lovett is lower class, or perhaps as a business and property owner, at the bottom of the middle-class spectrum, and despite its origins in folk culture, the waltz was quickly gentrified in the nineteenth century (Giordano 2007, 101–6). Neither does its traditional affect suggesting love or amorous accord seem to apply here. Though it is later revealed that Lovett is in love with Sweeney Todd, there's no hint that she yet knows who Todd is—that discovery is usually played out during the following number ("Poor Thing"). All of this is to say that unlike the congruent use of low-register topics for servants Martha and Dickon in *The Secret Garden*, the waltz does not match obvious aspects of Lovett's character or the current dramatic action in its most prominent associations. The use of the waltz during Lovett's description of her unpalatable meatless meat pies suggests instead a psychological reading: the somewhat elevated ballroom topic lends a genteel sheen of self-effacement to this number, while it simultaneously betrays Lovett's social ambition that comes to light later in the first act. Here, the social context of the waltz interacts with character and plot to communicate subtext. The topic's associations stand in opposition to the character and her words, and a potential subtextual reading is created through that difference.

Mrs. Lovett and Sweeney Todd make use of another kind of waltz at the end of act 1 in "A Little Priest." Todd has narrowly missed his opportunity to exact revenge on Judge Turpin (who banished Todd on a baseless charge, raped his wife, and took Todd's daughter Johanna as his ward). Todd then decides that, as a substitute, he will slit the throat of almost any man who comes into his shop for a shave because, he reasons, all men are guilty of or complicit in evil. Mrs. Lovett, in turn, offers to use the corpses of the slain to fill her meat pies, thereby proposing a symbiotic relationship for the pair. "A Little Priest" follows their decision and is a comic number in which Todd and Lovett joke about what kind of pie all different manner of men will make (e.g., the priest is "too good at least," and the green pie must have been a grocer). The song stands outside the dramatic action of the show, and the accompanying topic is the Bowery waltz. Different from a romantic waltz meant for dancing, the Bowery waltz was quicker with vamp-like accompaniments and was often used in early Broadway show, vaudeville, and British music-hall numbers of the late nineteenth and early twentieth centuries (Bennett 1986, 19; Gottfried 1993, 138; see example 3.3).[12]

Thus, "A Little Priest" becomes a music-hall performance that serves the broader work in a number of ways, not least of which is to put the audience more at ease with the murder and cannibalism about to be put on display in act 2. The number and the Bowery waltz in particular also contribute to the characterization of Todd and Lovett, though. Authors Puccio and Stoddart (2000) have posited that the waltz in this number "brings the protagonists together" in "a kind of romance" (124–26), but

**Example 3.3.** Accompaniment figure for "A Little Priest," mm. 93–96, piano reduction.
"A Little Priest" from *Sweeney Todd*. Words and music by Stephen Sondheim.


this assumes a solely romantic reading of the topic. I argue that the Bowery waltz brings the pair together not just as a couple, but also as a comic team and is appropriate to the vulgar subject matter: music halls such as the type this song would have been appropriate for were lower- and lower-middle-class entertainments and were spaces set apart for alternatives to Victorian values and morals (Kift 1996, 2). For Todd, the number is clearly an expression of his anger toward the politically and economically powerful, and it softens the reality of his solution to his own lack of power.[13] Mrs. Lovett's participation is not quite as straightforward. She is, after all, an aspiring social climber and does not seem to harbor the same deep-seated anger toward those of a higher social station. She uses the Bowery waltz as a vehicle for satire but simultaneously wishes to raise her own station. As such, she is a more conventional music-hall participant (and member of civilized society) than Todd; she uses the topical space to make herself indispensable to him, ensuring, she hopes, her own economic, social, and romantic security. The topic, then, allows appropriate space for Lovett's and Todd's conflicting motivations.

The waltz topic is used again later by the show's villain (if we're sympathetic to Sweeney Todd), Judge Turpin, who sings a waltz rhythmically similar to "The Worst Pies in London" in his song "Johanna." Both have a characteristic emphasis on beat two, which, though it seems to contradict the usual emphasis on beat one, was fairly typical of midcentury ballroom waltzes. But the topic does not seem to group Turpin and Lovett together in their characterization. Lovett's waltzes are comic, and although they betray her social ambition and desensitization to violence, they are not wicked or depraved (her scheme with Todd notwithstanding). In

**Example 3.4**. "Johanna," piano-vocal reduction, mm. 25–30.
"Johanna (Judge's Version)" from *Sweeney Todd*. Words and music by Stephen Sondheim. 

"Johanna," the Judge sings about his beautiful young ward. He secretly watches her through a keyhole, as he rationalizes marrying her and flagellates himself to sexual climax.[14] This waltz is made musically more sinister via troping with the *ombra* topic. The music matches many of Clive McClelland's topical indicators for *ombra* (2014, 282), including restless, repetitive accompaniment, moderate tempo, flat minor key, fragmented melody, sudden structural and dynamic contrasts, and low tessitura (see example 3.4).

"Johanna," indeed, embodies the darker side of the waltz; its nineteenth-century detractors saw the dance as scandalous and dangerous in its intoxicating fixation on (or even obsession with) whirling repetitive floor patterns and the dancing partner's eyes and body (McMillan 2006, 11–12; Giordano 2007, 103–6). Turpin thus turns the waltz on its head: yes, it perhaps signals his amorous motivations, and he is certainly the character with the highest social standing in the show. But the waltz topic is also associated with polite society, with social acceptability, and with partnership. Here it is perhaps a commentary on his place in society: Although, external to the plot of the show, Turpin embodies the typical associations of the waltz, he is revealed to secretly use his position of power selfishly and maliciously. The waltz highlights the dissonance between his *actual* character and the *perception* of his character by members of his own social class. The troping of music topics combined with the dramatic situation might even be described as grotesque. As Esti Sheinberg has explained, the grotesque is born from a "contradictory semantic pair," usually the ludicrous and the horrifying in modern aesthetics (2000, 207–10). The use of the waltz to accompany Turpin's inappropriate lust might by itself be ludicrous, but its pairing with his sexualized self-violence could be further read as horrifying and thus grotesque.[15] Turpin is thus read as grotesquely duplicitous, wanting to satisfy his social position and his lust in a monstrous way.

Judge Turpin later shares a more contextually appropriate topic with his civic companion, Beadle Bamford. Both characters sing the same metrically off-kilter contredanse toward the end of the first act in the numbers "Pretty Women, Part 1" and "Ladies in Their Sensitivities." Although mostly in $\frac{5}{8}$ time, a recomposition in $\frac{2}{4}$ makes clear the contredanse characteristics (see examples 3.5a–b).

The contredanse's affect is happy with, according to Allanbrook, an air of "civilized comedy" (1983, 59). It was also considered to be democratic,

**Example 3.5a.** "Ladies in Their Sensitivities," melody, mm. 5–8.
"Ladies in Their Sensitivities" from *Sweeney Todd*. Words and music by Stephen Sondheim. 

**Example 3.5b.** Recomposition in $\frac{2}{4}$ meter reveals conventional contredanse.

egalitarian, or bourgeois (depending on the listener's political and social inclinations), because it was a group dance that was easy to learn compared to the earlier eighteenth-century *danse noble* repertoire (Clark 1995; McKee 2012, 91). Turpin's contredanse clearly indicates his happiness and self-satisfaction in announcing his impending marriage to Johanna. In the Beadle's version, he suggests to Judge Turpin that perhaps Johanna isn't excited about their marriage because the Judge has let his appearance go. The Beadle has no obvious reason to feel joyous except for perhaps being happy for the Judge's marriage announcement. Keeping in mind the light-hearted affect of the contredanse, I interpret the Beadle's use of it as a means of saying something the Judge may not want to hear—the Beadle is softening the news. The contredanse provides a natural space in which the Beadle can meet the Judge as an equal, as long as the Judge is willing to participate. The contredanse here also gives the audience insight into how the Beadle handles the Judge. One could easily assume him to be nothing but a sycophant from his characterization earlier in the show. But in this number, it's revealed that he has a strategy for manipulating the Judge. A "bourgeois joke" may have a part to play here as well—the Beadle suggests that with a shave and some cologne, Johanna will "bow to [Turpin's] every will." But the topical context might imply that the Beadle realizes this is an unlikely scenario, while the Judge, it seems, is not "in" on the joke.

## *NOSTALGIA, THE WALTZ, AND BLENDED STRATEGIES IN* THE FANTASTICKS

Similar to *The Secret Garden*, topics in *The Fantasticks* tend to generalize about characters—styles and topics separate the principal characters into two sets of groups. Instead of sorting by class, though, they are separated by age and otherness. The young lovers, Luisa and Matt, sing mostly in a modern idiom with extended chords, quartal/quintal harmonies, and surprising, chromatic chord progressions. Their music sounds somewhat Bernstein-esque and less like that of traditional musical comedies. In the following excerpt from Matt's number "I Can See It" (example 3.6), pervasive extended chords that create both additional perfect intervals and dissonant seconds are used in linear succession in a large-scale, nonfunctional motion from the tonic C major down a sixth to E major. In mm. 104–108, each bar's principal harmony is decorated through oscillation with its dominant.

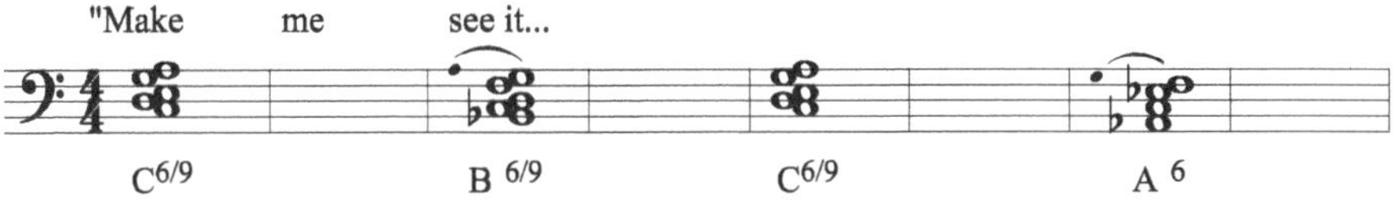

**Example 3.6.** "I Can See It," harmonic reduction, mm. 96–108.

**Example 3.7.** "Plant a Radish," end of introduction, mm. 9–10a.

Matt and Luisa's fathers, Bellomy and Hucklebee ("Bell" and "Huck"), on the other hand, predominantly use topics derived from vaudeville, operetta, and traditional musical comedy.[16] "Never Say No" uses tango and polka rhythms and almost sounds as if it would be at home in Victor Herbert's operettas. "Plant a Radish" is a clear polka, using the principal rhythmic cell 2/4 ♪ 𝄿 ♬ ♫.[17]

The latter song is in a moderate to quick duple meter with a reversed typical surface rhythm (often in polkas, the uneven figure comes on beat two; see Bennett 1986, 10). The song's introduction further signals vaudeville and the early twentieth century by leading the voice in with a popular stock progression from the time (example 3.7).

In comparison to the lovers' music, the fathers' topics mark them as older, from a different generation, and perhaps as comic. The polka, pervasive in their numbers together, was very popular in the mid and late nineteenth century, but it had mostly disappeared from American ballrooms by about 1906 (Giordano 2007, 173). Polka rhythms were used in popular songs, too, but again, this practice had mostly ended by the early twentieth century, after which polkas were primarily found in operetta (McMillin 2006, 11). Further, Bell and Huck's duets and topics—like Todd and Lovett's in "A Little Priest"—work together to define the pair as a comic vaudeville team. They are thus set apart from Matt and Luisa as older by being out of fashion and almost as rightly belonging to a different type of show. The lovers' music, on the other hand, sounds newer and fresher and is clearly meant to convey their energy and their longing for new experiences.

El Gallo, who doubles as the show's narrator, has mostly "exotic" or "othered" topics throughout the show—with the exception of "Try to Remember"—including the bossa nova ("It Depends on What You Pay"), the blues ("I Can See It"), and a Bowery waltz ("Round and Round"). El Gallo's topics mark him as an outsider, perhaps in an unpalatable way for present-day audiences, but acceptable at the time the show was written. Topics across the show thus separate the characters into broad groups. As was true in *The Secret Garden*, these topics present no immediate cross-domain oppositions—their groupings might simply be thought of as oppositional to one another.

Despite the overarching use of topical generalization in the show, some particularization is at work through the waltz topic. The waltz is used in three different numbers and therefore lends itself to comparison with their respective dramatic and musical contexts. Thereby, the topic creates oppositions across the work *and* interacts meaningfully among different domains within these numbers; thus, the topical-interpretive strategy blends generalization and particularization.

The waltz frames the show in that it is the first and last topic we hear (excluding the overture and bows/exit music). In the show's most famous song, "Try to Remember," lyrics and topic work together to set up a strong appeal to nostalgia—to a time when the listener was young and perhaps experiencing love for the first time. But the dreamy lyrics refer to a time that never really existed: when was "life so tender that no one wept except the willow?" Youth is only viewed this way through memory. The waltz does double duty here in supporting these lyrics by referring both to the past and to love. By combining both of these associations together, along with the lyrics, the waltz serves as a signal for nostalgia. Musical construction is a sonic analogue for the waltz here as well (see Zbikowski 2008). The main four-bar harmonic progression $\mathrm{I}|\mathrm{I}^{6}|\mathrm{IV}^{5-\!-6}|\mathrm{V}^{7}$ elides over and over again into its next iteration, with some phrases providing contrast via the descending fifths sequence ($\mathrm{iii}|\mathrm{vi}|\mathrm{ii}|\mathrm{V}|\mathrm{I}|\mathrm{IV}^{6-\!-5}|\flat\mathrm{VII}|\mathrm{V}$), which also tends to sound circular. The constant elision negates any sense of goal directedness and reminds the listener of the constant, dizzying spiral motion of the waltz as danced. The connection to this physical aspect of the dance creates a sense of haziness surrounding our memories, further supporting the feeling of nostalgia.

Triple meter is in fact not used again in the show at all until the second act's "Round and Round." This waltz is distinctly different from "Try to Remember" in that it has a "Bowery" or "carnival" feel to it. Pairing this more comic version of the topic with El Gallo's "courting" of Luisa is entertaining, energetic, and potentially nostalgic, but there is little association with love. The lyrics mention carousels, nonstop dancing, and romance, but nothing approaching a meaningful relationship between the two characters—for example: "We'll kick up our heels to music and dance! Until my head reels with music. Just like a lovely real romance. All we'll do is daily dance." Of course, Luisa soon learns this way of living is unsustainable. The waltz here has been, as in *Sweeney Todd*, turned on its head and made almost grotesque through the implication that the waltz compels dancers never to stop, leading to exhaustion.[18] By the end of the number, character and audience are left to question if the love and youthful nostalgia promised in the opening number are really possible outcomes for the show.

The last appearance of a waltz is in "They Were You," the final new number heard in the show (the last two numbers are reprises). In this song, the waltz returns to the style of the opening number, but now recast as a love duet. To be sure, the waltz topic is conventional for this setting, but "They Were You" is musically simple, not at all like the sweeping, operatic "You Are Love" from *Show Boat* or even like much of the rest of Matt and Luisa's music. In further contrast to the opening number, the musical analogue for the physical circular gestures is gone. Its emotional effect comes from the pairing of the pleasant, almost prototypical waltz with the lyrics: "Ev'ry secret prayer, ev'ry fancy free / Ev'rything I dared both for you and me / All my wildest dreams multiplied by two / They were you, they were you, they were you." Matt and Luisa both acknowledge that they were looking for more—excitement, adventure, and romance—but have come to realize that what each was really searching for could be found in the other. Thus, a sort of nostalgic or naïve understanding of love or of a partner is not necessarily a detriment—it can remind us of why we fell in love in the first place. "They Were You" interacts specifically with lyrics and drama at this moment in the work to support Matt and Luisa's true love through its associations with a couple's physical intimacy and amorous accord, but also with its other in-show uses, which contextualize it. The waltz as a topic, then, takes center stage in *The Fantasticks* both generically as a kind of theme for the show against which other music is measured, and also strategically in each of its iterations, suggesting specific dramatic interpretations.

## CONCLUSION

In sum, *The Secret Garden* and *Sweeney Todd* serve as poles on a continuum of topical-interpretive strategies in musical theater works. Musical topics in *Sweeney Todd* lead me to interpretations of character, subtext, and motivations, whereas in *The Secret Garden*, they act more as broad markers for characters and the metaphoric plot in which they participate. *The Fantasticks* falls somewhere on a continuum of particularization and generalization by blending the two strategies together. My sense is that when topics are identifiable, both generalization and particularization might be at work at different moments in a given show, although generalization seems to be the dominant strategy.[19] In other words, shows might, in general, be more similar to *The Fantasticks* in that they use a combination of these two strategies. Generalization, as I have tried to show, depends on topical associations that correlate closely with characters, lyrics, and dramatic situations, usually only providing oppositions to other kinds of music used in a work. But the readings I have proposed in this chapter demonstrate that generalization can provide fascinating insights into a work as a whole and into its broader sociocultural contexts.

Additionally, there are a lot of unexplored questions regarding the use of topics in musical theater: Can music commonly associated with Broadway, such as the foxtrot or soft-shoe, be used as a topic, or are these styles too standard in the repertoire to carry external sociocultural meaning? Do the "golden-era" Broadway musicals—those from about 1930 to 1960—have potential topical readings, or are these perhaps the origins of meaning for later shows? Have generalizing strategies in musicals contributed to broadly recognized cultural associations between certain kinds of music and characters or dramatic situations? How might the music of shows using rock and other popular styles signify? I am certain, though, that just as accumulated musical experiences translated into meaningful dramatic references for eighteenth-century opera audiences, so too do topics orient our understanding of the Broadway musical.

## NOTES

1. I presented a version of this paper at several conferences in the spring of 2017, and I am grateful for the input and insights from many colleagues, especially Vasili Byros, Yayoi Uno Everett, Lawrence Zbikowski, J. Daniel Jenkins, and Paul Sherrill. I have incorporated their suggestions throughout this chapter.

2. In Peircean semiotics, signs create meaning in three basic ways: icons, indexes, and symbols. Iconic signs refer to their signified through similarity or resemblance; indexical signs signify via a direct connection to the signified; and symbols signify through conventional or arbitrary association. Classic examples include portraits as icons, smoke indexing fire, and words themselves as symbols (see Chandler 2007, 36–37). Mirka's description of the topical semiotic process is somewhat different from that of Raymond Monelle (2000, 2006) because Mirka limits her examination of topics, for the purposes of her volume, to their point of musical origin. Monelle's project involved delving into the musical depiction of literary ideas and natural sounds, and so the creation of meaning is somewhat more complex. Given that topics in musical theater are generally also musical in origin, Mirka's explanation of the way topics signify serves well.

3. Laird (2011) explicitly recognizes and enumerates many different musical styles and dance types that have been used in Broadway shows, and he associates the "classic Broadway sound" with Tin Pan Alley (38). This mixing of styles also occurred in the Broadway show's immediate predecessors: vaudeville, music hall, and operetta. Indeed, in some ways, the American musical itself is an amalgamation of elements from these precursors (see, for instance, Grant 2004, 119; Preston 2008, 27–28).

4. I have elsewhere made similar claims about the role musical topics play in creating characterization in Handel's Italian-language operas (see G. Decker 2011, 2013, 2020).

5. The waltz was indeed a very common rhythmic characteristic in songs for musical theater and its immediate predecessors (see Bennett 1986, 10–22; Grant 2004, 124–26; McMillan 2006, 11–12; Laird 2011, 33–41). One may wonder if such a ubiquitous song type might be topical, as it could be perceived as part of the unmarked, typical flow of a Broadway score. While this may be the case, especially for earlier shows, I contend that its frequent use would only enhance its generalizing characteristics. Further, its potential for particularization would have increased after its period of most intense conventional social usage.

6. *Show Boat* presents numerous problems surrounding race and the show's construction, plot, and production, not the least of which is its stereotypical depiction of Black people. For a recent discussion in addition to T. Decker 2013,

see Bradley Rogers's examination of the exploitation of Black bodies in the show and the problematic ways the show tries to absolve itself of racism (2020, chapter 4). For related discussions (focusing especially on the 1936 film), see Smith 2005, 10–24, and Stanfield 2000, who takes a critical look at the problematic ways in which blackface and its subsequent abandonment are used as markers for white social progress in the show.

7. The origins of the tune, lyrics, and meaning of various sets of lyrics for "Yankee Doodle" have stirred much debate (see Lemay 1976; Murray 1999; Abelove 2008). Several sources place the origin of the tune much earlier than the 1750s, but the lyrics with which many are familiar today ("Yankee Doodle went to town . . .") were apparently first published in 1852 (Murray 1999, 207). Murray guesses, though, that these lyrics originated in some form in the eighteenth century, especially because of the reference to "macaroni" (1999, 207–8). The other set of commonly known lyrics ("Father and I went down to camp . . .") were certainly written in the mid-eighteenth century. As for "Billy Boy" ("Oh, where have you been, Billy Boy, Billy Boy . . ."), 1776 is the earliest date given for this family of lyrics in Waltz and Engle 2016 (s.v. "Billy Boy").

8. "A Fine White Horse" also uses horn fifths and some traditional musical galloping gestures as a kind of leitmotif to refer to the horse Martha describes. This kind of direct, almost pictorial musical association can be found at other points throughout the show, but since it is not the focus of this chapter, I do not delve into this issue further.

9. Dorian—along with Ionian, Mixolydian, and Aeolian—is a typical diatonic mode for English folk songs (Karpeles 1973, 32), although I would argue that any modal or obviously pentatonic melody would signal folk music for today's audiences.

10. The lament and the *stile concitato* were used in seventeenth- and eighteenth-century opera almost exclusively for noble characters, and so they continue to carry associations with an elevated register. But I think for most present-day listeners, they may also be understood more generally as compositional techniques from classical music; I conjecture that this more general association also implies an elevated register with audiences today.

11. The musical dichotomy I have posited also suggests, then, that Martha and Dickon see Mary as a catalyst for change in the Craven family—potentially part of their "secret knowledge" not available to upper-class characters.

12. For reference, commonly known Bowery waltzes include "Take Me Out to the Ball Game" and "In the Good Old Summertime," as Mark Grant has pointed out (2004, 124).

13. Music-hall songs often functioned to help the lower classes laugh at their own plight, while sometimes concurrently offering solutions to these problems (Kift 1996, 37). "A Little Priest" serves both purposes for Todd, albeit in a grotesque way (see below).

14. The scene is uncomfortable to watch and was cut from the original Broadway production ostensibly for time, but Sondheim later implied that perhaps director Harold Prince thought it too perverse for audiences (Horowitz 2003, 136–37).

15. There also is a physical opposition between the staging of Mrs. Lovett's waltz and Judge Turpin's that contributes to the grotesque reading: in "The Worst Pies in London," Lovett is usually bustling about the stage while she tries to convince Todd to try one of her pies. In "Johanna," Turpin makes the waltz more grotesque through a lack of movement—he hunches over and gets down on his knees, with most of his physical movement coming from self-flagellation. Indeed, much of the content and structure of the entire show might be described as grotesque, according to Sheinberg's definition.

16. The use of music truly at home in musical comedy or precursors to the musical does, at first glance, seem to contradict Mirka's understanding of topics as "taken out of their proper context" (2014, 2). How can the use of this music in a Broadway show be topical? My argument for a topical reading is twofold: First, many of the styles used in early musical comedies originate outside the Broadway theater (e.g., the polka or the foxtrot), so in one sense, they have already been placed into new contexts. Second, by the time *The Fantasticks* premiered in 1960, the traditional musical comedy was one subgenre on a spectrum of structural possibilities for musical theater works, and so the kinds of music used in a given show were no longer standardized.

17. Assigning novelty or otherwise stylistically incongruous songs to secondary or featured characters is a long-standing device in musical theater.

18. Sheinberg has posited that triple meter lends itself to becoming grotesque through the feeling of "whirling, uncontrollable motion" (2000, 221).

19. This kind of reading, I submit, might also be useful to those eighteenth-century operas whose topics have traditionally been understood as correlating with characters and dramatic moments exactly, providing exactly the kind of facile reading musicologists and literary theorists usually wish to ignore.

## WORKS CITED

Abelove, Henry. 2008. "Yankee Doodle Dandy." *Massachusetts Review* 49 (1/2): 13–21.

Allanbrook, Wye Jamison. 1983. *Rhythmic Gesture in Mozart: "Le Nozze di Figaro" and "Don Giovanni."* Chicago: University of Chicago Press.

Bennett, Anthony. 1986. "Music in the Halls." In *Music Hall: Performance and Style*, edited by J. S. Milton Keynes, UK: Open University Press.

Burford, Freda, and Anne Daye. "Contredanse." *Grove Music Online. Oxford Music Online.* Oxford University Press (accessed 25 May 2017).

Chandler, Daniel. 2007. *Semiotics: The Basics.* 2nd ed. London: Routledge.

Clark, Maribeth. 1995. "The Contredanse, that Musical Plague." In *Proceedings of Bor-*

*der Crossings: Dance and Boundaries in Society, Politics, Gender, Education, and Technology*, compiled by Linda H. Tomko. Society of Dance History Scholars.

Decker, Gregory J. 2011. "The Language of Baroque Opera: Topic, Structure, and Characterization in Handel's Italian-Language Operas." PhD diss., Florida State University.

Decker, Gregory J. 2013. "Pastorals, Passepieds, and Pendants: Interpreting Characterization Through Aria Pairs in Handel's *Rodelinda*." *Music Theory Online* 19 (4).

Decker, Gregory J. 2020. "Dance Music and Signification in Handel's Opera Seria." In *Singing in Signs: New Semiotic Explorations of Opera*, edited by Gregory J. Decker and Matthew Shaftel. New York: Oxford University Press.

Decker, Todd. 2013. *Show Boat: Performing Race in an American Musical*. New York: Oxford University Press.

Giordano, Ralph G. 2007. *Social Dancing in America: A History and Reference*. Vol. I. Westport, CT: Greenwood Press.

Gottfried, Martin. 1993. *Sondheim*. New York: Harry N. Abrams.

Grant, Mark N. 2004. *The Rise and Fall of the Broadway Musical*. Boston: Northeastern University Press.

Gregory, E. David. 2010. *The Late Victorian Folksong Revival: The Persistence of English Melody, 1878–1903*. Lanham, MD: Scarecrow Press.

Hatten, Robert. 1994. *Musical Meaning in Beethoven: Markedness, Correlation, and Interpretation*. Bloomington: Indiana University Press.

Horowitz, Mark Eden. 2003. *Sondheim on Music: Minor Details and Major Decisions*. Lanham, MD: Scarecrow Press.

Karpeles, Maud. 1973. *An Introduction to English Folk Song*. London: Oxford University Press.

Kift, Dagmar. [1991] 1996. *The Victorian Music Hall: Culture, Class and Conflict*. Translated by Roy Kift. Cambridge: Cambridge University Press.

Laird, Paul R. 2011. "Musical Styles and Song Conventions." In *The Oxford Handbook of the American Musical*, edited by Raymond Knapp, Mitchell Morris, and Stacy Wolf. Oxford: Oxford University Press.

Lemay, J. A. Leo. 1976. "The American Origins of 'Yankee Doodle.'" *William and Mary Quarterly* 33(3): 435–64.

McKee, Eric. 2012. *Decorum of the Minuet, Delirium of the Waltz: A Study of Dance-Music Relations in 3/4 Time*. Bloomington: Indiana University Press.

McMillin, Scott. 2006. *The Musical as Drama: A Study of the Principles and Conventions Behind Musical Shows from Kern to Sondheim*. Princeton, NJ: Princeton University Press.

Mirka, Danuta, ed. 2014. *The Oxford Handbook of Topic Theory*. New York: Oxford University Press.

Monelle, Raymond. 2000. *The Sense of Music: Semiotic Essays*. Princeton, NJ: Princeton University Press.

Monelle, Raymond. 2006. *The Musical Topic: Hunt, Military, and Pastoral.* Bloomington: Indiana University Press.

Murray, Stuart. 1999. *America's Song: The Story of "Yankee Doodle."* Bennington, VT: Images from the Past.

Preston, Katherine K. [2002] 2008. "American Musical Theatre Before the Twentieth Century." In *The Cambridge Companion to the Musical*, 2nd ed., edited by William A. Everett and Paul R. Laird. Cambridge: Cambridge University Press.

Puccio, Paul M., and Scott F. Stoddart. 2000. "'It Takes Two': A Duet on Duets in *Follies* and *Sweeney Todd.*" In *Reading Stephen Sondheim: A Collection of Critical Essays*, edited by Sandor Goodhart. New York: Garland Publishing.

Rogers, Bradley. 2020. *The Song Is You: Musical Theatre and the Politics of Bursting into Song and Dance.* Iowa City: University of Iowa Press.

Scott, Derek B. [1989] 2001. *The Singing Bourgeois: Songs of the Victorian Drawing Room and Parlour*, 2nd ed. Burlington, VT: Ashgate.

Sheinberg, Esti. 2000. *Irony, Satire, Parody, and the Grotesque in the Music of Shostakovich: A Theory of Musical Incongruities.* Aldershot, UK: Ashgate.

Smith, Susan. 2005. *The Musical: Race, Gender and Performance.* London: Wallflower Press.

Stanfield, Peter. 2000. "From the Vulgar to the Refined: American Vernacular and Blackface Minstrelsy in *Showboat.*" In *Musicals: Hollywood and Beyond*, edited by Bill Marshall and Robynn Stilwell, 147–56. Exeter: Intellect Books.

Tawa, Nicholas E. 1980. *Sweet Songs for Gentle Americans: The Parlor Song in America, 1790–1860.* Bowling Green, OH: Bowling Green University Popular Press.

Waltz, Robert, and David G. Engle. 2016. *The Traditional Ballad Index: An Annotated Bibliography of the Folk Songs of the English-Speaking World.* Fresno: California State University, Fresno. http://www.csufresno.edu/folklore/BalladSearch.html (accessed 5 June 2017).

Zbikowski, Lawrence. 2008. "Dance Topoi, Sonic Analogues, and Musical Grammar: Communicating with Music in the Eighteenth Century." In *Communication in Eighteenth Century Music*, edited by Danuta Mirka and Kofi Agawu. Cambridge: Cambridge University Press.

# 4 A Phenomenological Approach to Music Theater Rhyme

RICHARD PLOTKIN

## INTRODUCTION

The cornerstone of contemporary musical theater is the tight-knit process of book-writing, lyric-writing, and music composition. While a single author occasionally assumes all roles (e.g., Jason Robert Brown's *The Last Five Years* or Michael R. Jackson's *A Strange Loop*), more often than not two or three collaborators are involved in creating a work (Marsha Norman, for instance, wrote the book and lyrics for *The Secret Garden* with Lucy Simon's music, and Stephen Sondheim collaborated with a variety of book writers when he took charge of both music and lyrics in his later works). The fact that musical theater songs are often the result of a collaborative process runs counter to typical analytical approaches to them, which do not often account deeply enough for the enormous influence every creator and every sound has on the other parts. Instead, analysis of song often disassembles the collaborative: lyrics are analyzed as components of a larger plot (the book), and the story of the lyrics serves to feed back into the final analysis of the song, supported by additional thoughts on harmony and musical form. There is nothing inherently wrong with this approach—many impactful and insightful analyses are framed in this manner—but treating the relationship of lyrics and composition as much more intimately intertwined can lead to fruitful new insights.[1]

Lyrics are not poems—not even when the lyric was a poem in its first incarnation. They always take place in song and cannot successfully be analyzed like poetry. To meaningfully confront this problem, I propose here a method to address the *musical* aspects of the words. I draw heavily from William Caplin's work on musical form (1998) and make extensive use of his terminology regarding sentences, periods, and hybrid themes; basic ideas, contrasting ideas, and continuations; and thematic functionality and larger formal units. If Caplin's work is entirely unfamiliar to the reader, some of this material will certainly be obscured behind that terminology.[2] I also acknowledge the problematic overlap of terminology: "sentence" means one thing in the analysis of musical form and another in the identification of a grammatical unit, and there are similar problems with the terms "meter" and "form." Where it could be unclear which I'm referring to, I will use explicit (albeit cumbersome) language to reduce ambiguity.

Caplin's conception of musical form and phrase structure, which incorporates the language of functional harmony, can be seen as a means of conveying musical expectation—a dominant expects a tonic, a half-cadence projects an authentic cadence, and a presentation promises a continuation. This conception can be expanded for song. I suggest that lyrics—not *words* but *words-with-music*—are themselves musical phenomena, integrated parts of a complete *Klang*. In this chapter, I primarily consider where and how lyric *rhyme* propels *musical* expectations.

As an introduction, consider the music in example 4.1a, taken from the opening of a reprise to "Sixteen Going On Seventeen" from Rodgers and Hammerstein's *The Sound of Music* (1959). Formally, this is a typical sentence, with a basic idea (b.i.) repeated to form a presentation, and an authentic cadence at the end of the continuation.[3] The basic ideas from the presentation are rhymed—"ring it" and "sing it"—and the continuation and cadential functions are rhymed—"stay" and "away." In example 4.1b, I have altered the lyrics to implement a different pattern of rhyme: the first b.i. rhymes with the continuation—"rings" with "wings"—and the second b.i. rhymes with the end of the phrase—"play" with "away."

Example 4.1b is a nontrivial change because our expectations for the resolution of the theme are substantially altered. In 4.1a, "ring it" is rhymed when the b.i. is repeated, and once that rhyme succeeds, we have no further need for "ring it" to be rhymed. When we hear "stay" in the

Example 4.1a. "Reprise: Sixteen Going On Seventeen," *The Sound of Music* by Richard Rodgers and Oscar Hammerstein II.

Example 4.1b. Modified lyrics.

continuation, it is positioned as far from the start of the continuation as "ring it" was from the start of the presentation, it is rhymed in a similarly balanced manner, and when the continuation ends, we have no further need for "stay" to be rhymed. In 4.1b, the need for "rings" to be rhymed is not resolved until the end of the continuation function. And during this longer wait for a rhyme, we are *also* asked to begin waiting for a rhyme to "play." Consider the quantitative difference in our expectations—our *needs*—for rhyme to occur: at the middle of m. 5 in 4.1a (indicated by a star), we have no need for resolution coming from unanswered rhyme; at the star in 4.1b, we simultaneously have *two* unfulfilled needs for rhyme. Although the harmonic and form-functional components of the theme are the same, 4.1b presents an altered musical experience. In both versions, the end of the presentation is a moment of anticipation for continuation; but whereas in 4.1a the anticipatory potential is limited to form and harmony, in 4.1b the presence of two unfulfilled rhymes gives the continuation an uncomfortable kinetic surge, imbuing an intensity to the underlying harmonic and formal structure of the passage not present in 4.1a.[4]

What I want to draw from this simple example is that *rhyme creates expectations for resolution*. The way those expectations are created, and the myriad ways in which they are satisfied, denied, and often toyed with, influences not just the poetic experience of the words, but also the overall *musical* experience.[5]

There are, of course, less trivial examples, and exploring those requires a more robust technical foundation. The text that follows incrementally establishes analytical terminology and notation, and applies the newly established tooling to musical examples. The material is organized to first present common lyric-musical patterns, then terminology based on those common patterns, and then analytical examples making use of the technical foundation. The examples include applications of the theory to a fully conventional excerpt and a less-conventional excerpt, and conclude with an example that more deeply explores the implications of how expectations for lyric rhyme grow and adjust dynamically with the musical experience.

## LYRICAL RHYME

### *Proper Rhyme and Well-Crafted Song*

Well-crafted song exhibits narrative clarity, and one key aspect of narrative clarity is good prosody. In the context of a song, prosody refers to how music supports (or undermines) the natural sound of the lyrics. An example of a challenging exercise in prosody: try setting the words of the Lord's Prayer to the tune of the Beatles' "Let It Be."[6] It is a tall order to lightly modify the lyrics so that the rhythm in the words becomes naturally supported by the music, and if done incorrectly, the lyrics become unintelligible. Narrative clarity through rhyme—which itself is an aspect of prosody—is an essential component of a lyricist's skill set. A lyricist uses rhyme to help a listener parse the story of the song, and rhyme influences the larger poetic structure. Most importantly, lyricists are taught that rhyme sets powerful aural expectations for the listener.

Within the scope of music theater, well-crafted songs use proper rhymes extensively. A proper rhyme is any pair of words or phrases that share all sounds and stress patterns from a stressed vowel through to the end of a sequence of syllables. Pairs of sounds that match in this way but share an identical starting consonant (or lack of consonant) are not proper rhymes, they are *repetitions* or *identities*. A *homeoteuleton*, also called a "near rhyme" or "slant rhyme," is close to a rhyme but deficient in some manner (for instance, *time* and *mine* are in the category of homeoteuleton since they do not share the same final consonant). William Harmon's deep study on the taxonomy of rhyme says that "[proper] rhyme occurs in a range between mere repetition and mere homeoteleuton" (1987, 369). Stephen Sondheim says, "using near-rhymes is like juggling clumsily" (2010, XXVII)[7] and in no uncertain or equivocating terms calls out as lazy all songwriters who don't execute proper rhyme (2010, XXV–XXVI). That's not to say that *everything* in a song must rhyme. In the musical examples that follow, there are fabulous uses of deliberate repetition and moments that intentionally substitute non-rhymes to create a specific effect. Notwithstanding deliberate exceptions, the regular practice of proper rhyme, and the regular criticism of deficient rhyme, creates an unambiguous framework for the discussion that follows. There is no room to quibble about sort-of-rhymes; either words rhyme, or they do not. This level of certainty gives us the ability to lay a strong analytical foundation; we should treat the primacy of proper rhyme as axiomatic.[8]

### *Rhymed Words in Small Themes*

The union of formal types and rhyme types is essential to my analysis. Here, I want to familiarize the reader with some patterns common to small thematic musical units. What follows is certainly not an exhaustive list of possibilities, but an enumeration of some relatively standard rhyme progressions occurring in small and symmetric sentences, periods, and hybrid themes (see example 4.2).

Primarily two types of rhyme are common to small themes:[9] end rhymes and interior rhymes. An *end-rhymed theme* has a rhyme that is completed at the very end of a theme; in a typical thematic structure of 4-measure phrase + 4-measure phrase (4+4), the words at the end of each phrase would rhyme. The following represent standard end-rhymed themes: a period in which a four-measure antecedent rhymes with its consequent ("It All Fades Away," 4.2a) and a sentence in which a four-measure presentation rhymes with its continuation phrase ("I Get to Show You the Ocean," 4.2b). Another typical end-rhymed theme is a sentence in which the second phrase contains a rhyme between the continuation and cadential functions ("One Hand, One Heart," 4.2c). Note that 4.2c is considered end-rhymed because the rhymed word occurs at the end of the full theme; "end-rhymed" does not require a 4+4 subdivision as exemplified by 4.2a and 4.2b. Hybrid themes also follow these common patterns, such as a rhymed antecedent with a non-consequent conclusion ("Cabaret," 4.2d).

An *interior-rhymed theme* has a rhyme that is completed prior to the end of the theme. This often involves a 2+2 subdivision of a phrase with introductory or medial placement. Sometimes, an interior rhyme is within the melodic-motivic repetition of a presentation ("My Favorite Things," 4.2e); at other times, there is a rhyme between the two ideas of the antecedent ("Some Other Time," 4.2f). Themes that *only* have an interior rhyme often use the word at the end of the theme for an inter-theme rhyme or repetition; in the case of "Some Other Time," the song's title is repeated at the end of each stanza. Of the examples given, 4.2a and 4.2e are interior-rhymed *and* end-rhymed, though they represent distinct combinations of formal types and rhyme types. Example 4.2e is a sentence with a rhymed presentation, followed by a separately rhymed continuation (like 4.2c).

Finally, "Something's Coming" (4.2g) is an exceptional instance of two interior rhymes, along with a different, and repeated, end rhyme. The presentation is rhymed (like "My Favorite Things") and is followed by an interpolation that enlarges the first half of the theme by four measures, ending on "shows." The fragments of the continuation are also rhymed with each other, where the second fragment is a two-measure expansion that creates space for the second interior rhyme. The end of the continuation rhymes "rose" with the interpolation that closes the presentation phrase, mimicking the broad structure of many other end-rhymed themes (4.2a, 4.2b, and 4.2d). Yet this rhyme does not feel completed until "rose" is followed by "knows." The incomplete feeling of "rose" is brought about by a metric hemiola that compresses the continuation and places the rhyme five beats out of alignment with the placement of "shows." Later in this chapter, I give other examples of how such misalignments affect our sense of musical resolution, even when the misalignment is largely one of rhyme.

In each of the excerpts, essential formal components are bracketed and labeled. The rhyme most relevant to the style being showcased is wrapped in a dashed box, and other rhymes are underlined. If there are multiple basic ideas (b.i.) or contrasting ideas (c.i.) in a passage, a subscript numeral is added to the description of the rhyme for clarity; the subscript numerals do not imply a separate idea or functional role.

**Example 4.2a.** Period with rhymed antecedent/consequent (c.i.$_1$/c.i.$_2$): "It All Fades Away," *The Bridges of Madison County*, music and lyrics by Jason Robert Brown.

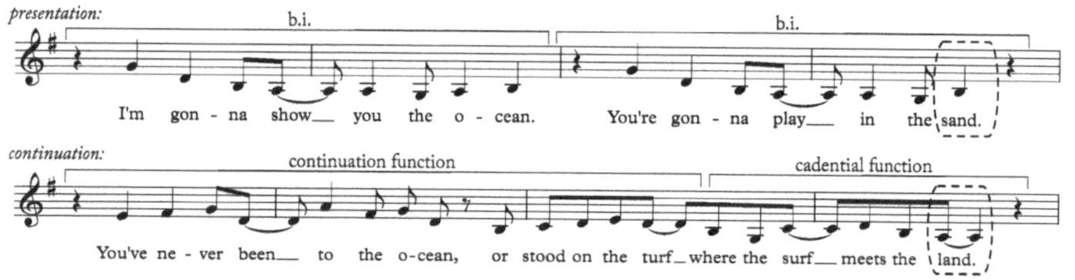


**Example 4.2b.** Sentence with rhymed presentation/continuation phrase (b.i.$_2$/cadential): "I Get to Show You the Ocean," by Georgia Stitt.

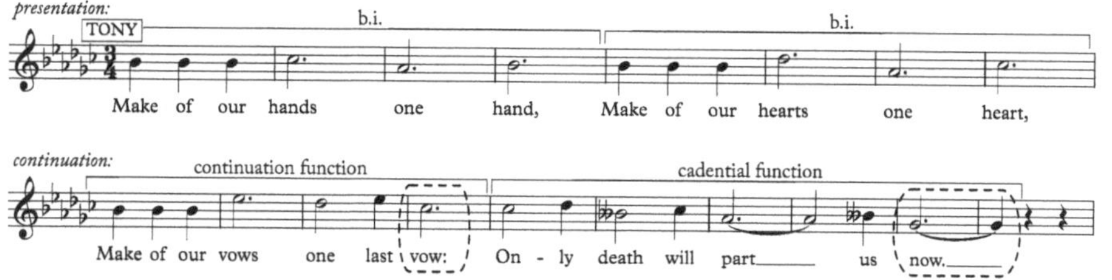


**Example 4.2c.** Sentence with rhymed continuation/cadential: "One Hand, One Heart," *West Side Story*, music by Leonard Bernstein and lyrics by Stephen Sondheim.

**Example 4.2d.** Hybrid theme (antecedent + continuation): "Cabaret," *Cabaret*, music by John Kander and lyrics by Fred Ebb.

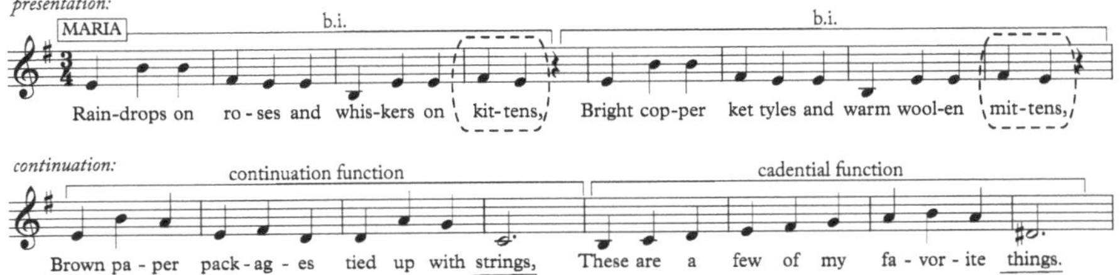


**Example 4.2e.** Sentence: "My Favorite Things," *The Sound of Music*, music by Richard Rodgers and lyrics by Oscar Hammerstein II.

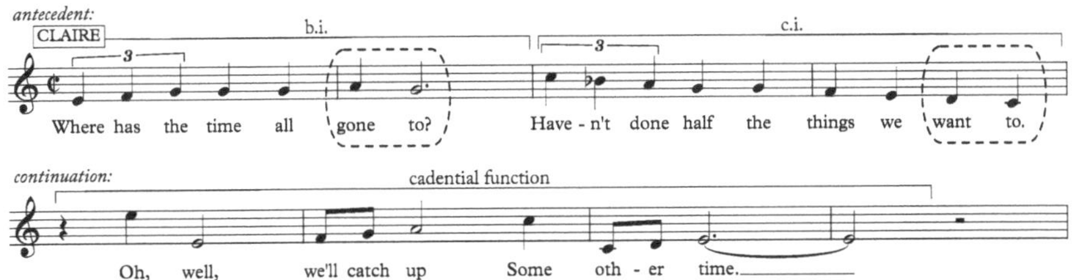


**Example 4.2f.** Caption: Hybrid theme (antecedent + cadential): "Some Other Time," *On the Town*, music by Leonard Bernstein and lyrics by Betty Comden and Adolph Green.

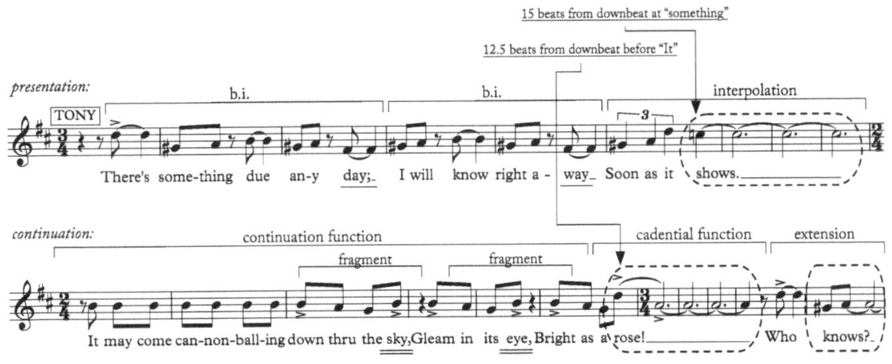


**Example 4.2g.** Deviant, symmetrical theme (sentence with interpolation, expanded continuation): "Something's Coming," *West Side Story*, music by Leonard Bernstein and lyrics by Stephen Sondheim.

## *A Hypothesis on Preferences for Rhyme*

Example 4.3 shows a compound period with "away" at the end of the antecedent rhymed by "say" at the end of the consequent. Were we to simply mark the moment that "say" appears as the moment that "away" is rhymed, we would be neglecting something more powerful that happened during this musical phrase: "away" *promised* that it would be rhymed, and "say" convincingly provided a manner of closure—linguistic and musical—to that promise. Why do we expect that "away" *should* rhyme, and why do we portend its resolution to the end of the subsequent phrase?

I think the answer lies in our learned preferences for a musical style. I propose, then, a subjective set of rules about our preferences (Preference Rules, or "PRs"), informed by my experience with musical theater songs, that describe different situations in which we either expect or prefer to hear rhyme.[10] I name each rule for the convenience and efficiency of referring back to it later. These preference rules will probably be most meaningful in the realm of musical theater, or in similar music in which there exists an expectation for proper rhyme. They are as follows:

- PR-GRAM: **Prefer rhymes at the terminus of a GRAMmatical unit.** A rhymed word is expected to occur at the end of a grammatical unit (the end of a sentence, the end of a subclause, the end of a prepositional phrase, etc.). This applies to both the word to be rhymed and the word that rhymes the former. Both Harmon (1987) and Tsur (1996) take

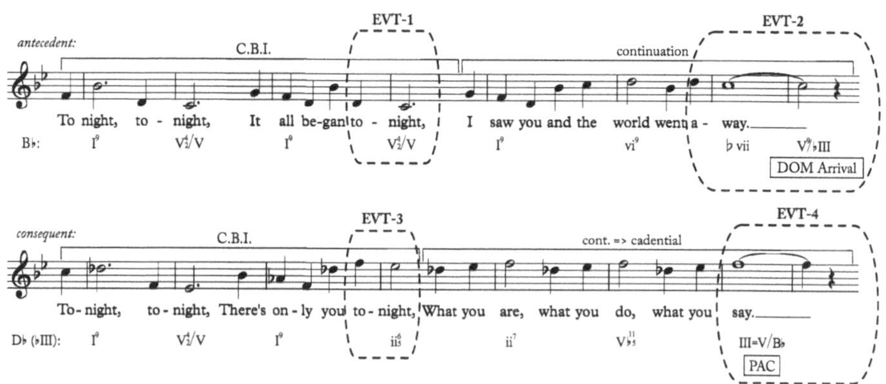


**Example 4.3.** Compound period: "Balcony Song," *West Side Story*, music by Leonard Bernstein and lyrics by Stephen Sondheim. *Note: In this example, EVT-n designates events that will be discussed further into the chapter.*

rhyme at an ending as part of its essential nature, and both argue for an even more intense accounting of rhyme based on parts of speech; in lyrics, although not all rhymes are at the end of grammatical units, we should still treat this as a strong preference.

- PR-FEET: **Prefer rhymes after similar counts of poetic FEET.** All things being equal, a rhymed word is likely to occur with the same (poetic-)metric placement as the word being rhymed. Consider Shakespearean rhymed verse, usually found as rhymed couplets in iambic pentameter: there are exactly five feet in each line, and the rhymed words each occupy the last of those feet. A technique such as substitution (exchanging one or more feet for different feet, often in different quantity) will influence our acceptance of rhymes that violate this rule, and the temporal (PR-DUR) and accentual (PR-GROUP) manifestations of *musical* rhythm and accent will also exert an influence on our acceptance of nonmatching counts of stresses.
- PR-GROUP: **Prefer rhymes at the terminus of a rhythmic GROUP.** This is the musical counterpart to PR-GRAM. Rhythmic groups can be of many sizes; a range from four notes (like the fragments in "Something's Coming" [4.2g]) up to the size of a phrase is a reasonable expectation.
- PR-DUR: **Prefer rhymes after similar DURations.** This is the musical counterpart to PR-FEET. Often there are similar numbers of feet over a similar number of measures, but sometimes very different quantities of feet are worked out over the same number of measures, where the change is usually tied to the emotion of the character or the meaning of the song.
- PR-MEL: **Prefer rhymes in similar MELodic-motivic material.** All things being equal, rhyming arrival often occurs within a *similar* melodic-motivic setting. PR-GROUP is *implicit* in this rule; we expect the rhyme to be at the end of this melodic-motivic material. The strongest example would be a rhymed pair of basic ideas in a presentation, and the next best example would be a rhymed pair of contrasting ideas in a period, where the music of the latter c.i. is mostly like the first c.i. A counterexample would be when a rhyme pairs a c.i. with a b.i. in a period, which usually confirms PR-FEET but denies PR-MEL.
- PR-FORM: **Prefer rhymes in similar FORM-functional material.** All things being equal, rhyming often occurs within similar form-functional material. PR-GROUP is *implicit* in this rule; we expect the

rhyme to be at the end of this form-functional material. In concert with PR-MEL, the strongest example would be a rhymed pair of basic ideas in a presentation, and the next best example would be a rhymed pair of contrasting ideas in a period. Unlike PR-MEL, PR-FORM does not need the music to be similar in a rhymed pair of contrasting ideas. Finally, as far as this particular PR is concerned, it's useful to consider continuation function and cadential function situated in a fairly equal formal manner, and similarly to consider the phrases of a thematic unit as roughly equivalent. In other words, we would find this preference satisfied by rhyming the end of two measures of continuation function with the end of the subsequent two measures of cadential function, and we would find this preference satisfied by rhyming the end of a presentation and the end of the subsequent continuation.

- PR-SIM: **Prefer SIMilar rhyme patterns in similar musical settings of stanzas.** Internal to a song, we expect similar music to achieve rhyme in similar ways. If a song has an AABA refrain, and the first A section is an end-rhymed period, then the expectation is that the second and third instances of A will also be end-rhymed periods.

## *A PHENOMENOLOGY OF RHYME*

Having now established some language for expressing hypothetical rhyming preferences, I can turn to an exploration of our *experience* of those preferences being satisfied or denied. Indeed, to better comprehend lyrical rhyme, we must understand the architecture of the system in which it is experienced. The core experience of rhyme is tripartite: (1) initially, you hear a word (or combination of words) that should be rhymed; (2) music and lyrics pass, leading you to a moment in which you expect the appearance of a rhyme to the initiating word; (3) finally, you (probably) hear a rhyme to the initial word. It's usually straightforward to identify the instant in which a word *has been* rhymed, but it is less straightforward to determine why a word marks a point of initiation for rhyme-expectation. Examining musical excerpts using the preference rules helps to elucidate this murkier undertaking.

### *Applying Preference Rules*

In the examples that follow, phenomenology is used to express and examine a listener's experience of a song over time. The presentation of phenomenological experience follows the approach presented in Lewin 1986. "Events" are simply things that happen. "Context," in this set of examples, is the window of musical measures through which the event should be viewed—and in the majority of cases below, the context simply expands linearly over time, tracking the manner in which a listener would experience the music (first mm. 1–4, then mm. 1–8, which adds mm. 5–8 to the prior context of mm. 1–4). "Perceptions" are the possible experiences of an event in a given context, and perceptions can be statements of expectation, reorientation, and denial (among other possibilities). "Percepts" are the collections of perceptions for a given event and context.

Returning now to the "Balcony Song" (example 4.3), the theme is a compound period. A harmonic analysis shows the antecedent moving to the dominant of ♭III, and the consequent concluding with a PAC on *its* III, which brings the entire phrase to a conclusion on V of the home key of B♭. The grammatical endings occur at each of the moments called out by a dashed enclosure and are sequentially labeled with **EVT-n**. Each of these moments may create or resolve an opportunity for rhyme (based on PR-GRAM) whether or not that opportunity is fulfilled. In the phenomenological chart, table 4.1, I have captured a concrete set of percepts based on the preference rules from above. Since the events are identified and labeled in example 4.3, I have not included an additional column for musical details. Absent from the chart are instances of PR-GROUP and PR-SIM—the former because it is, in this excerpt, implicit in PR-MEL and PR-FORM, and the latter because this is the start of the refrain, so there is no similar setting to which this stanza could be reasonably compared.

The first percept, **p1**, says that we expect "tonight" to be rhymed at the end of the next grammatical unit, after a similar number of poetic feet and beats, and after similar melodic-motivic and form-functional material. These expectations point to the possibility of an interior-rhymed theme (like examples 4.2e–4.2g), where 4.2e is an example that satisfies all of these at the end of its presentation. In fact, if the last two words of this antecedent were changed such that the lyric read, "Tonight, tonight, It all began <u>tonight</u>, I saw you and the world *was* <u>*alight*</u>," **p1a**, **p1b**, and **p1c** would be satisfied at EVT-2.

Table 4.1. Phenomenological chart based on the above preference rules

| Percept | Event | Context | Perceptions |
|---|---|---|---|
| **p1** | EVT-1 | mm. 1–4 | **p1a**: "tonight" will rhyme the next grammatical unit [PR-GRAM]<br>**p1b**: "tonight" will be rhymed at the end of approximately 5 more poetic feet [PR-FEET]<br>**p1c**: "tonight" will be rhymed at the end of approximately 16 more beats [PR-DUR]<br>**p1d**: "tonight" will be rhymed at the end of a similar melodic-motivic unit [PR-MEL]<br>**p1e**: "tonight" will be rhymed at the end of a similar form-functional unit [PR-FORM] |
| **p2** | EVT-2 | mm. 1–8 | (**p1a** modification, reoriented to the next grammatical ending)<br>(**p1b** modification, reoriented to 5 feet from the start of the second half)<br>(**p1c** modification, reoriented to 16 beats from the start of the second half)<br>(**p1d**, NOT denied, waiting for possible match)<br>(**p1e**, NOT denied, waiting for possible match)<br>**p2a**: "away" will rhyme the next grammatical unit [PR-GRAM]<br>**p2b**: "away" will be rhymed after approximately 10 more poetic feet [PR-FEET]<br>**p2c**: "away" will be rhymed at the end of approximately 32 more beats [PR-DUR]<br>**p2d**: "away" will be rhymed at the end of a similar melodic-motivic unit [PR-MEL]<br>**p2e**: "away" will be rhymed at the end of a similar form-functional unit [PR-FORM] |
| **p3** | EVT-3 | mm. 1–12 | (**p1a**, strong denial; the next grammatical unit is already designated to **p2a**)<br>(**p1b**, denial; same word forms an identity, not a rhyme)<br>(**p1c**, denial)<br>(**p1d**, denial)<br>(**p1e**, denial)<br>(**p2a** modification, reoriented to the next grammatical ending) |
| **p4** | EVT-4 | mm. 1–16 | (**p2a**, confirmation)<br>(**p2b**, confirmation, 10/11 feet)<br>(**p2c**, confirmation)<br>(**p2d**, denial; not the same melodic-motivic material)<br>(**p2e**, confirmation) |

The percepts **p1d** and **p1e** say that we expect "tonight" might be rhymed at the end of a matching melodic-motivic and/or form-functional unit. These are expectations that are unique to the musical context of a lyric, and it's worthwhile discussing how such expectations might be formed. At EVT-1, we have just experienced the compound basic idea (c.b.i.) of a compound antecedent, and even if we don't yet know that it's a compound antecedent—indeed, even if the subsequent phrase is not a consequent—within this small four-measure moment we can be certain that we've heard something *motivic* and something the *characteristic length* of a musical idea. With that hearing, our formal experience of this moment implies both a phrase that has not yet ended and a phrase part that has the possibility of being repeated. These cues lend themselves to an expectation that there could be a matching unit that is similarly situated as the first half of a phrase; those cues turn our preferences PR-MEL and PR-FORM into the expectations of **p1d** and **p1e**.

By the mere fact that it does not rhyme EVT-1, EVT-2 fails to satisfy the expectations set forth in **p1a**, **p1b**, and **p1c**. The first c.b.i. is in a special position, such that we might be willing to see **p1a**, **p1b**, and/or **p1c** satisfied with the *next* beginning; with this possibility, the three percepts are reoriented toward the possibility of being confirmed at EVT-3. As far as **p1d** and **p1e** are concerned, we heard neither a matching melodic unit nor a matching formal unit, so those expectations remain active until such a match is no longer a possibility. Since it does not rhyme EVT-1, EVT-2 also generates a new set of expectations for "away," based on its own position in the antecedent: **p2b** will wait ten more feet, and **p2c** thirty-two more beats, before a match is likely.

To validate that the time span in which we consider PR-FEET and PR-DUR for EVT-2 is longer than those spans for EVT-1, I've created the following, excessively odd variation of the lyric, in which a rhyme for "away" occurs at the end of the consequent's c.b.i., and a rhyme for "tonight" occurs at the end of the consequent's close:

> Tonight, tonight, It all began <u>**tonight**</u>, I saw you and the world went <u>away</u>,
> Tonight, tonight, *is better than the <u>day</u>*, What you are, what you do, *is so **bright***

This lyric sounds strange not because there are words that don't rhyme, but because there are words that don't rhyme *in the right places*. Since we are ruining the lyric (or perhaps I should say that we are respecting the original lyric by showing how it could have been wrong), we might try this one as well, and note that it seems less bad than the one above:

> Tonight, tonight, It all began tonight, I saw you and the world went away,
> Tonight, tonight, *I hope that you will* stay, What you are, what you do, what you say

The latter lyric, rhyming "away," "stay," and "say," is *not* less awful at "stay" (where the prior lyric landed "day"). Instead, it's made slightly less bad because "stay" projects another four-measure expectation to the end of the consequent, and in this latter lyric, *that* expectation is satisfied with "say."

The third percept of table 4.1 is interesting in that its denial of all aspects of **p1** is due not only to the lack of a proper rhyme, but also to the lack of further anticipated places where any of the expectations in **p1** might readily be satisfied. If the music turns out to be structured normatively (as this music does), then the expectations for rhyme from EVT-2 already occupy the space any reorientation of **p1** might attempt to shift toward. EVT-4 confirms the majority of expectations expressed in **p2**.

### *The Progression of Expectation*

The "Balcony Song" of example 4.3 is a normative musical theater setting, and I would anticipate similar norm-conforming music, such as example 4.2a, to exhibit quite similar phenomenological patterns. The next example looks at what might happen in music that is *nearly* normative.

In the opening of Olaf's "In Summer" lyric from *Frozen* (example 4.4a), there is a trio of monosyllabic rhymes ("buzz," "fuzz," and "does") within the formal structure of a musical sentence. Both "buzz" and "fuzz" occur at the end of grammatical units, and at the end of each of the sentence's basic ideas, such that if we agree that an expectation for rhyme is established at "buzz," "fuzz" would successfully resolve that expectation. On the other hand, "does" presents some analytical problems: it occurs mid-clause rather than at the end of a grammatical unit. And it does not occur at the end of a musical unit: continuation and cadential functions are fused in an expanded cadential progression, and the only moment of musical closure is on "summer" at the end of the phrase. The poetic-metrical placement of "does" is identical to the placement of "fuzz," occurring on the stress of

**Example 4.4.** "In Summer," *Frozen*, by Kristen Anderson-Lopez and Robert Lopez. *Note: R=½N, meaning that, for the purposes of analyzing form, ½ of a notated measure in this example is the equivalent of a full measure in normative examples.*

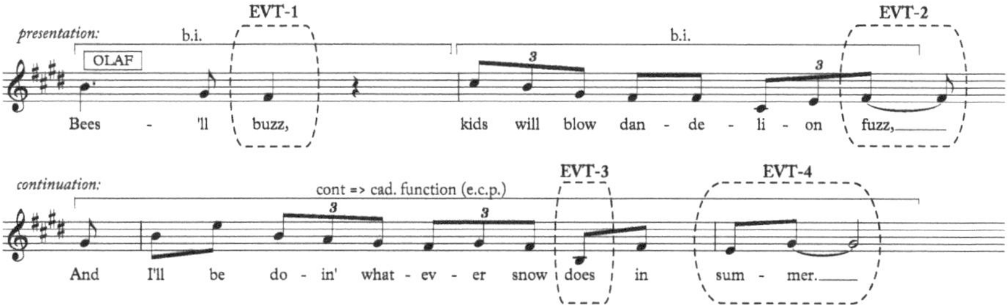


**Example 4.4a.** Trio of monosyllabic rhymes within the musical sentence.

**Example 4.4b.** Quartet of rhymes.

**Example 4.4c.** Same music as 4.4b, but with a trio of rhymes.

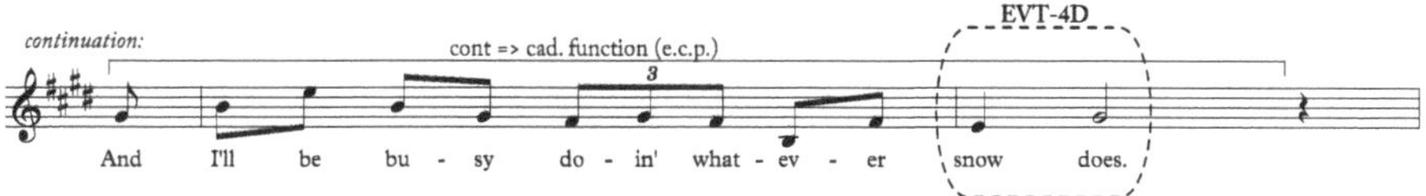


**Example 4.4d.** Shifts the rhyme to the end of the thematic unit.

the fourth foot, but the music does not provide enough feet after "does" for an additional rhyme. Perhaps most problematic when evaluating "does" is that the expectations of a rhyme for "buzz" are already resolved. What possible expectations are satisfied or created by "does" when all existing expectations have seemingly been dealt with?

To understand the possibilities at the moment of "does," Table 4.2 offers a phenomenological assessment. To get around the thorny issue of expressing expectation based on what *actually* happens in the music, I've also written a few alternates to the latter half of this thematic unit. Example 4.4b creates a quartet of rhymes, rhyming "because" with "does," and ending on a half cadence. Example 4.4c adopts the music of 4b, but has only a trio of rhymes (like the actual song). Example 4.4d shifts the rhyme to the end of the thematic unit.

Let's start by assuming EVT-3 (in examples 4.4a, 4.4b, and 4.4c) creates some set of expectations for future rhyme (**p3**). Perhaps this is not how we would normally process the music of 4.4a, yet $\mathbf{p4_B}$ at EVT-4b *confirms* all the expectations that were posited by **p3**. If these expectations can be confirmed, then they *must* exist for 4.4a and 4.4c, even if such expectations are ultimately denied in those examples.

Once we've established the possibility of these perceptions, we can take a more analytical approach to comparing 4a and 4c, both of which deny **p3** at EVT-4 and EVT-4C, respectively. Of course, the actual music (4a) is thoroughly acceptable, and the latter is intentionally and abominably bad (4c). Curiously, the distinguishing characteristic between these two excerpts is not the lack of rhyme, but the lyrical and musical content *leading to* the non-rhyme. This indicates that the expectations of **p3** are not strongly set at the end of m. 3, but instead progressively increase in intensity from m. 3 to the final moments of m. 4. In 4.4b and 4.4c, *as the music in m. 4 unfolds*:

- PR-MEL is intensified because we are in the process of hearing similar melodic-motivic material;
- PR-FEET is intensified because we are hearing more poetic feet . . . bringing us ever closer to our expected tally of four feet;
- PR-DUR is intensified as we get closer to our tally of four more beats; and
- PR-GRAM is intensified as we wait in greater suspense for the grammatical closure promised at the start of m.3.

The unrhymed end of 4.4c, as compared to 4.4a, cannot distinguish itself as a stronger denial of the rhyme itself—either there is rhyme, or there is not. The distinction is that 4.4c is a denial of that rhyme from much farther along on the path toward a rhyme, where the deprivation of rhyme is then felt much more deeply.

One last point to consider is how 4.4a succeeds in satisfying us with its rhyme. Notably absent from 4.4a is a rhyme at a moment of grammatical or musical closure, a miss on PR-GRAM and PR-GROUP. Those are rather exceptional misses—*every* excerpt from example 4.2 satisfies these preferences. Example 4.4d alters the music to satisfy these preferences, but in doing so fails to satisfy PR-MEL, which seems to miss a strong melodic implication for the rhyme. So 4a satisfies PR-MEL, and then *quickly* closes down the musical unit:

- There is a single poetic foot after "does."
- There is a trivial beat-and-a-half to the final syllable.
- There is quick grammatical closure.
- There is quick cadential closure to the expanded cadential progression (e.c.p.).

This quick closure is essential to the success of the passage, because it shunts the progression of expectations that would otherwise emerge, as in 4c; simultaneously, the rhyme's lack of alignment with grammatical and musical closure prevents it from taking part in the closure of the theme.

### *Expectations Over Time*

The prior example described a phenomenon in which the *intensity* of a preference or expectation for rhyme can increase over time, where the change in intensity alters the musical experience. The most notable difference between example 4.4a (the real music, of superb craft) and example 4.4c (an abomination) was the duration from the mid-continuation rhyme to the end of the phrase. This final example is a detailed study on the subject of changing intensity, and it presents a full assessment of what preferences-over-time might look like for *every possible rhyme* in the music of "I Get to Show You the Ocean" (example 4.2b).

Example 4.5 illustrates each grammatical ending of example 4.2b connected to the next, no matter how feasible or unreasonable. For each connection, six of the preference rules (omitting PR-SIM) are evaluated until the moment at which all six preferences fail to be satisfied (indicated by an "X"), or until a proper rhyme occurs (which only takes place in **5f**). Each dash in the chart represents one of the thirty-two beats in the excerpt. Look first at the six-beat space from "ocean" to "sand." This is a period with a note-for-note repetition of the b.i.; and until the moment that the rhyme

Table 4.2. Phenomenological chart of "In Summer"

| Percept | Event | Context | Perceptions |
|---|---|---|---|
| p1 | EVT-1"*buzz*" | mm. 1 | **p1a**: "buzz" will be rhymed at the end of the next grammatical unit [PR-GRAM]<br>**p1b**: "buzz" will be rhymed at the end of approximately 2 more poetic feet [PR-FEET]<br>**p1c**: "buzz" will be rhymed at the end of approximately 4 more beats [PR-DUR]<br>**p1d**: "buzz" will be rhymed at the end of a similar melodic-motivic unit [PR-MEL]<br>**p1e**: "buzz" will be rhymed at the end of a similar form-functional unit [PR-FORM] |
| p2 | EVT-2"*fuzz*" | mm. 1–2 | (**p1a**, confirmation)<br>(**p1b**, denial, 4 feet, not 2)<br>(**p1c**, confirmation)<br>(**p1d**, weak confirmation; altered but similar melody)<br>(**p1d**, confirmation)<br>**p2a**: "fuzz" could be rhymed at the end of the next grammatical unit [PR-GRAM]<br>**p2b**: "fuzz" could be rhymed after approximately 4 more poetic feet [PR-FEET]<br>**p2c**: "fuzz" could be rhymed at the end of approximately 4 more beats [PR-DUR]<br>**p2d**: "fuzz" could be rhymed at the end of a similar melodic-motivic unit [PR-MEL]<br>**p2e**: "fuzz" could be rhymed after approximately 6 more poetic feet, taken at the phrase level [PR-FEET]<br>**p2f**: "fuzz" could be rhymed at the end of approximately 8 more beats, taken at the phrase level [PR-DUR]<br>[I've chosen to account for projections of both equally sized 1-measure units (**p2c** and **p2d**) and equally sized 2-measure units (**p2e** and **p2f**). This is a less commonly fulfilled expectation, though multiple examples certainly exist ("Surrey with the Fringe on Top" from *Oklahoma!* and "Wouldn't It Be Loverly?" from *My Fair Lady* come to mind). It is most typical, I think, when the music moves relatively quickly (cut time or R=2N) and when the continuation of a sentence begins with the melodic-motivic material of the basic idea. These examples all happen to be three-item lists + reveal, defined as type *STL1b* in Callahan 2013.] |

| | | | |
|---|---|---|---|
| p3 | EVT-3"*does*" (a)"*because*" (b, c)[4d is not included here] | mm. 1–3 | (**p2a**, denial)<br>(**p2b**, confirmation)<br>(**p2c**, confirmation)<br>(**p2d**, confirmation)<br>(**p2e**, unlikely)<br>(**p2f**, unlikely)<br>**p3a**: "does"/"because" will be rhymed at the end of *this* grammatical unit [PR-GRAM]<br>**p3b**: "does"/"because" will be rhymed at the end of approximately 4 more poetic feet [PR-FEET]<br>**p3c**: "does"/"because" will be rhymed at the end of approximately 4 more beats [PR-DUR]<br>**p3d**: "does"/"because" will be rhymed at the end of a similar melodic-motivic unit [PR-MEL]<br>[No expectation of PR-FORM exists because there's no *normative* possibility of a second continuation. If an evaded cadence were to lead to a restatement of the continuation, we might retroactively attain this possibility.] |
| $p4_A$ | EVT-4"*summer*" (a) | mm. 1–4 | "summer" does not rhyme with "does"<br>(**p3a**, denial)<br>(**p3b**, denial)<br>(**p3c**, denial)<br>(**p3d**, denial) |
| $p4_B$ | EVT-4B"*does*" (b) | mm. 1–4 | "does" rhymes with "because"<br>(**p3a**, confirmation)<br>(**p3b**, confirmation)<br>(**p3c**, confirmation)<br>(**p3d**, confirmation) |
| $p4_C$ | EVT-4C"*enjoy it*" (c) | mm. 1–4 | "enjoy it" does not rhyme with "because"<br>(**p3a**, denial)<br>(**p3b**, denial)<br>(**p3c**, denial)<br>(**p3d**, denial) |
| $p4_D$ | EVT-4D | mm. 1–4 | "does" rhymes with "fuzz"<br>(**p2a**, confirmation)<br>(**p2b**, denial)<br>(**p2c**, denial)<br>(**p2d**, denial)<br>(**p2e**, confirmation)<br>(**p2f**, confirmation) |

doesn't land, everything in the music indicates that a rhyme *could* be made. Were "sand" to be replaced with a rhyme for "ocean," like "devotion," the rhyme would satisfy a great deal of progressively built-up preference for that rhyme. In the instant that such a rhyme does *not* arrive, at beat 15, **5b** begins building a new expectation toward a rhyme for "ocean." Unlike the previous expectations, notice here that PR-MEL of **5b** is cut off at the third beat of the fifth measure, because at this moment in time we are certain that this is no longer a melody that fits into our concept of sameness with the b.i. Similarly, as soon as the fifth measure starts, we receive harmonic confirmation that this is not a loosely sentential unit with three b.i.'s, and therefore is not a matching formal unit. The crescendo-like blocks above the staff are graphical representations of the number of beats supporting the preferences indicated: "sand" and "land" rhyme and thus satisfy preferences after a cumulative tally of sixty-seven beats (divided over sixteen beats and six preference possibilities).

Despite the numeric values provided in example 4.5, I only intend to indicate a rough heuristic, and not any sort of formal mathematical framework. Example 4.5 illustrates a method for creating a specific, nuanced reading of the different preferences as they are confirmed or denied over time, as it will sometimes be analytically useful, in other excerpts, to capture *when* in the music different preferences falter.[11] The numeric values mean little on their own, but offer us some insight when compared: "land" is a satisfying moment when it rhymes with "sand" (**5f**), and "ocean" not being rhymed at that moment is neither dissatisfying nor confusing (**5c**), because there is substantially more material suggesting that "land" will rhyme.

Example 4.6 distills and compresses the possibilities presented in example 4.5. Lines are shown underneath the music to indicate the creation of an expectation. The expectation satisfied by proper rhyme, from "sand" to "land," is indicated with a line leading to a boxed *PR*. *Connection A*, from "ocean" to "ocean," invokes two expectations. When "sand" appears at the end of the presentation, the first expectation is reoriented toward a new expectation for a rhyme at the end of the continuation func tion. This line concludes with a boxed *ID*—indicating an identity (word repetition, not a rhyme) that closes down the expectation. In the case of *Connection A*, closure is denied through repetition, and in the case of *Connection B*, closure is satisfied by proper rhyme.

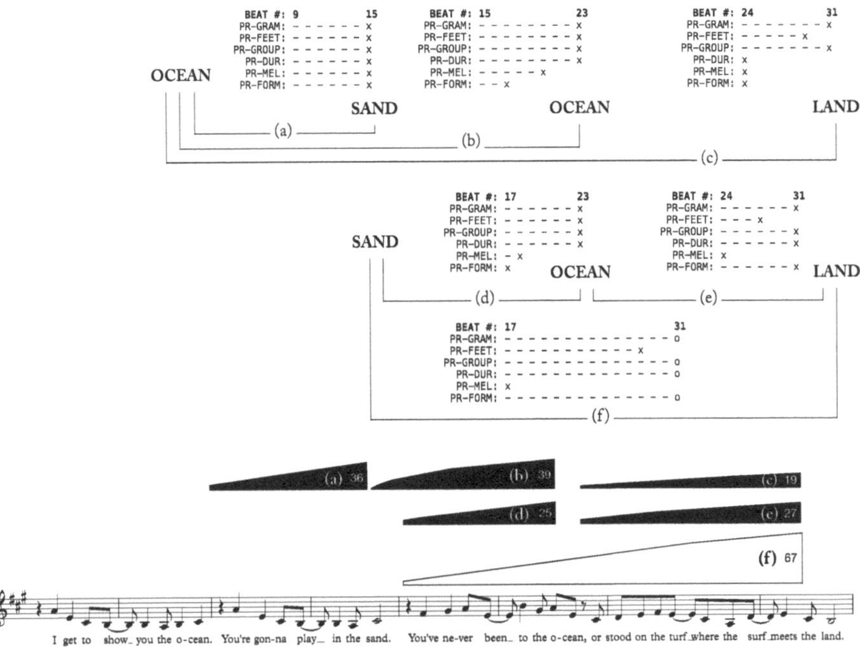


**Example 4.5.** Illustration of each grammatical ending of example 4.2b connected to the next.

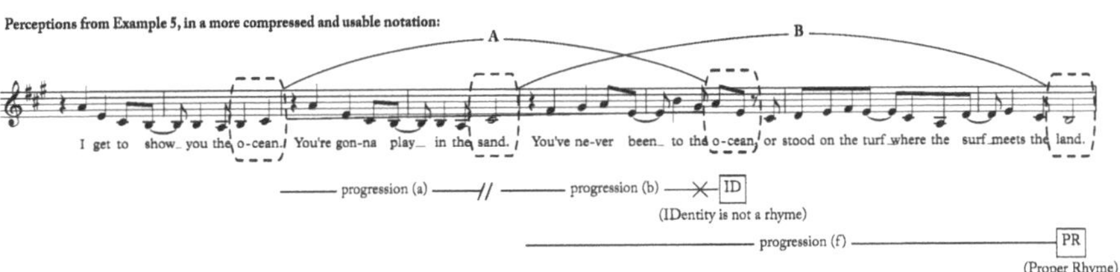


**Example 4.6.** Distillation and compression of the possibilities presented in example 4.5.

## *CONCLUSION*

My own collaborative discussions involve a give and take between composer and lyricist as we try to achieve the sound and structure that the lyricist desires in a musically convincing way. Landing jokes comes to mind as a particularly challenging feat—timing is *everything*. The mechanics of musical form laden the comedic poet with a beat and a harmonic rhythm.

If you use a too-quirky chord to punctuate a joke, you kill the joke. If you let a rhyme land in the wrong spot, you kill the joke. If the words don't come out at a natural rate of speech, you kill the joke. There is never a separation of words from the music.

The hypothesis presented at the outset of this chapter is that musical theater song lyrics can be analyzed as part of the music to which they are set—that lyrics are an integrated, inseparable part of the music. Expectations, and their satisfaction or denial, are intrinsic to music, to lyric, and to our comprehension of both as they come at us together. Treating lyrics in a phenomenological manner that can be simultaneously applied to, or looked at alongside, a musical analysis, can allow us to unpack that beautiful marriage of vocal and non-vocal elements that make songs overflow with humanity.

## NOTES

1. Stephen Rodgers has taken a delightful approach to poetic setting and formal design in "Sentences with Words" (2014). Though the approach I take here is distinct from his, I believe these are compatible studies. One could, for instance, use the approach that follows to give additional context to Rodgers's already musically sensitive analysis of *Die schöne Müllerin*.

2. For the unfamiliar reader, I highly recommend the first few chapters of Caplin's *Classical Form* (1998) or his even more accessible textbook, *Analyzing Classical Form* (2013).

3. The terminology around "continuation" in sentences can be a bit confusing. The "continuation" is the entire latter half of the sentence. This latter half incorporates both "continuation function" and "cadential function." In this study, I consistently refer to the phrase as "continuation," and explicitly refer to the function as "continuation function."

4. The excess potential in 4.1b is also at odds with the musical sentiment. This results in decreased "emotional prosody," indicating a misalignment of the nature of the words with the nature of the music.

5. This work is deeply indebted to the guidance and training I've been fortunate to receive from Jason Robert Brown, Marsha Norman, Elise Dewsberry, Scott Guy, John Sparks, Frederick Freyer, Patrick Cook, Adam Mathias, and Sara Wordsworth.

6. This suggestion is similar to challenges presented to me by Scott Guy in New Musicals Inc.'s *Lyric Lab*.

7. In full, Sondheim says "Using near rhymes is like juggling clumsily: it can be fun to watch and it *is* juggling, but it's nowhere near as much pleasure for an

audience as seeing all the balls . . . being kept aloft with grace and precision. In the theater, true rhyme works best on every level . . ."

8. Other styles of music might have different thresholds for sounds that satisfy the expectation for rhyme. That consideration is outside of the corpus used in this text, and there may still be a lesser effect from not-quite-rhyme events, but it certainly seems appropriate to give a nod to the idea that genre-specific criteria could be applied.

9. Caplin uses the term "theme" to express a form-functionally complete musical unit like a sentence or period; a conventional theme has two "phrases," like a period having an antecedent phrase and a consequent phrase. But other writers prefer to refer to the period as a "phrase," and to the antecedent and consequent as "sub-phrases." This is confusing! I am choosing Caplin's terminology throughout, but if you prefer, you may read my use of "phrase" to mean "sub-phrase."

10. I believe this could be further extended by examining a cross-domain mapping between the grammatical domain and the musical domain, where each domain can provide cognitive reinforcement to the other—for instance, a rhymed word landing on a cadence tends to enhance a feeling of closure. To some extent, I have developed the preference rules from my understanding of the work of Reuven Tsur (cognitive poetics; 1996) and Candace Brower (music cognition; 1993).

11. I not only think it is far from being a metric, it also fails to capture the impact of a failed rhyme on the next moment. For me, this particularly stands out when "sand" does not rhyme with "ocean," for at that moment we reorient ourselves to expect a possible rhyme at the end of the continuation; I think there is more pressure created for the rhyme to resolve than example 4.5 is able to indicate.

## WORKS CITED

Brower, Candace. 1993. "Memory and the Perception of Rhythm." *Music Theory Spectrum* 15(1): 19–35.

Callahan, Michael. 2013. "Sentential Lyric-Types in the Great American Songbook." *Music Theory Online* 19(3).

Caplin, William. 1998. *Classical Form: A Theory of Formal Functions for the Instrumental Music of Haydn, Mozart, and Beethoven*. New York: Oxford University Press.

Caplin, William. 2013. *Analyzing Classical Form: An Approach for the Classroom*. New York: Oxford University Press.

Harmon, William. 1987. "Rhyme in English Verse: History, Structures, Functions." *Studies in Philology* 84(4): 365–93.

Lewin, David. 1986. "Music Theory, Phenomenology, and Modes of Perception." *Music Perception* 3(4): 327–92.

Rodgers, Stephen. 2014. "Sentences with Words: Text and Theme-Type in *Die schöne Müllerin*." *Music Theory Spectrum* 36(1): 58–85.

Sondheim, Stephen. 2010. *Finishing the Hat: Collected Lyrics (1954–1981) with Attendant Comments, Principles, Heresies, Grudges, Whines and Anecdotes*. New York: Knopf.

Tsur, Reuven. 1996. "Rhyme and Cognitive Poetics." *Poetics Today* 17(1): 55–86.

## LIST OF MUSICAL WORKS

Anderson-Lopez, Kristen, and Robert Lopez. 2014. "In Summer," *Frozen*. New York: Hal Leonard.

Bernstein, Leonard, Betty Comden, and Adolph Green. 1944. "Some Other Time." *On the Town*. New York: Boosey & Hawkes.

Bernstein, Leonard, and Stephen Sondheim. 1957. "Balcony Scene," "One Hand, One Heart," and "Something's Coming." *West Side Story*. New York: G. Schirmer.

Brown, Jason Robert, and Marsha Norman. 2014. "It All Fades Away." *The Bridges of Madison County*. New York: Hal Leonard.

Kander, John, and Fred Ebb. 1966. "Cabaret." *Cabaret*. New York: Times Square Music Publications Co.

Rodgers, Richard, and Oscar Hammerstein. 1959. "My Favorite Things," and "Reprise: Sixteen Going on Seventeen." *The Sound of Music*. New York: Williamson Music.

Stitt, Georgia. 2007. "I Get to Show You the Ocean." *This Ordinary Thursday: The Songs of Georgia Stitt*. Geocate Music.

5

# The Changing Rhythms of Bridges and Ends

RACHEL SHORT

## INTRODUCTION

Musical theater songs are best known for their choruses, which repeat melodies and motives and breed familiarity. Bridges, by their very name, connote little more than connecting material, but their function, or musical and lyrical role, is almost always far more dramatically important than that. This chapter explores ways that bridges and other contrasting sections diverge from the more familiar music that surrounds them, with a particular focus on rhythmic and textual changes that not only provide much-needed contrast, but contribute to characterization and narrative arcs. I focus on ballads, tracing how types and placement of sections with different rhythms have changed over the ninety years that "bridge" *Show Boat* and *Hamilton*.

The songs I discuss in this chapter all feature sections where melodic rhythms deviate significantly from those found elsewhere in the song. In songs from more contemporary musicals, rhythmically contrasting sections—which heretofore had predominantly been bridges—often appear as ending sections. I lay out four different strategies for rhythmically differentiating sections, highlighting select examples for each strategy. These rhythmic strategies demonstrate that rhythm and lyric are inextricably linked. Therefore, in these emotionally charged sections, rhythmic changes support textual changes that create dramatic or rhetorical contrast and character development. The lyrics are the driving force, and the changing rhythms bring them into relief.

In this study, I focus on ballads because they are sung by, and feature emotional journeys of, individual characters.[1] Narrowing the scope in this way allows me to compare numbers that tend to serve similar structural-dramatic purposes within shows and that use similar formal structures. Of course, individual performances of a song can differ greatly in their rhythmic interpretations.[2] To ensure consistency, I work from published show scores or sheet music.[3]

## *BRIDGES AND OTHER CONTRASTING SECTIONS*

In Tin Pan Alley tunes and early musical theater songs (c. late 1920s and after), the standard bridge, also known as the "release" or "middle eight," is the **B** section of an **AABA** form, often called thirty-two-bar song form.[4] More than just new musical material, a singer's lyrics often change in style or focus during a bridge, which functions as the apex of the dramatic arc within the thirty-two-bar scope. Charles Hamm (1983) argued that this standardized form "represent[ed] a final step in a formal evolution that had taken place over a time span of more than a century."[5]

The repetition inherent in this form worked well for audience engagement. Scott McMillin (2006) notes that "music gains meaning through the accretion of repeated combinations of phrases and rhythms" (31). He argues that the repetition in **AABA** forms "would be intolerable in conversation, but it is normal and even enjoyable in a lyric and musical structure, that celebrates doing things again and again." The prevalence of **AABA** form is in part due to its combination of pleasurable musical repetition and the contrast in the bridge.

As the structure of Broadway shows shifted, and their constituent styles of music changed over the years, the formal structure of individual songs also morphed. After around 1950, a thirty-two-bar **AABA** refrain had become less standard. Composers began playing with this formal expectation, making the eventual achievement of an **AABA** song form part of the drama of a song or scene.[6] Formal sections with contrasting rhythmic profiles also began to appear outside of **AABA** forms as independent, transitional sections, often between verse/chorus repetitions. Another option was for rhythmic cells from the bridge to return at the end of a song, with final—not transitional—function. In recent musical theater music, entire sections with contrasting rhythms are often placed at a song's end to create final emphasis.

Scholars usually describe the contrast that bridges provide in terms of harmonic characteristics, or discussions of rhythm are subsumed into the "bigger picture" of prolongational analyses, melodic design, and/or phrase structure.[7] Bridges do differ from their surrounding sections through a combination of all these means, but much can be lost by glossing over rhythms. Rhythmic details are important in these songs because they are so salient, especially when they differ significantly from prior sections. Rhythmic changes affect the speed, pattern, and accentuation of the way lyrics are sung, which can highlight dramatic moments. Often, contrasting sections demonstrate changes in a character's perspective to create a dramatic arc. The character might change their mind, consider another viewpoint, voice their challenges another way, or come to a decision. These perspective changes can affect the lyrics, which generally interrelate with the rhythms.

In this chapter, I'll consider four categories to classify the different ways rhythmic elements can define musical sections: *rhythmic density*, *phrase beginnings*, *rhythmic distribution*, and *syncopation*. These four main attributes interact and overlap with one another and with other rhythmic elements,[8] but I consider them separately for ease of comparison. Rhythmic density measures how many notes occur proportional to each beat; many quick attacks can subdivide a beat to create dense, complex rhythms, or longer-held notes may span multiple beats for a more open effect. The second category, phrase beginnings, distinguishes between phrases that begin on the downbeat and those that begin with anacruses, which vary in length and stress. Less frequently, the vocal line may feature a "loud rest" on the downbeat, often with great dramatic effect (London 1993).

The third category, rhythmic distribution, describes rhythmic density across longer musical time spans. Distribution of rhythmic figures over phrases varies greatly: some rhythms feature relatively even attack points, yielding mostly equal note durations in a measure or phrase; some phrases or rhythmic cells are what I call "front-loaded," meaning that they are more dense at the beginning, while others are "back-loaded," with longer notes occurring earlier on and with greater density toward the end.

Both types of uneven distribution can affect the quality of transitions: back-loaded phrases have a kinetic effect, ramping up energy to lead into the next section, whereas longer notes tend to sound more final, signaling rhetorical—if not harmonic—closure.[9] The fourth category accounts for the amount and type of rhythmic syncopation. A bridge may differ from surrounding sections simply in its use of syncopated rhythms (or a change in their frequency), or the contrast may come in the kinds of syncopation used (i.e., at the level of the beat, the beat division, the beat subdivision, or spanning multiple beats). These four types of rhythmic changes create significant deviations to delineate bridges and other departures, and they create emotional interest and support the dramatic narrative.

## *RHYTHMIC DENSITY*

Rhythmic density refers to the number of attacks proportional to each beat. In a dense passage, frequent beat subdivisions or complex rhythms fill musical phrases with plentiful movement. In contrast to dense passages, some sections have longer notes that span multiple beats, creating a more open sensation. Changes in rhythmic density create rhythmically and dramatically contrasting bridges in **AABA** refrains; an early example of this is "Over the Rainbow" (*The Wizard of Oz*, Harold Arlen and E. Y. Harburg, 1939),[10] in which the dense bridge contrasts the more open **A** sections. Sometimes, the **A** sections are more dense than the bridge. "Can't Help Lovin' Dat Man" (*Show Boat*, Jerome Kern and Oscar Hammerstein II, 1927) and "On the Street Where You Live" (*My Fair Lady*, Frederick Loewe and Alan Jay Lerner, 1957) both feature **B** sections with open and steady rhythmic profiles, contrasting denser, more syncopated **A** sections.[11]

In "Over the Rainbow," after rhythmically sparse **A** sections, the contrasting bridge is set apart by quickly moving eighth notes that double the rhythmic density to provide rhythmic contrast and support the dramatic arc (see example 5.1a). In **A** sections, the character Dorothy wonders about a place "Some-*where* o-ver the *rain*-bow" with large motivic leaps and long note values that begin the backloaded phrases.[12] In the bridge, she changes perspective, daydreaming of a hopeful future ("some-day") and allows herself to imagine what that place will be like when she gets there ("where troub-les melt like *lem*-on drops, a-way a-bove the *chim*-ney tops"). The **B** section's brief anacrusis begins a rocking motion of motivic fluttering eighth-note alterations set to smaller melodic intervals. These fluctuations return at the end of the song for a final closing "tag" section, often performed with a deceleration that seems to stretch three downbeats to six, as the singer focuses again on her longings, echoing the **B** section in lyric perspective and rhythmic content.

Contrarily, the **A** sections of "Can't Help Lovin' Dat Man" and "On the Street Where You Live" are more dense than the open and smooth **B** sections.[13] In "Can't Help Lovin' Dat Man," the character Julie is describing—through a diegetic song—how her love will endure "no matter what" her man does. As shown in example 5.1b, the **A** section's greater rhythmic density comes from its syncopated and front-loaded phrases. Swung eighth notes and slight anticipations of beat three create a sense of accelerated motion ("Fish got to swim—and birds got to fly—. I gotta love—one man till I die—") before slowing for the declamatory titular hook, which adds one more anticipatory syncopation: "Can't *help* lov-in' dat man—of mine."

While a seemingly simple diegetic song, it has hidden depth, helped in part by the rhythmic character. Unusually, the bridge is not the first contrasting rhythmic section heard. After singing **A1** and **A2**, dialogue interrupts the song, before Julie begins again to sing the "whole thing." The introduction is a twelve-bar swung section, showing Julie's ability to sing the blues (which foreshadows her later "unmasking").[14] Contrasting both the bluesy introduction and the **A** section, the rhythms in the **B** section are more open. The first two measures of the **A** sections are nearly twice as dense as those of the **B** section. The second half of **B** is slightly back-loaded, helping create forward momentum into **A3**. While both **A** and **B** begin on the downbeat, the syncopations from **A** are smoothed out in **B** into four straight quarter notes before an upward slur, or scoop ("When he *goes* a-way | Dat's a *rain*-y day."). Even within the decreased density of the **B** section, the embedded anticipatory syncopation helps show Julie's ability to portray the hidden depth of the blues, and the consistent quarter notes draw attention to lyrics that express one of the show's tragic elements.

Through the "golden age" of musical theater,[15] the rhythmic content of bridges still tended to differ significantly from surrounding **A** sections; often these "soaring" bridges featured a more even distribution of rhythmic density with steadier, smoother rhythms and a greater focus on the downbeat, combining rhythmic and textual changes to support the dramatic arc of the song.[16] In *My Fair Lady*, the **A** sections of Freddy's ballad "On the Street Where You Live" are full of front-loaded motions, with no

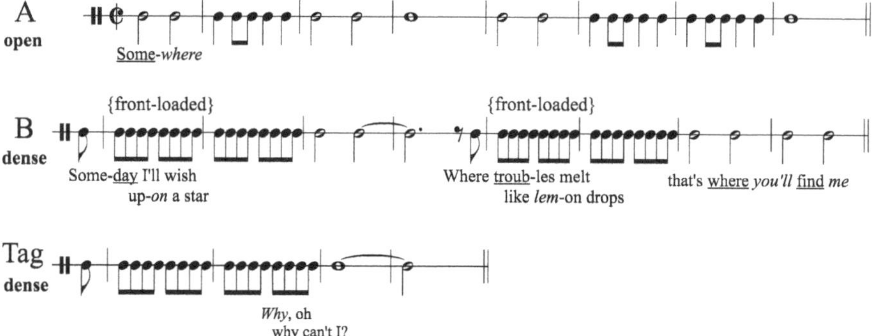


**Example 5.1a.** "Over the Rainbow" (*The Wizard of Oz*, Harold Arlen and E. Y. Harburg, 1939).

**Example 5.1b.** "Can't Help Lovin' Dat Man" (*Show Boat*, Jerome Kern and Oscar Hammerstein II, 1927).

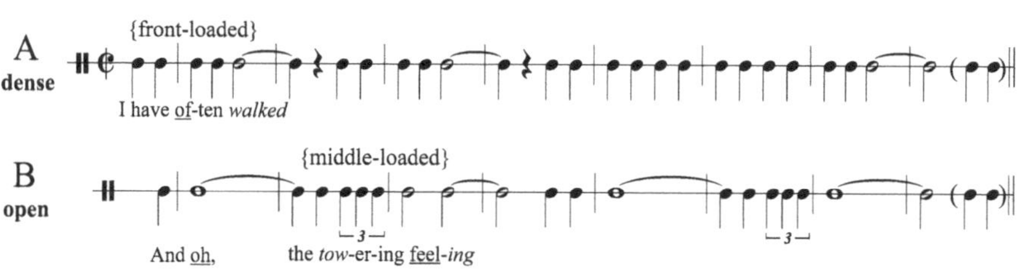


**Example 5.1c.** "On the Street Where You Live" (*My Fair Lady*, Frederick Loewe and Alan Jay Lerner, 1957).

held notes until the middle of the measure ("I have of-ten *walked* down this street be-*fore*" (see example 5.1c). The contrasting **B** sections feature soaring long notes tied into descending triplets, a contrasting density change and back-loaded rhythmic distribution that corresponds to a textual one: Freddy begins by describing how Eliza's presence charms her location, but in the bridge, he focuses on how her presence charms *him* ("And oh, the *tow*-er-ing feel-ing just to know some-*how* you are near!").

## *PHRASE BEGINNINGS*

A focus on phrase beginnings distinguishes sections where phrases and internal motives begin on the downbeat and those that begin with an anacrusis, or pickup.[17] Less frequently, but with striking effect, the vocal line may feature a "loud rest" on the downbeat. Phrase beginnings, of course, occur with other rhythmic techniques, but they are the most easily isolated of the four rhythmic techniques described here. Often, **A** sections feature strong downbeat entrances that contrast with the anacruses that begin **B** sections, such as in "Younger than Springtime" (*South Pacific*, Richard Rodgers and Oscar Hammerstein II, 1949) and "Being Alive" (*Company*, Stephen Sondheim, 1970). The opposite can happen: outer framing sections begin with an anacrusis and central sections with a downbeat entrance, as in "What More Can I Say" (*Falsettos*, William Finn and James Lapine, 1990/1992).[18] "Someone to Watch Over Me" (*Oh, Kay!*, George Gershwin and Ira Gershwin, 1926) provides an example of **A** phrases that begin with a conspicuous rest to contrast the anacrusis that begins the **B** phrase.

The downbeat entrance of the **A** section in Lieutenant Joe Cable's **AABA** ballad "Younger than Springtime" (example 5.2a) is followed by quick-moving rhythms. The front-loaded phrase is slightly fragmented by downbeat rests in the second measure as he describes the girl he loves ("Youn-ger than *spring* time _ are *you*"). In contrast, the lengthy, legato **B** phrases begin with a long anacrusis (ana.) that prepares the rest of the phrase to set declarative lyrics evenly distributed on the downbeats as he sings of her attributes ("And when your youth and joy in-vade my arms"). The lyrics here transition from descriptions of Cable's beloved, Liat, to his action of embracing her. This textual departure in the bridge causes a change in perspective in the final **A**: Joe is now the subject ("Young-er than *spring*-time _am *I*") because he has been transformed through Liat's embrace.

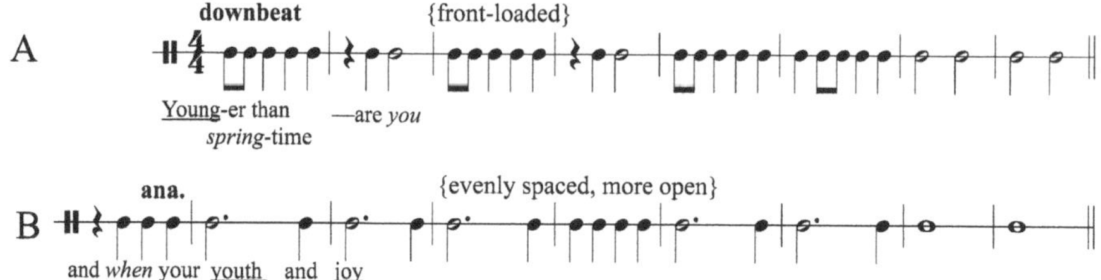


**Example 5.2a.** "Younger than Springtime" (*South Pacific*, Richard Rodgers and Oscar Hammerstein II, 1949).

While still inspired by Golden Era successes from Rogers and Hammerstein (R&H) and others, Broadway shows in the 1960s and 1970s began to transform in theme and organization. The traditional "book" musical gave way to nonlinear "concept" or "frame" musicals with decreased focus on romance, exploring more "modernist concerns about alienation and identity" (Swain 2002, 41). In tandem with these structural, dramatic, and narrative changes, composers started to incorporate more diverse musical styles, especially pop-rock.[19] Some composers infused typical Broadway forms with syncopations influenced by contemporary popular music, and standard **AABA** forms began loosening and expanding. When other formal layouts were used, they also contained rhythmically contrasting sections similar in musical and dramatic function to earlier bridges.[20] Whether in **AABA** song form or some variant, the framing sections often incorporated more complex, dense, and front-loaded rhythms. Central sections contrasted this complexity with more open rhythms smoothly spaced across lengthy phrases to correspond to the dramatic climax in the center of the song, and phrase beginnings heralded this rhythmic contrast.

In "Being Alive" the rhythmic changes stress Bobby's developing search for connection using two main rhythmic motives. Beginning his impersonal observation in **A**, the syncopated motive that starts the phrase on the downbeat is repeated and fragmented ("Some-one to *hold* you too close," example 5.2b).[21] As he is unsure of what he wants, the early musical phrases are left incomplete and trail off into embedded dialogue: not until the end of the fourth time he restarts **A** ("Some-one to *crowd* you with love") do the things he is missing "add up" to enough emotional weight that he can complete the phrase—and the section—with the repeated triplet pickup motive "*be*-ing a-live." The **A** section ends with this anacrusis

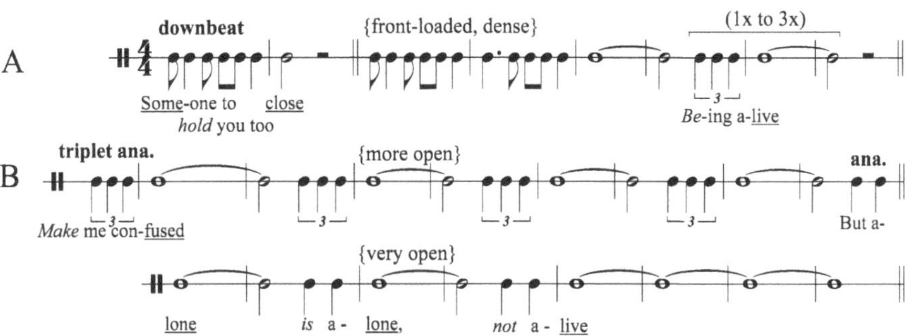


**Example 5.2b.** "Being Alive" (*Company*, Stephen Sondheim, 1970).

motive that is later developed in the bridge. As he has decided he is now ready for a relationship, the song restarts in a new key with his pleading request for connection ("Some-body *hold* me too close" and "some-bod-y *hurt* me too deep"). All phrases in **A** are now complete and end with the triplet pickup motive ("*make* me a-live"). Through Sondheim's "procliv-ity toward motivic compression" (Swayne 2005, 103), the triplet motive also begins **B** and repeats throughout the majority of the section, paired with lengthy notes, causing **B** to be far less rhythmically dense than **A**. The switch in dramatic focus is heightened by the triplet pickup ("*Make* me con-fused, *mock* me with praise"). The end of **B** features an anacrusis without triplets ("*But* a-lone; *is* a-lone; *not* a-live"). The number begins hesitantly, interrupted by dialogue, with rhythmic and melodic motives developed and combined into progressively longer phrase lengths that correspond to Bobby's emotional growth.[22]

In the 1980s and 1990s, some smaller and more traditional musicals continued to feature solo numbers with sections still set apart by rhyth-mic contrasts. However, the differentiated sections are not always bridges in a traditional **AABA** format. Sometimes an **AABA** form is embedded within a larger song structure, as in the **AABACAA'** of "What More Can I Say" (example 5.2c), where the **C** section functions as a traditional bridge, and the varied phrase beginnings of both **B** and **C** contrast the **A** sections.

The **A** section phrases begin with an anacrusis that leads to held notes that accent the downbeat. Interspersed short anacrustic notes create a feeling of halting stops and starts as the character considers the past ("it's been hot, *al*-so ver-y sweet, and I'm not *u*-su-al-ly in-dis-*crete*"). The end of **A1** elides into the anacrusis beginning of **A2** ("*What* more can I say").

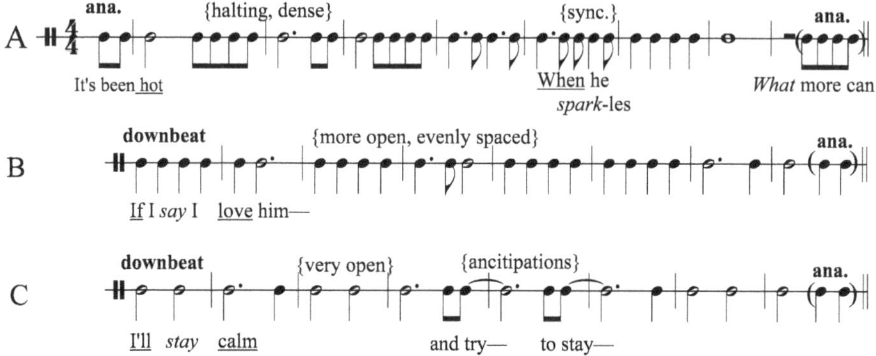


**Example 5.2c.** "What More Can I Say" (*Falsettos*, William Finn and James Lapine, 1990/1992).

As the singer shifts focus to his inner feelings, the **B** features an entrance directly on the downbeat before a smoothly distributed phrase ("If I *say* I love him—, you might *think* the words come *cheap*"). In its expanded **AAB-ACA<A′** form, the added **C** section has an even stronger "release" effect than **B** with a downbeat entrance and decrease in density that accompany his personal decision ("I'll *stay* calm, un-tie *my* tongue and try—to stay—both kind and young"), and an abrupt key change prepares the last **A**.[23]

While beginning a phrase with loud downbeat rests happens across many types of musical theater music, the Gershwins' "Someone to Watch Over Me" is quite striking. After a loud downbeat rest, the front-loaded **A** sections are characterized by pairs of quickly flowing dotted quarter notes and sixteenth notes (often sung as swung eighth notes, see example 5.2d). The beginning lyrics are set to a melodic line that matches their hopefulness with a rising contour ("_There's a *some*-bod-y I'm"), before a gently syncopated rhythmic cell repeats three times in a stepwise descending sequence ("long-ing to *see*"). The following downbeat rest and declarative quarter notes clearly express the singer's yearning as they set the titular hook ("_Some-*one* who'll watch *o*-ver me"). In contrast to the rests and lilting rhythms from before, the decisiveness of these concluding rhythms helps accentuate the end of each **A** section.[24]

**B** starts with a long anacrusis of evenly distributed quarter notes before a higher-level syncopated rhythmic cell (an augmentation of **A**'s syncopation) repeats five times ("_Al-*though* he may not *be* the man some—girls"). While the total rhythmic density is not a drastic change between the **A**

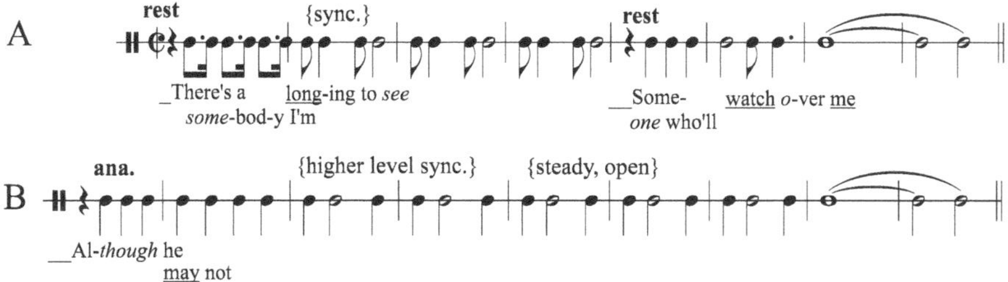


**Example 5.2d.** "Someone to Watch Over Me" (*Oh, Kay!*, George and Ira Gershwin, 1926).

and **B** phrases, the rhythmic contrast comes from front-loaded motion changing to smooth distribution, and from the different ways the phrases begin: starting with a rest for **A** and a long anacrusis for **B**. To aid his consideration of the song as a ballad, not a rhythmic tap-dance tune as it was originally supposed to be, Alec Wilder argues that the rhythmic qualities of the release lead it to be "freer, less spastic; in fact, [it] soars like a ballad" (1972, 137). As Deena Rosenberg notes, the rhythmic contrast in the bridge allows for a change in perspective, allowing the singer to move from "describing an emotional void to focus on a specific man and her reactions to him"; the mode of address then subtly changes in **A3**, from a report on the character's state of mind to an "overt plea, bringing the listener into the text of the song" (1997, 150–51).

## *RHYTHMIC DISTRIBUTION*

Rhythmic distribution describes the location of rhythmic density across longer musical time spans, portraying where in the phrase or motive the density occurs. This distribution varies greatly across musical styles and between sections in the same style: some rhythms feature fairly even attack points that create strings of mostly equal note durations; some phrases or rhythmic cells are more dense at the beginning, which I call "front-loaded," while longer notes occurring earlier with greater density toward the end create "back-loaded" phrases. Uneven rhythmic distribution creates specific transitional affects; the kinetic effect of a back-loaded phrase can ramp up energy to lead into the next section, or rhetorical and harmonic closure is often signaled by phrases that end with longer notes.

For example, in "This Nearly Was Mine" (*South Pacific*, R&H, 1949), the front-loaded **B** contrasts with the smother and slightly back-loaded or "middle-loaded" **A**.

Within a song form, whether **AABA** or some variant, the **A** sections are often more front-loaded, dense, and rhythmically complex. These contrast with central sections that are relatively more open, with rhythmic distribution that is smoothly spaced, like the steady bridge in "Some Enchanted Evening" (*South Pacific*, R&H, 1949), or the open and back-loaded bridge in "Soon It's Gonna Rain" (*The Fantasticks*, Harvey Schmidt and Tom Jones, 1960). Alternately, the inner **B** sections can have steadier and more evenly distributed rhythms than the outer sections. In "If I Loved You" (*Carousel*, R&H, 1945) the **A** section rhythms have greater back-loaded density than the evenly distributed **B** sections, and in "Far from the Home I Love" (*Fiddler on the Roof*, Jerry Bock and Sheldon Harnick, 1964), dense, front-loaded **A** sections contrast with the smoother **B**. Even large-scale musicals from the 1980s include songs where changes in rhythmic distribution create rhythmically contrasting sections, such as "Soliloquy/Javert's Suicide" (*Les Misérables*, Claude-Michel Schönberg and Alain Boublil, 1985). From across diverse musical styles, these examples demonstrate that changes in rhythmic distribution support textural changes at decisive moments, helping to shape a song's dramatic arc.

*South Pacific* (R&H, 1949) includes three ballads in **AABA** form with rhythmically contrasting **B** sections, including the aforementioned general density changes from **A** to **B** sections in "Younger than Springtime" (example 5.2a). The **A** section of "Some Enchanted Evening," sung by Emile de Becque as he describes meeting a lover, consists of two main repeating rhythmic motives (example 5.3a); the front-loaded *a1* begins on the downbeat (the titular "Some en-chant-ed *eve*-ning, you may see a *strang*-er"). Motive *a2* also features front-loading rhythms, albeit of a different type: a large anacrusis with over-the-beat-level triplets and beat-level syncopation ("that *some*-how you'll see her—a-gain and—a-gain"). The **B** section is much shorter (six versus sixteen measures), with simple rhythms that are evenly spread across the motivic cell *b* as the lyrics change to rhetorical questioning ("Who can ex-*plain* it, who can tell you *why*?"). After **A3**, **B** material recurs in expanded form to create the final tag, the downbeats and smooth phrase highlighting the prescriptive actions ("Once you have *found* her, nev-er let her *go*").

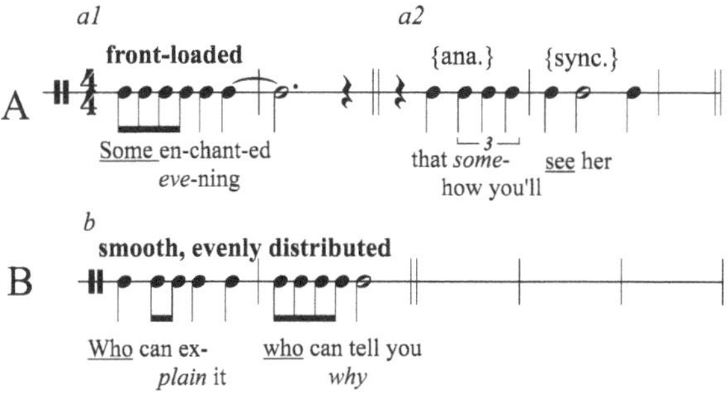


**Example 5.3a.** "Some Enchanted Evening" (*South Pacific*, Richard Rodgers and Oscar Hammerstein II, 1949).

Emile also sings the waltz-ballad "This Nearly Was Mine" in the second act (example 5.3b). Here, the bridge similarly provides contrast through rhythmic distribution, flipping the density of the first two measures of each phrase between the middle-loaded **A** ("One dream in my heart") to the front-loaded **B** ("Close to my heart she came"). In the full version of the song, greater rhythmic contrast comes in the lesser-known **C** section, which connects two full **AABA** refrains. As his focus shifts from the past into his abiding, vivid dreams ("So clear and deep are my fan-cies—"), the music surges forward to accompany his awakened desires. While the increase in total musical density is only slight, the rhythmic distribution creates a driving sensation through a motivic anacrusis, a denser second measure, and anticipating the fourth downbeat.[25]

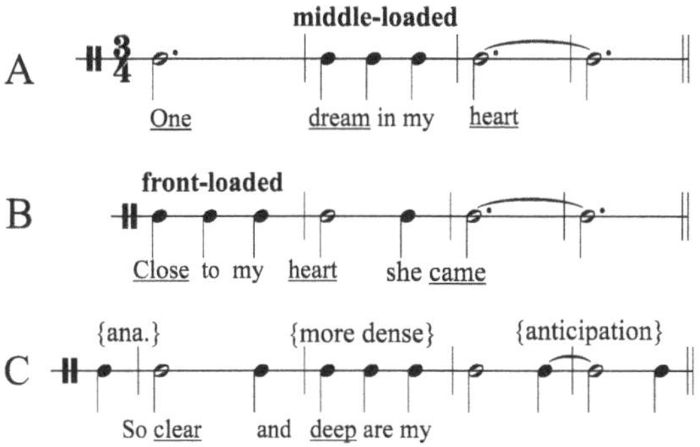


**Example 5.3b.** "This Nearly Was Mine" (*South Pacific*, Richard Rodgers and Oscar Hammerstein II, 1949).

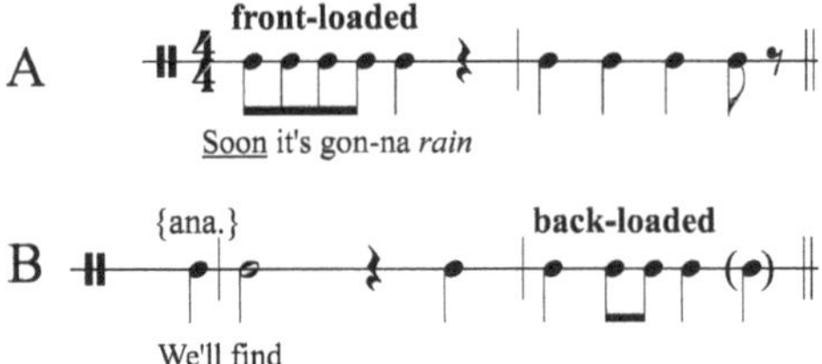


**Example 5.3c.** "Soon It's Gonna Rain" (*The Fantasticks*, Harvey Schmidt and Tom Jones, 1960).

The **AABA** chorus in *The Fantasticks*' "Soon It's Gonna Rain" also finds contrast through rhythmic distributions that change in the bridge section. **A** starts with front-loaded eighth notes that seem to quickly move away from the downbeat (example 5.3c, "Soon it's gon-na *rain*"). In the more open **B** section, the two characters discuss purposeful actions to plan for their house (and their budding relationship): a short anacrusis begins a back-loaded rhythmic motive that repeats in ascending sequential fashion ("We'll find four limbs and a *tree*, we'll build four walls and a *floor*, we'll bind it o-ver with *leaves*").

While rhythms can be clearly distributed on one end of a phrase, contrast can also come from juxtaposing phrases with evenly spaced rhythms against phrases with more irregular note groupings. In "If I Loved You" (**AABA**), the rhythms in **A** have a halting, fragmented quality with more middle-loaded density than the evenly distributed **B**—a rhythmic distribution change that helps communicate changes in the character's focus. The **A** sections begin with the conditional statement "If *I* loved you—," made more uncertain by placing the word "you" on the weak second beat, before quarter notes tied into triplets create a tripping effect that sets a melodic octave descent (example 5.4a).[26] The **B** section's rhythms are slightly less dense, but the contrast is more through a change to smoother rhythmic distribution than a change in overall density. Even though the tonal center has moved from the surety of the tonic area to vi, the open rhythms of **A** smooth into a steady pattern that heightens the feeling of clarity. This supports the lyrics that no longer begin with "if." The character's uncertainty is gone and the declamatory bridge allows the characters to reveal their actual feelings ("long-*ing* to tell you").[27] Similar to the bridge in "Younger than Springtime," a change in the characters' focus here also highlights the dramatic transformation through rhythmic differentiation.

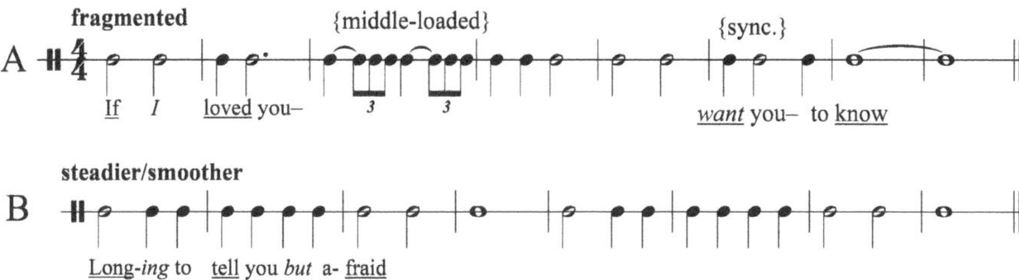


**Example 5.4a.** "If I Loved You" (*Carousel*, Richard Rodgers and Oscar Hammerstein II, 1945).

In "Far from the Home I Love" (**AABA**), the character Hodel attempts to make her father understand her in the front-loaded **A**; she sings one densely flowing bar before repeating a motivic cell with agogic accents on the third beat (example 5.4b, "How can I *hope* to make you un-der-*stand* why I *do* what I *do*"). In the bridge, the overall density is quite similar, but the smoother and more evenly spaced rhythms contrast the front-loaded density from **A**. The changed rhythms in **B** correspond to a dramatic change in the melodic contour—from sudden descent to slowly rising—as the character describes the unexpected change in her situation ("Who could *see* that a man would *come* who would change the *shape* of my dreams?"). This changing density distribution is evident on the measure level as well as the phrase level: in **A**, rhythmic cells are front-loaded: in **B**, rhythms slightly increase in density on the fourth quarter note in each bar.

In the 1980s, economic, sociocultural, and stylistic changes in Broadway and American culture at large gave rise to the "megamusical," which,

**Example 5.4b.** "Far from the Home I Love" (*Fiddler on the Roof*, Jerry Bock and Sheldon Harnick, 1964).

though sung-through, did include solo songs.[28] These "set pieces" are often a part of larger scenes, frequently repeated in different contexts (with different lyrics) through the show. Sections in these numbers are still often set apart by rhythmic contrasts. However, differentiated sections are not always bridges in a traditional **AABA** format. End sections in particular are often set apart: these differentiated ending sections have characteristics similar to traditional bridges and feature contrasting rhythms, often for dramatic effect. In *Les Misérables*, which is sung-through, the song initially sung by Valjean as part of the long opening scene ("Prologue: What Have I Done?") is repeated in its entirety in act 2 as "Soliloquy/Javert's Suicide."[29] The rhythmic density gradually lessens from densely packed beginning sections through the open final section as the character's emotions change from anger to confusion and finally despondency.

The song's form is **ABCBD**: the sparser **C** section functions as a bridge and the unevenly distributed **D** as a contrasting concluding section. Each section deploys a few brief rhythmic cells, one to two bars in length, that repeat insistently.[30] As shown in example 5.4c, the three main cells in **A** are similarly dense and consist mostly of driving sixteenth notes. (The first lyrics of each cell are: (a) "Who is this man—"; (b) "_Damned if I'll live"; (c) "There is no-thing on *earth* that we share.") The **B** section switches to longer eighth notes in legato phrases that begin either just before, or almost a whole measure before, the hypermetric downbeats, shown with accents. (The first lyrics are: (d) "_How can I *now* al-low this man"; (e) "_This des-p'rate *man* whom I have hun-ted.") The rhythmically contrasting bridge/**C**, continuing the slower eighth notes, has a loud rest on the downbeat and longer rests between rhythmic cells (lyrics: (f) "_And my thoughts fly a-part."). After repeating the anacrusis from **B** ("_And must I *now* be-gin to doubt?"), the final **D** section has the shortest rhythmic cell to this point, as static and repetitive sixteenth-note pairs lead to beats one and three. The fragmented rhythms set fragmented lyrics, and pitches noodle unremittingly around the dominant scale degree as he stares hopelessly into the void ("I am reach-ing but I *fall*"). His final long note initially seems dissonant, but is soon transformed by swelling orchestral music with a drastic key change that accompanies the underscored return of his prior ballad, "Stars."

**Example 5.4c.** "Soliloquy/Javert's Suicide" (*Les Misérables*, Claude-Michel Schönberg and Alain Boublil, 1985).

### *SYNCOPATION*

While there is some form of syncopation in most musical theater styles, recent shows tend toward more frequent and complex syncopation.[31] This happens at various levels: the beat, beat divisions and subdivisions, or spanning multiple beats. Frequently, rhythmic contrast happens from changes in syncopation: either changes in the frequency of syncopated rhythms, or from the types of syncopation used. This can occur in more traditional "sung" ballads as well as rap-infused music that veers toward semi-spoken text. Changes in syncopation often highlight changed lyric focus within an emotional journey, such as the angst-ridden and densely syncopated bridge of "Fine, Fine Line," (*Avenue Q*, Robert Lopez and Jeff Marx, 2003). In non-**AABA** forms, sections with drastic rhythmic contrasts are often reserved for the song's end in order to correspond to a character's final realizations or decisions, such as the closing sections of "Inútil" (*In the Heights*, Lin-Manuel Miranda, 2008) and "Hurricane" (*Hamilton*, Miranda, 2015).[32] In these ballads, highly syncopated rhythms in central sections contrast declarative straight rhythms in the culminating sections. While in different locations than earlier bridges, these sections with changing rhythms similarly support dramatic development through musical change.

In "Fine, Fine Line," the **A** sections start with a brief anacrusis that leads to a slightly syncopated melody. Here, four-measure phrases are split by gentle beat anticipations and rests into three asymmetrical subphrases as Kate describes a precarious and potentially romantic relationship ("There's a <u>fine</u>, fine line—; be-tween a <u>lov</u>-er—; and a friend—," example 5.5a). When Kate switches focus in the **B** section to directly address her estranged lover, her tone changes from reflection to anger and the rhythms provide contrast with increased syncopation and density. After beginning with a loud rest, the syncopation highlights the off-beats, as four-bar phrases are filled with one connected thought ("__And I don't *have* the time—to waste on you—an-y-more—").

Miranda's *In the Heights* could be classified as a Latino/a "integrated" musical, with its infusion of soul, R&B, and Latin rhythms into traditional theater conventions and forms. Although a number of songs lie outside traditional **AABA** form, they still exhibit meaningful rhythmic contrasts. The ballad "Inútil" (**ABABC**) does so using a contrasting end section that

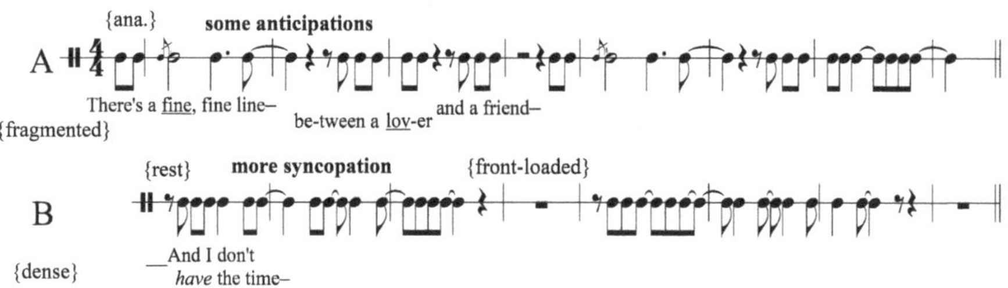


**Example 5.5a.** "Fine, Fine Line" (*Avenue Q*, Robert Lopez and Jeff Marx, 2003).

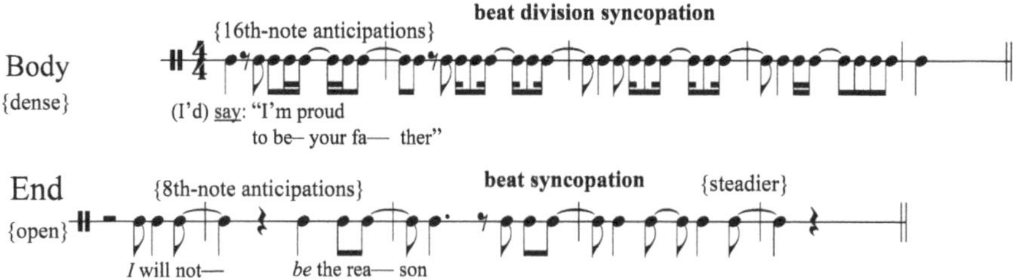


**Example 5.5b.** "Inútil" (*In the Heights*, Lin-Manuel Miranda, 2008).

decreases in rhythmic density and changes syncopation levels. The main body of the number (**AB**)—in which Kevin apologetically explains to his family how he views their relationship—is dense: syncopation subdivides the beat and phrases that start with rests obfuscate the downbeat (example 5.5b, "I'm *proud* to be your fa—ther, 'cuz *you* work so much har—der"). Syncopation moves to the beat-division level to provide space and add weight to his final decision ("*I* will not— *be* the rea— son *that* my fam— 'ly *can't* suc-ceed—").

Similarly to "Inútil," the ballad "Hurricane" sets apart the ending section with changes in syncopation, this time fully removing the subdivided syncopation that has been normative. The number's form is **ABCAB'D**,[33] with sections **A** through **C** featuring subdivided syncopation. As Alexander Hamilton surveys his current situation (that is, how to handle the exposing of his affair with Maria Reynolds), his phrases mostly start with downbeat rests, and anticipatory syncopation before other strong beats. Example 5.5c shows the densely syncopated body sections (**A1** "_In the eye of a *hur*-ri-cane there is qui—et for *just* a mom—ent, a yel-low sky—"

**Example 5.5c.** "Hurricane" (*Hamilton*, Lin-Manuel Miranda, 2015).

and slightly denser **A2** "_When I was sev-en-teen a *hur*-ri-caine—"; and **B** "I wrote—my way <u>out</u>"). Also starting with a loud rest, the **C** section functions as a typical bridge: as he changes focus to himself, it provides rhythmic contrast through a change to rhythmically dense spoken rap ("_I wrote my way out of hell— I wrote my way to re-vo-<u>lut</u>-ion"). After repeated **A** and modified **B** sections, the ending (**D**) section eliminates all syncopation, creating declarative rhythms to help Hamilton express his controversial decision ("<u>This</u> is the eye of the *hur*-ri-cane, this is the <u>on</u>-ly way I can pro-*tect* my leg-a-cy").

Yonatan Malin observed that "syncopations embody a kind of tension, and we may interpret this as the yearning or desire of a musical persona" (2008, 67). Writing about electronic dance music, Mark Butler similarly acknowledges that "certain types of rhythms are defined by a dynamic tension between our perception of a note's position and our sense of where it *should* be. This interplay creates a kind of gravitational pull toward the beat, a sort of negative emphasis on the position from which the note is displaced" (2006, 87, italics in original). In "Hurricane," the tension created by rhythmic syncopation is released in the final section, creating a musical depiction of the calm eye of the storm that the lyrics describe. At this moment in the song, Hamilton is making a drastic decision that will affect the rest of his life, and the drama is heightened by the markedly contrasting rhythms.[34]

## *OTHER TECHNIQUES FOR CONTRASTING RHYTHMS*

While varied rhythmic density, phrase entrances, rhythmic distribution, and syncopation are the most distinctive and effective ways to create rhythmic contrast, there are other discrete methods. These include changing meters, as in "Days" (*Fun Home*, Jeanine Tesori and Lisa Kron, 2015),[35] and changes in articulation, as in "I Believe in You" (*How to Succeed in Business without Really Trying*, Frank Loesser, 1961)—rhythmic techniques that can be used in tandem with various other procedures to create contrasting sections.

*Fun Home* often features frequent drastic meter changes within songs. For example, "Changing My Major" begins in $\frac{4}{4}$ and changes to a $\frac{3}{4}$ waltz for the titular chorus.[36] The meter changes in "Telephone Wire" signify specific changes in time: Alison narrates in the present and remembers the

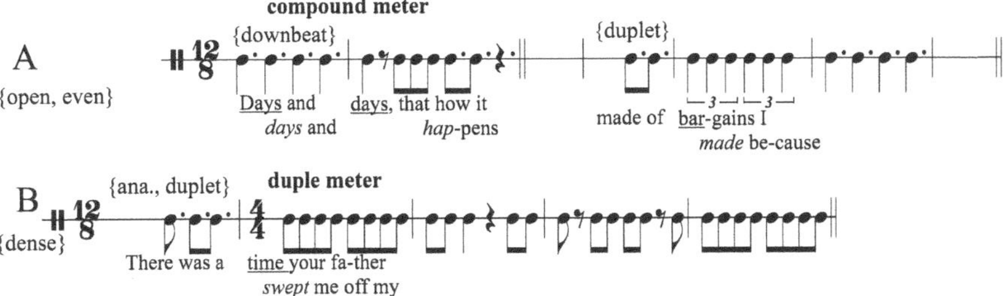


**Example 5.6a.** "Days" (*Fun Home*, Jeanine Tesori and Lisa Kron, 2015).

past. There are many verse/chorus formats (e.g., "Ring of Keys," "Changing My Major," and "Edges"), and also some **AABA** forms. "Days" is an **AABA** song in which the major rhythmic contrast comes from changes in meter, rhythmic density, and downbeat focus (example 5.6a). The **A** sections in $\frac{12}{8}$ are open and evenly distributed ("<u>Days</u> and *days* and <u>days</u>, that's how it *hap*-pens"), with occasional duplets and over-the-beat triplets. In **B**, the intermittent duplets take over as the meter changes to $\frac{4}{4}$; the increase in density and the added anacrusis together create rhythmic contrast as the character changes focus to specific memories of the past ("There was a <u>time</u> your father *swept* me off my <u>feet</u> with words").

"I Believe in You" features an **AABA** structure with twenty-four-bar **A** sections (two compound basic ideas and a continuation with the title lyric).[37] In **A**, the lengthy anacrusis of the presentation leads to a downbeat arrival, which, while notated as a whole note, is often sung short and staccato as the character engages in self-description. (example 5.6b, "You *have* the <u>cool</u>, <u>clear</u>, <u>eyes</u> of a <u>seek</u>-er of *wis*-dom and <u>truth</u>"). Paired triplets create a surge in density in the fourth bar, creating an overall back-loaded distribution. A similar anacrusis characterizes the relatively front-loaded continuation, where the notes are held longer but still sharply accented at the repeated title lyric ("Oh *I* be-<u>lieve</u> in <u>you</u>. *I* be-<u>lieve</u> in <u>you</u>"). The vocal articulations in the **A** sections contrast with those in the legato and smooth bridge (**B**), which features a dramatic downbeat entrance and sweeping legato phrases, contrasting articulations that correspond to a dramatic change of perspective in the lyrics and key area ("<u>And</u> *when* my <u>faith</u> *in* my <u>fel</u>-low *man*—, <u>all</u> but *falls*—a-<u>part</u>").

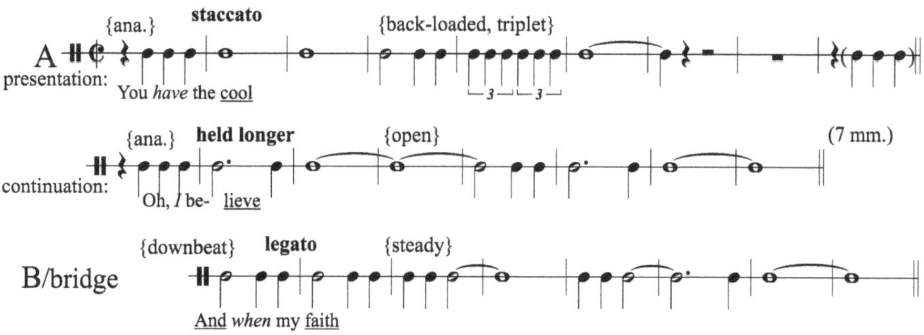


**Example 5.6b.** "I Believe in You" (*How to Succeed in Business without Really Trying*, Frank Loesser, 1961).

## *CONCLUSION*

The examples in this chapter highlight various rhythmic elements, but they only scratch the surface of the wide variety of rhythms in Broadway ballads. Rhythmically contrasting sections are used to support a dramatic arc, enhance emotional expression, or reflect change in the character's perspective. Formally, these sections can serve as an internal bridge or establish a final decisive moment. The contrasts discussed herein are achieved though changes in four musical parameters: rhythmic density, phrase beginnings, rhythmic distributions, and the amount and level of syncopation. These alterations occur at predictable locations within ballads, though that expected juncture has changed over time; the more recent style of a rhythmically contrasting section at the end of a ballad, as in "Hurricane" and "[Javert's] Soliloquy," harkens back to some older songs where rhythms from contrasting bridges returned at their songs' end, as in "Over the Rainbow." Regardless of location, musical and lyrical contrasts help convey pivotal moments in the story. From diverse musical styles and eras, these examples all show how changes in rhythmic elements support the emotional journey of the character through the ballad.

## NOTES

1. In the context of musical theater, a ballad is a song in which music and lyrics work together to explore a character's emotional journey. This is often

a slower or lyrical solo with a romantic or personal focus, and usually occurs at pivotal moments within the context of the show. Grant (2004) traces the beginning of this congruence to Al Jolson, who "inadvertently turned the theater song into a dramatic soliloquy that powerfully speaks the interior of a specific person or character" (22–23). Grant also connects the widespread use of foxtrot rhythms in these songs to the foxtrot's ability "to accommodate and highlight narrative lyrics" (137).

2. See Hamm (1994) for a discussion of how genre can be shaped by changes in performers' interpretations and audience perception.

3. Occasionally, well-known individual performers, original cast recordings, and standard performance practices can help elucidate common rhythms as they are usually sung and inform analyses.

4. Alec Wilder (1972) uses terms "main strain" for the **A** sections and says the "release" is "almost always new material" (56). Hamm (1983) also uses the term "release" (363). Forte (1995) considers the main part of song the *refrain*, which he breaks into a *ternary* **ABA** sequence: Chorus 1, Bridge, Chorus 2, with Chorus 1 encompassing sixteen bars and the other two eight bars each.

5. As Hamm explains, in standard Tin Pan Alley songs, the lesser-known introductory verses were optional, and choruses—or "refrains"—were usually made up of four equal-length sections using either **AABA** or **ABAC** patterns. He mentions how Kern, Gershwin, and Rodgers expanded the harmonic language of Tin Pan Alley tunes, probably owing to their classical music experience (1983, 327–90, particularly 358–59 and 368). Appen and Frei-Hauenschild (2015) also trace the rise of **AABA** song form through the 1920s, exploring in detail the placement of the "hook." Note that McMillin (2006) calls the hook, or invariant lyric, the "refrain" (109). Summach does as well, considering it part of the strophe, and he separates out the more common "tail refrains" from "head refrains" (2011, [7]).

6. See McMillin's discussion of *Carousel*'s bench scene (2006, 135–39), and the ensemble number "Everybody's Got the Right to Be Happy" in *Assassins* (197–200).

7. Hamm notes the instability and "tonal adventures" of B sections (1983, 363). Graziano explores "the expansion of harmonic possibilities" in bridge sections of AABA form, noting the "surprise" of moving away from the comfort of the tonic (2014, 96, 104). This focus on harmonic contrast in bridges appears in analyses of other musical styles as well, such as Keith Waters's study on bridges in Debussy (2012). Brian Jarvis and John Peterson posit that the level of contrast in bridges is "expected," which they contrast with the "unexpected" contrast of detours, including uncommon features such as completely new keys, new characters, or "dramatic tempo changes" (2020, 9:40). Steve Larson (2003), Jarvis and Peterson (2019), and Alec Wilder (1972) speak of the transitional, directed motion of bridges that connect other sections. Allen Forte (1995) is interested in how rhythms help unify a piece, not in how they can differ and create contrast in sec-

tions. Michael Buchler compares bridges with "a sense of musical status" in two songs, looking at their (lack of) harmonic motion, unachieved modularity goals, and static melody (2008, 49–50). Joseph Swain (2002) focuses on harmonic relationships, cadences, and phrase lengths, such as his discussion of phrase lengths in "If I Loved You" (129–30) and "Where's the Mate for Me" (34), and the disruption of harmonic rhythms in "Wouldn't It Be Loverly" (200). Geoffrey Block (2009) privileges melodic aspects over harmonic aspects, particularly melodic intervals, as in his assertion that Kern chose to represent the river in *Show Boat* through the melodic interval of a fourth (27–33). In his study of the composer Stephen Schwartz, Paul Laird (2014) also explores recurring melodic motives, even as small as "three descending pitches."

8. Other considerations include tempo and meter changes, articulation, the length of rhythmic motives (which is tied into phrase length), and registral accents.

9. Bridges tend to end in half cadences, chains of secondary dominants, deceptive cadences, or other means of harmonic instability that necessitate tonic return.

10. Unless otherwise noted, the dates used are those of the first Broadway or cinematic production.

11. My discussion in this section considers the overall note-content of a phrase, whether generally "dense" or "open" (sparse). Changes in rhythmic density can occur in tandem along with changes in rhythmic patterns, changes in syncopation, and the way the density is distributed through the phrase, which will be explored later in more detail.

12. From here forward, underlined lyrics denote words that land on downbeats, italics signify mid-measure on-beat attacks, underscores show downbeat rests, and the em dash shows the anticipated accent of beats.

13. The song's performance tempo is up for debate. Grant considers it a "fox-trotted blues" (2004, 140); Wilder is also unsure that it is a ballad (1972, 57). While the song later evolves into a danced ensemble number, I consider Julie's solo presentation to be a ballad.

14. Scholars have discussed what they see as blues elements of the song, especially as the character singing it has then-hidden Black heritage. Banfield notes how this is a model for a diegetic song, yet it does more: "Julie knows a blues . . . and her singing of it prefigures her unmasking; thus not just the singing of the song but the recognition of musical and lyric style actually becomes an issue in the plot" (1993, 184). The song is brought back for further diegetic use later in the show. Appen and Frei-Hauenschild cite the song as an example of how the **AABA** form itself was associated with African Americans in the early years of its popularity. McMillin similarly notes that while "it is Julie's song, called for in the pantry of the showboat, it is Kern's song, too, and as Kern's song it is saying something Julie cannot say as a book character" (2006, 105–9). Swain agrees: it is not just a "prop"

song since Julie is singing about herself and her situation (2002, 51). See also Greg Decker's discussion in this volume of the music in *Show Boat* as a marker for race.

15. As for most eras, the dates of the "golden age" are blurry; new trends began in the 1950s, even as more traditional musicals continued to be written well past 1960.

16. Grant describes "On the Street Where You Live" as the show's "most soaring melodic line" with a compass of an eleventh—which he finds unusual, as the range of Broadway music had shrunk by then to help singers act on the lyric (2004, 27). I use the term "soaring" not just to delineate melodic contours that stretch a larger span—like the apex and nadir that Forte traces (1995, 26)—or jump to a single high note, like the melodic arc Grant discusses (25), but also to discuss longer phrases featuring multiple high notes with longer durations. These often begin directly on the downbeat, providing metric, registral, and agogic accents.

17. An anacrusis is an unstressed note or set of notes that begin the phrase or gesture before the downbeat.

18. The 1992 Broadway musical *Falsettos* was a combination of the two off-Broadway one-acts: *March of the Falsettos* (1981) and *Falsettoland* (1990).

19. The incorporation of pop-rock into Broadway scores has variously been the subject of sharp critique and seen as a popular inevitability. For example, Swain claims that when rock music began to influence musical theater, some considered this "death to the music drama," as "simpler harmonic plans deriving from the blues, energized by insistent downbeats in fast tempo" took the place of "periodically phrased and yet supple, flexible melodies" (2002, 415–17). His critique is partially based on the rhythmic content of rock styles: he argues that rock is not a dramatic vehicle itself, because the driving beat and sound "best express powerful but static emotions" (417). Grant complains that "the rhythm was made the melody, and the rhythmic groove became the new building block of the song," and songwriters would simply altar the groove instead of creating differences with melody and harmony (2004, 151–53). On the other hand, Coleman writes that in the early 1960s, the traditional musical seemed hopelessly out of touch with contemporary America and was "escapist and nostalgic" (2017, 356). Pop-rock styles began to fill the "chasm" between the musical language of musical theater and of the culture at large (Swain 2002, 415).

20. For example, in *Chorus Line* (Marvin Hamlisch and Edward Kleban, 1975), the form in "Music and the Mirror" is **A'ABCABB'**, with front-loaded **A** sections, strong downbeat agogic accents in **B** and a denser **C** providing rhythmic contrast; in the overall form **ABBABCB'A'** of "If I Were a Rich Man" (*Fiddler on the Roof*, 1967), the striking rhythmic contrast comes in the **C** section that begins with a loud rest ("_ the most im-*por*-tant men in <u>town</u>"), which differs from the front-loaded **A** sections that begin on the downbeat ("<u>If</u> I were a *rich* man"), while the **B** sections begin with an anacrusis ("I'd *fill* my <u>yard</u>").

21. "Being Alive" also features modified section lengths with repetitive rhyth-

mic cells developing into longer phrases, similar to those in "What I Did For Love" and "Music and the Mirror" (*Chorus Line*, Marvin Hamlisch and Edward Kleban, 1975).

22. A1 and A2 last twelve and fourteen bars, respectively, the **B** section lasts a standard symmetrical sixteen measures, and the final **A3** extends to eighteen measures. See Banfield (1993, 68–71) and Swayne (2004) for further discussion of Sondheim's **AABA** phrase explosion. While even in R&H it is common to expand the final **A**, the slow growth to achieving full phrases with subsequent expansion found in Sondheim is unique.

23. This key change (from F to G♭, signified with <) would seem to be a simple step-up modulation, but it is poignantly set up earlier in the melody. Through modal borrowing, the chromatic predominant iv in the first **A** section supports $\flat\hat{6}$ in the melody. While usually the **A** anacrusis starts $\hat{3}$–$\hat{4}$–$\hat{5}$, for the final chorus it is modified to $\hat{3}$–$\hat{4}$–$\flat\hat{6}$, which becomes $\hat{5}$ in the new key.

24. The entire line repeats for **A2**, this time ending in a conclusive perfect authentic cadence. **A3** is mostly the same as **A2**, but with an optional tag for the final climax.

25. This accompanies a drastic key change. While the **AABA** sections were in C major, with a strong emphasis on F major (IV) in the bridge, the **C** section starts in E minor, or iii, journeying through E♭ major and G major before returning to C major.

26. Block contrasts these "hidden triplets," which seem to demonstrate the hesitation of the subjunctive lyrics, with the "Many a New Day"–type triplets (*Oklahoma!*) on stronger metric beats (2009, 205).

27. The **AABA** form in "If Loved You" is only achieved after an introduction in which quickly alternating rhythmic patterns lessen in density to herald the beginning of the actual song. The bench scene is noted as a thoroughly "integrated" scene encompassing interwoven dialogue, transitional music, and the main refrain in **AABA** form. For more on this, see McMillin (2006, 137–39) and Block (2009, 199–206).

28. Scholars and critics alike have tended to view megamusicals with skepticism, implicitly arguing that popularity and artistic value were bad bedfellows for most musicals after *Oklahoma!*. Criticism of these shows often centers on the dramatic and narrative implications of the sung-through score (see for example Swain 2002; Grant 2004; McMillin 2006). Sternfeld (2006) is one of the few academics who engages these shows critically. See also Hutchinson's recent (2020) analysis of music from *Sunset Boulevard* and *Miss Saigon*.

29. I choose to examine Javert's version of the number in part because it is better known and recognized. Swain (2002) notes the contrafactum, and Prece and Everett note how "Valjean and Javert share much of the same music, thus demonstrating that they represent two sides of the same human condition" (2008, 248–49). On the other hand, Sternfeld argues that both *Les Misérables* and *Phantom of the Opera*

use "most of [their] set numbers as fodder for manipulations and recurrence, rather than as character-defining signature tunes" (2006, 260), noting that musical repetition constitutes one of three main characteristics of megamusicals (27).

30. Other Javert and Valjean numbers similarly use small, repeating rhythmic cells to create contrast and build intensity. See for example Valjean's "Who Am I," which similarly uses repeating rhythmic cells that decrease in rhythmic density, and Javert's "Stars," which builds in rhythmic density to the declarative bridge (**C**, "And so it must be, for so it is *writ*-ten," in **ABABCA'**).

31. Syncopation at the subdivision level is especially common in recent musicals, corresponding to the increased syncopation in contemporary music that it is closely linked with. For more on this, see both Temperley's discussions of syncopation (1999, 2019) and Condit-Schultz's 2019 study of the increased frequency and varieties of syncopations in recent *Billboard* hits.

32. The move from bridge to end echoes similar sections in earlier megamusicals.

33. Alternately, the **AB** sections could be combined for an overall **ABA'C**, but I see them as separate sections because of their relative length and thematic differences.

34. Hatten (1994) discusses musical markedness: how musical opposites can create meaning through comparison. Markedness goes further than general contrast, as it requires one to invoke generic and contextual expectations.

35. The show premiered on Broadway in 2015, but first opened off-Broadway in 2013.

36. See also Rachel Lumsden's chapter on *Fun Home* in this volume.

37. The full song has an extended introduction sung by the ensemble and a combined finale, but my remarks focus on the central solo by the lead character.

## WORKS CITED

Appen, Ralf von, and Markus Frei-Hauenschild. 2015. "AABA, Refrain, Chorus, Bridge, Prechorus—Song Forms and Their Historical Development." *Samples. Online Publikationen Der Gesellschaft Für Popularmusikforschung/German Society for Popular Music Studies e.V.* 13.

Banfield, Stephen. 1993. *Sondheim's Broadway Musicals*. Ann Arbor: University of Michigan Press.

Block, Geoffrey Holden. 2009. *Enchanted Evenings: The Broadway Musical from Show Boat to Sondheim*, 2nd ed. New York: Oxford University Press.

Buchler, Michael. 2008. "Modulation as a Dramatic Agent in Frank Loesser's Broadway Songs." *Music Theory Spectrum* 30 (1): 35–60.

Butler, Mark Jonathan. 2006. *Unlocking the Groove: Rhythm, Meter, and Musical Design in Electronic Dance Music*. Bloomington: Indiana University Press.

Coleman, Bud. 2017. "New Horizons: The Musical at the Dawn of the Twenty-First

Century." In *The Cambridge Companion to the Musical*, 339–55. Cambridge Companions to Music. Cambridge: Cambridge University Press.

Condit-Schultz, Nat. 2019. "Expanding and Contracting Definitions of Syncopation: Commentary on Temperley 2019." *Empirical Musicology Review* 14 (November): 81.

Forte, Allen. 1995. *The American Popular Ballad of the Golden Era, 1924–1950*. Princeton, NJ: Princeton University Press.

Grant, Mark N. 2004. *The Rise and Fall of the Broadway Musical*. Boston: Northeastern University Press.

Graziano, John. 2014. "Compositional Strategies in Popular Song Form of the Early Twentieth Century." *Gamut: Online Journal of the Music Theory Society of the Mid-Atlantic* 6 (2).

Hamm, Charles. 1983. *Yesterdays: Popular Song in America*. New York: W. W. Norton & Co.

Hamm, Charles. 1994. "Genre, Performance and Ideology in the Early Songs of Irving Berlin." *Popular Music* 13 (2): 143–50.

Hatten, Robert S. 1994. *Musical Meaning in Beethoven: Markedness, Correlation, and Interpretation*. Bloomington: Indiana University Press.

Hutchinson, Kyle. 2020. "Retrospective Time and the Subdominant Past: Tonal Hermeneutics in Contemporary Broadway Megamusicals." *Music Theory Online* 26 (2).

Jarvis, Brian Edward, and John Peterson. 2019. "Alternative Paths, Phrase Expansion, and the Music of Felix Mendelssohn." *Music Theory Spectrum* 41 (2): 187–217.

Jarvis, Brian Edward, and John Peterson. 2020. "Detour or Bridge? Contrasting Sections and Storytelling in Musical Theatre." *SMT-V* 6 (2) (March).

Laird, Paul R. 2014. *The Musical Theater of Stephen Schwartz: From Godspell to Wicked and Beyond*. Lanham, MD: Rowman & Littlefield.

Larson, Steve. 2003. "What Makes a Good Bridge." *Tijdschrift Voor Muziektheorie* 8: 1– 15.

London, Justin. 1993. "Loud Rests and Other Strange Metric Phenomena (or, Meter as Heard)." *Music Theory Online*. 0 (2).

Malin, Yonatan. 2008. "Metric Analysis and the Metaphor of Energy: A Way Into Selected Songs by Wolf and Schoenberg." *Music Theory Spectrum* 30 (1): 61–87.

McMillin, Scott. 2006. *The Musical as Drama: A Study of the Principles and Conventions Behind Musical Shows from Kern to Sondheim*. Princeton, NJ: Princeton University Press.

Prece, Paul, and William A. Everett. 2008. "The Megamusical and Beyond: The Creation, Internationalization and Impact of a Genre." In *The Cambridge Companion to the Musical*, 246–65. Cambridge: Cambridge University Press.

Rosenberg, Deena. 1997. *Fascinating Rhythm: The Collaboration of George and Ira Gershwin*. Ann Arbor: University of Michigan Press.

Sternfeld, Jessica. 2006. *The Megamusical*. Bloomington: Indiana University Press.

Summach, Jay. 2011. "The Structure, Function, and Genesis of the Prechorus." *Music Theory Online* 17 (3).

Swain, Joseph P. 2002. *The Broadway Musical: A Critical and Musical Survey*, 2nd ed. Lanham, MD: Scarecrow Press.

Swayne, Steve. 2004. "So Much 'More': The Music of 'Dick Tracy' (1990)." *American Music* 22 (1): 50–63.

Swayne, Steve. 2005. *How Sondheim Found His Sound*. Ann Arbor: University of Michigan Press.

Temperley, David. 1999. "Syncopation in Rock: A Perceptual Perspective." *Popular Music* 18 (1): 19–40.

Temperley, David. 2019. "Second-Position Syncopation in European and American Vocal Music." *Empirical Musicology Review* 14 (1–2): 66–80.

Waters, Keith. 2012. "Other Good Bridges: Continuity and Debussy's 'Reflets Dans l'eau.'" *Music Theory Online* 18 (3).

Wilder, Alec. 1972. *American Popular Song: The Great Innovators, 1900–1950*, edited by James T. Maher. New York: Oxford University Press.

# PART 2

# Chapters That Engage a Single Work

# 6 *Three Notions of Long-Range Form in* Guys and Dolls

*MICHAEL BUCHLER*

*Guys and Dolls* opened on Broadway on November 24, 1950, apparently to uniformly positive reviews from New York's often-grumpy press corps. Specifically, raves appeared in the *New York Times*, the *New York Daily News*, the *New York Herald Tribune*, the *New York World Telegram*, the *New York Post*, the *New York Journal American*, the *Daily Mirror, International News* [Wire] *Service*, the *Sunday News*, *Colliers Magazine*, the *Saturday Review*, and the *New Yorker*.[1] In 1950 and over the years since, both critics and scholars have hailed it as a "perfect musical."

In the immediate wake of the show's premiere, John Chapman (theater critic for the *New York Daily News*) wrote:

> I did not want to leave the theatre after the premiere last night and come back here and write a piece about the show. I wanted to hang around, on the chance that they would raise the curtain again and put on a few numbers they'd forgotten—or, at least, start *Guys and Dolls* all over again. For here is New York's own musical comedy—as bright as a dime in a subway grating, as smart as a sidewalk pigeon, as professional as Joe DiMaggio, as enchanting as the skyline, as new as the paper you're holding.
>
> . . . In all departments, *Guys and Dolls* is a perfect musical comedy. (November 25, 1950)

Some historians have been similarly enthusiastic: David Ewen claimed that *Guys and Dolls* "is the model of what an ideal musical comedy should be. Like different parts of a solved jigsaw puzzle, each part is made to fit neatly into the complete picture and is basic to the over-all pattern" (Ewen 1958, 189). And Gerald Bordman declared that *Guys and Dolls* attained "tonal and structural cohesion rare in the annals of the American Musical Theatre" (Bordman 2001, 631).

What does it mean to be a "perfect musical comedy?" The idea of *perfection* might seem quaintly romantic today, especially as it appears to be uniformly wrapped up in bygone ideals of organic unity, something that many musicals from the past fifty years have flouted in creative and, at times, postmodern ways. But in the golden era of book-driven, single-composer musicals, traditional notions of musical and dramatic unity were heavily valued and critically praised on Broadway. As Stacy Wolf commented, "starting in the mid-1940s, the critical judgment of a musical depended on how well the show's elements were formally integrated" (Wolf 2011, 9).

In this chapter, I investigate notions of the "perfect" midcentury musical comedy from several perspectives: (1) character development in an archetypal two-couple romantic comedy; (2) large-scale musical form, investigating the placement and character of songs and incidental music; and (3) the placement and meaning of duets. Theorists' discussions of musical form are not generally nourished by the interaction and development of characters or by the categorization of songs according to their dramatic function and show order. However, the ways in which a composer portrays their characters through musical topics, styles, and more discrete musical features (harmony, rhythm, orchestration, . . .) have just as much to do with *form* (writ large) as does the interplay of themes and tonal areas in classical instrumental music. In this chapter, I aim to broaden our notions of form and better capture each constituent song's raison d'être.

## *AN ARTFUL ARRANGEMENT OF DRAMATIS PERSONAE*

In some ways, *Guys and Dolls* resembles Mozart's da Ponte operas, especially *Marriage of Figaro* and *Cosí fan Tutte*. They all feature two central couples, one of which is more significant than the other, and they also stress a contrast between high and low culture: *Cosí* and *Guys and Dolls* both involve a central wager; *Figaro* and *Guys and Dolls* both feature sympathetic minor characters who facilitate the relationships. The latter two also both include a minor character who keeps watch as illicit activities take place.

I see echoes of da Ponte's dramatic archetypes in *Guys and Dolls*, but I make no claim that either Abe Burrows or, least of all, Damon Runyon actively felt that influence.[2] Burrows was, by most accounts, the show's primary book author (the initial contracted librettist, Jo Swerling, left the project during its creation), and Runyon wrote the famous short stories that served as posthumous sources of the show's characters and some its plot points.[3] *Guys and Dolls* projects far greater dramatic clarity than those two operatic examples, and, though it is distinctly comic, the musical avoids da Ponte's sometimes inelegant silliness. Indeed, Frank Loesser claimed that he wanted people to take the characters seriously and not create a work of slapstick.[4]

## *MAPPING THE DRAMA*

To understand how a drama functions, it can be useful to draw comparisons to an archetype and map out various characters' relations with one another. This brings the overall plot into sharper focus and helps make sense of each character's motivation and, more importantly for this project, the songs they sing. Imagine an abstract dramatic model for a (heteronormative) two-couple romantic musical comedy. Many such shows were written in the 1940s and 1950s, including *Oklahoma!*, *Kiss Me, Kate*, *The Pajama Game*, and *The Most Happy Fella*. Generally speaking, during their dramatic expositions either the two men or the two women (or occasionally both) are friends, and at least one of the couples (occasionally both, as in *Guys and Dolls*) are in conflict, motivating the common first-act "I'm not in love with you" love duet (sometimes called the "conditional love duet") that anticipates the show's central romance.[5] Opposites always seem to attract, after all.

The two-couple romantic comedy often requires a third party—an agent—either to introduce the couples or to help bring resolution to one or both opposed pairs. Of course, if everything is copacetic from the outset, there is probably no drama and certainly no comedy, so we expect some combination of romantic conflict and agreement.

The cast of characters in *Guys and Dolls* falls almost neatly into two groups that help motivate the drama: the gamblers, who are pressuring Nathan to find a place for their craps game, and the Save-A-Soul Mission, which seemingly cannot find any souls to save on Broadway. The mission's tough and pragmatic regional head, General Mathilde B. Cartwright, has unexpectedly come to town and announced that she will close the failing mission. The earnest missionaries ask for a reprieve when Sky Masterson promises that he can fill the place with sinners, if only Sister Sarah agrees to travel with him to Havana, a trip that would satisfy Sky Masterson's crass bet with Nathan Detroit.

Figure 6.1 diagrams the dramatic framework of *Guys and Dolls* in terms of its characters' relationships to one another. At the risk of committing the cardinal theatrical sin of "too much exposition," I will walk through this graph, listing plot details. Sky Masterson and Sister Sarah Brown are unacquainted with one another as the show opens. After a bet necessitates their introduction, they quickly develop an adversarial relationship (dramatized by the duet "I'll Know"), but by the end of the first act, it is clear—even to them—that they have fallen in love (which they acknowledge in "I've Never Been In Love Before"). By contrast, Nathan Detroit and Miss Adelaide (who has no last name) are a loving couple who have been together for so long that he seems to take her for granted, and she is getting ready to give up on him unless he commits to marriage.

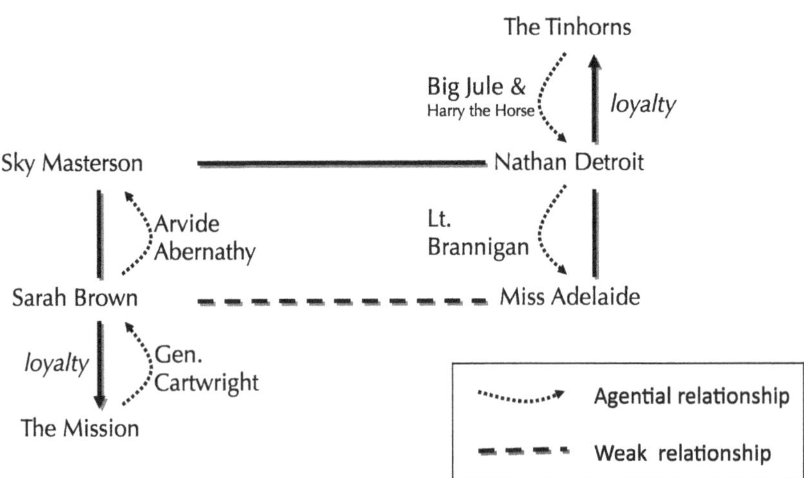


**Figure 6.1.** Dramatic framework of *Guys and Dolls*.

The friendship between Sky and Nathan binds the two couples. Their central $1,000 wager—that Sky cannot take Sister Sarah to Havana with him—motivates the unlikely romance between Sky and Sarah, but while the two principal men are competitive, they are not genuinely adversarial. They share the same aims—gambling and staying free and easy—and they both want the craps game to succeed. For at least the first half of the show, the women do not encounter one another. After all, one is a prim missionary, the other a burlesque performer. I have drawn the women's relationship with a dotted line. Except for a very brief encounter at the end of act 1, the women do not truly talk with (or, more significantly, sing with) one another until the very end of the musical, when they perform the show's final duet, "Marry the Man Today." In the film version, which excludes that duet, Sarah and Adelaide never meaningfully encounter one another until the final scene.

The dramatic state in the first half of act 1 features no relation between the women, an agreeable if competitive relation between the guys, and conflict within each couple. But, toward the end of act 1, the adversarial relationship between Sky and Sarah has turned loving, and Nathan (slightly under duress) has set a date for marrying Adelaide. However, we don't go to intermission thinking that all is well—not by a long shot.

Moving beyond the central four characters, figure 6.1 portrays the drama as a trio of balances that more accurately reflects how everything ties together in this complex but deeply integrated story. Sarah balances her concerns for the mission with her animosity for Sky. That animosity later turns to affection, then anger, then eventually forgiveness. Sky balances his desire to win a bet with his increasing affection for Sarah and his need to fill her mission hall as promised. Nathan is balancing the promises he made to his eager fiancée with the promises he made to his eager gamblers. Adelaide's place in this drama, though important, is more unilateral. She only cares about Nathan and whether he will or won't commit to her. She is therefore the only major character who is not really balancing two concerns.

Various secondary characters act as agents who create and/or help resolve the primary and secondary dramatic conflicts. Arvide Abernathy is Sarah's kindly and worldly grandfather who plays bass drum with the mission band.[6] When Sarah seems unwilling to forgive Sky for facilitating Nathan's decision to hold his craps game in the mission hall, Arvide sings her the touching and vaguely Celtic/folksy song "More I Cannot Wish

You," advising that finding her own true love is the most important thing she can do (as it was for most women in musicals from the first half of the century). Arvide counsels Sarah to follow her heart and he quietly warns Sky that if he fails to keep his end of the deal by filling the mission hall, everyone on Broadway will learn that Sky has "welshed" on a promise.

Lt. Brannigan, shown on the right side of the graph, indirectly serves as an agent by walking into a planning meeting for that night's craps game. All the tinhorns are wearing flowers in their lapels to identify themselves and gain admission to the game. When Brannigan asks what's going on, one of the gamblers inventively declares that it is Nathan's bachelor party, as he is finally going to tie the knot with Adelaide. Naturally, Adelaide is within earshot and overjoyed by the news, which consequently seals their fate. (This is the point in the 1955 film version where Nathan Detroit, played by Frank Sinatra, sings the song "Adelaide," which was composed for the movie and is not in the original show.)

Further motivating the drama, Big Jule, a larger-than-life thug visiting from East Cicero, Illinois, is disturbed that the game broke up when the cops arrived at the mission, and he demands that Nathan coordinate another game to allow him to win back his losses (this time with Jule's own crooked dice). Without Big Jule and his lieutenant, Harry the Horse, the important second craps game wouldn't take place and we would lose the motivation for Sky's climactic moment in the second act, not to mention the classic song, "Luck Be a Lady." And without General Cartwright's threats of closing the mission, Sarah would lose her altruistic reason for going to Havana with Sky, which is, after all, where she falls in love with him and where, thanks to the local rum drinks, she first confronts her repressed sexuality.

Capturing aspects of both a musical reduction and a transformational network, the atemporal dramatic model of *Guys and Dolls* in figure 6.1 helps to elucidate some of the larger oppositional issues that unfold over time and propel the drama. One of the primary conflicts is between religious and secular characters and institutions. Everyone on the chart's left side is religious, including Sky Masterson, whose hidden religious background gets revealed throughout the show in his scenes with Sister Sarah. Two key moments from act 1 are illustrative: in the first mission scene, Sky demonstrates that he can expertly cite biblical chapter and verse, and at the end of act 1, Sky, in his most vulnerable and romantic moment, reveals that his real name is biblical (Obadiah). Another opposition, as in da Ponte's work, is between social ranks (again demarcated by the left side versus right side of the same graph). In this case, religious characters correlate with higher ranks and gamblers/burlesque performers with lower ranks. A different sort of opposition separates those who approve of and those who disapprove of gambling—they're separated on the horizontal axis with Nathan and Sky (and everyone above them) as gamblers. Adelaide's vocabulary and her occupation mark her as distinctly low class, but she dreams of white picket fences and she sees Nathan's gambling as all that stands between her and blissful married life.

Lehman Engel, one of the most important conductors, chroniclers, and creative mentors during musical theater's so-called golden era, commented that Burrows and Loesser "balanced the musical with two sets of characters, each member as well as each couple telling [their] own tale. . . . There is no secondary plot or subplot—only two coexistent and closely related ones." Engel deemed this a "unique accomplishment" (2006, 95–96). My lengthy mise-en-scène explicitly draws out Engel's observation. In the remainder of this chapter, I examine ways that this high degree of interconnectedness motivates (or is motivated by) Loesser's local musical decisions and how those musical decisions and the order of songs shape the show's large-scale form.

## *DICHOTOMIES AND RELIGIOSITY*

As *Guys and Dolls* opens, we both hear and see a strong contrast between the missionaries and the gamblers. The overture is about half the length of a 1940s Rodgers and Hammerstein overture, and instead of launching directly into song, the curtain opens onto a fully choreographed (by Michael Kidd) modern dance sequence ("Runyonland") that vividly reveals the shady goings-on on Broadway. "Runyonland" leads directly into the famous "Fugue for Tinhorns." Thomas Riis described that song as "an instance of quintessential Loesser/Runyon humor to call the opening three-part round a 'fugue,' a nose-thumbing gesture for people who might want to point out that it fell short of being a true Baroque fugue" (2008, 85).

Because it is a round with entries at four-bar intervals, "Fugue for Tinhorns" is both harmonically simple and hypermetrically regular, but the syncopations, the pervasive use of accented dissonance, the mildly bluesy passing use of $\flat\hat{7}$, and the winding, seemingly continuous—indeed

Escher-like—descending lines mark this as a song that is both comedic and distinctly secular. The fact that it goes round and round portrays the tinhorns' continuous obsession with gambling. Like "Oh, What a Beautiful Mornin'" in *Oklahoma*, Loesser's "Fugue" sets the scene but doesn't contribute to the dramatic exposition.[7] Example 6.1 illustrates Loesser's inventive and deceptively simple contrapuntal structure by juxtaposing the three four-bar segments that are heard simultaneously. With nothing but tonic and dominant harmonies, Loesser's continuous descents ensure that tonic bars prominently feature $\hat{1}$, $\hat{3}$, and $\hat{5}$, while dominant bars feature scale degrees a step lower: $\hat{7}$, $\hat{2}$, and $\hat{4}$.[8] $\hat{6}$ is usually passing, but sometimes forms a dominant ninth. Harmony and counterpoint aside, what makes this tangled web of lyrics comprehensible and funny (the former is a prerequisite of the latter) is that the active and syncopated first four bars that feature creative lyrics ("I've got the horse right here . . .") are juxtaposed against the slower, unsyncopated, and lyrically repetitive assurances of "can do, can do." Though the parts of the tune are heard alternatingly by three different singers, Loesser's faster and more syncopated first four bars always stand out as primary—and that, of course, is where the cleverest lyrics lie.

At precisely the moment "Fugue for Tinhorns" winds its way to a cadence via a tacked-on coda that ends the round (not shown in example 6.1), sidewalk missionaries barge onto the scene with their quotidian march, "Follow the Fold." These first two songs both rely on limited harmonic palates, consisting largely of tonic and dominant harmonies, yet the contrast couldn't be clearer. The final tonic of the "faux learned" D♭-major "Fugue" is overrun by the missionaries' C-major march, creating an unmistakably stark opposition, both tonally and stylistically. The immediate tonal motion *down* a half step is also markedly the opposite of the usual intensifying gesture.[9] The austere Salvationist band plays and/or sings that same tune over and over again in the musical, always squarely, always in C major, and often a bit out of tune, diegetically portraying the missionaries' remarkable lack of persuasiveness. Is it any wonder that General Cartwright is threatening to close their branch? These evangelists have no fire and no savvy, and their rhetoric (both musical and linguistic) is clearly no match for that of the gamblers.

Soon after the mission band finishes their amateur rendition of this comically stale melody, we hear another of the cleverest tunes in the show—and it was a late edition. In an early draft of the script, Abe Bur-

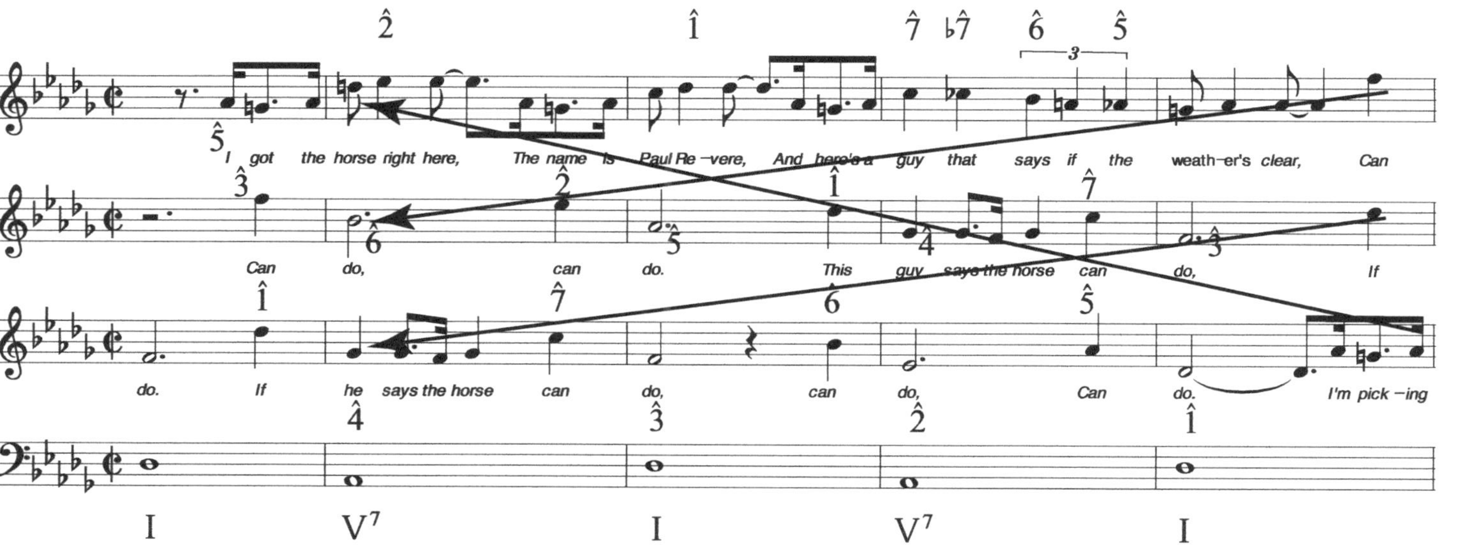


**Example 6.1.** "Fugue for Tinhorns," a three-voice canon with Escher-like descents. The first entry's twelve-bar theme is layered against itself to show the harmonic implications of the unfolding contrapuntal imitation.

"Fugue For Tinhorns" from *Guys and Dolls* by Frank Loesser. 

rows had purportedly described Nathan's game as "the oldest established permanent floating crap game in New York," and Loesser thought that was too rich a description to be relegated to a single spoken laugh line (S. Loesser 1993, 102). The men's ensemble number, "The Oldest Established," begins with a recitative-like verse, featuring relative rhythmic and metrical freedom and a melody of gradually ascending reciting tones. "The Biltmore Garage wants a grand" (B♭4) . . . "And they've now got a lock on the door" (C5) . . . "There's the stockroom behind McClosky's Bar" (D5). Unlike the endless descents in the "Fugue," which seem to portray an unabated and undirected conversation performed daily by rote, this ascent has a clear goal and, by ascending, Loesser helps to build tension that is gloriously diffused at the beginning of the refrain ("Why it's good old reliable Nathan . . .").

The refrain's acrobatic compound melody not only contrasts the verse, but offers two stylistic juxtapositions with the missionaries and their march. As in the opening "Fugue," the gamblers show that their lyrics demand syncopated rhythms. Also like the "Fugue," this is an ensemble number that opens by appropriating "high art" (classical recitative, in this case) into a vulgar landscape by using lyrics inspired by Damon Runyon's poetically low-class vernacular.

Loesser saves the memorable, if unwieldy, title lyric for the cadence, which he sets using ornamented suspensions that clearly invoke religiosity. Indeed, at the end of the final chorus, the score is marked "*Maestoso (quasi religioso)*."[10] Clearly, both the missionaries and the gamblers are reverent, but the objects of their reverence differ, as do their musical signifiers. We hear another ornate contrapuntal allusion to religion in Sky Masterson's revelatory song "My Time of Day," where religiosity is articulated by a surprising bit of diatonicism and an ornamented cadential gesture in the middle of an otherwise chromatic and episodic song (at the lyric: "And the street lamp light fills the gutter with gold."). Sky Masterson more explicitly casts the refrain of his most famous song, "Luck Be a Lady," as a prayer just before he rolls the dice. After an especially chromatic climactic moment ("you might forget your manners, you might refuse to stay"), that song's opening verse pauses and then concludes with a purely diatonic cadential progression underscoring the text: "and so the best that I can do is pray." And, of course, the big showstopper near the end of act 2 is the gospel song "Sit Down, You're Rockin' the Boat," which is sung by gamblers in the mission hall. Its religious markers directly counter the foursquare "Follow the Fold," and this livelier number leads both to the mission's salvation and to the genuine repentance of (at least some of) the gamblers.[11]

Throughout *Guys and Dolls*, music reveals that the gamblers aren't necessarily averse to religion, but they are simply unwilling to listen to the missionaries; the missionaries, on the other hand, cannot speak—or sing—convincingly to the tinhorns, but once a tinhorn starts singing the gospel, the others come around. Fauconnier and Turner's model for conceptual blending (as applied in Zbikowski 2002) seems made for this kind of moment. It involves taking aspects from two different generic—or conceptual—spaces and creating a product that represents more than the sum of its parts. To wit: the missionaries seem marked by local diatonicism, rhythmic/hypermetric squareness, stepwise motion, and a strong emphasis on tonic and dominant (not pre-dominant) functions.[12] The gamblers and Miss Adelaide, however, tend to be more chromatic, harmonically rich, and syncopated, and/or to use dotted rhythms and triple subdivisions of the beat (either triplets or compound time).

The missionaries also tend to stay in "safe" keys such as C, F, and B♭, while the gamblers more frequently sing in D♭ and G♭. And when the gamblers draw on religious tropes, they generally seem to be of a more Catholic or Lutheran variety, invoking ornamented cadences, plagal gestures, and textures with considerably more polyphony. In the gamblers' songs, religious markers also tend to lie in the verses. The livelier syncopated music heard in "The Oldest Established," "Luck Be a Lady," and "Guys and Dolls" (the title song) takes over in the choruses, but again these styles aren't strictly segregated.

The gamblers and the missionaries invoke separate religious musical tropes, but it's their frequency and placement throughout the show that help us understand them as formal makers. My reading of large-scale form in *Guys and Dolls* draws inspiration from Dora Hanninen's associational landscapes, a nontraditional and flexible structural approach that builds from well-defined "associational sets." Hanninen writes that "an associative set is not just a collection of segments but a *system of relationships among segments* that itself functions as a unit at a higher level of organization. Instead of privileging certain shared features as necessary and sufficient criteria for membership, an associative set recognizes the complexity of relationships among its individual segments and embraces the full spectrum of similarity and difference" (2012, 236).

This is not motivic analysis—at least not as we generally think of it—but rather something much more pliable that can accept any number of criteria for judging similarity. *Associative sets* are placed on *associative landscapes*, which offer a way of discussing form that moves far beyond the standard taxonomical designations such as "AABA" or "sonata form." Hanninen's set of tools inspires my large-scale readings of form, but I divert from her use in two important ways: (1) she does not bring culturally defined criteria such as musical topics and intersubjective meaning into the mix, and (2) her associative criteria are better defined than what I produce here, primarily because she limits her criteria to distinct musical categories, including notes, harmonies, intervals, rhythms, and timbres. Differences aside, my reading takes inspiration from the helpful questions she poses about the recurrence of musical ideas, including an associative sets' "scale of activity" (whether it enjoys widespread or merely localized appearances), whether they are common or rare within a work, and whether any patches of associative sets are distributed evenly or unevenly (Hanninen 2012, 174).

Table 6.1 shows the complete list of musical works in *Guys and Dolls* as printed in both the published vocal score and libretto. I have annotated it with the songs heard instrumentally [shown in square brackets] during dances, transitions, and tags. The numbers are the original song numbers used in the published vocal score. Perhaps most apparently, at the beginning of the show the missionaries are marked by their dogged recitation of the comically earnest "Follow the Fold." Using the vocal score numbers found on the left of this page, I have constructed some make-shift landscapes in figure 6.2.

The first timeline in figure 6.2 traces recurrences of "Follow the Fold." It is heard in a dense patch at the beginning of the show, roughly alternating with clever songs sung by the gamblers. Apparently, it's the only song that members of the Save-a-Soul Mission knew; it is habitual at first, recurring less often as the plot unfolds and the characters—and especially Sister Sarah—exhibit greater complexity.

The frequency of "Follow the Fold" is particularly salient in a show that reprises songs considerably less than most other shows of its era.[13] Casting a somewhat broader net, the next landscape in figure 6.2 charts all the places where religion—or at least morality—is conveyed by the music and/or text. The shadowed crosses ✞ are songs that are sung by the gamblers, although numbers 29 and 31a probably should be shaded both light and dark: they're the last reprises of "Follow the Fold" and they involve the group of newly enlightened gamblers as well.

A still *broader way* that we could think about these associations is that the more rhythmically square a song is, the more likely it is to be sung by (or to represent) Sarah Brown and the missionaries, whereas the more rhythmically free, syncopated, or simply jazzy the number, the more likely it is sung by the ne'er-do-wells or Miss Adelaide, whose songs often feature more natural speech rhythms. This is not an especially tightly defined classification, so I offer grains of salt along with this third landscape. Many of the light squares ❑ in this chart represent recurrences of "Follow the Fold." Song no. 23 is the very sweet "More I Cannot Wish You" that Arvide sings to Sarah. Many of the dark squares ■ are either duets that involve Sarah ("I'll Know" and "I've Never Been in Love Before") or they refer back to those duets.[14]

The fourth landscape in figure 6.2 shows that only the gamblers or Adelaide sing or are represented by pervasively nonsquare (for lack of a better term) numbers until no. 15, late in act 1. No. 14 is the diegetic background music that Sky and Sarah hear in Havana. It is a long passage of Latin dance music that gets more and more frenetic as the scene progresses (and finally ends when Sarah gets embroiled in what must be her first bar fight). Although Sky is not a Latino, he is worldly and it is music that represents an environment where he feels comfortable; however, it is also music that, along with the cocktails, helps Sarah loosen up. As she recovers outside the club, she sings her drunken and mildly swinging yet still rather saccharine song, "If I Were A Bell." That's song no. 15, the first light-colored circle that appears.

Song no. 28, the next one with a light dot, is "Sit Down You're Rockin' the Boat," where, especially in the most recent Broadway revival, the missionaries learn to worship up-tempo and with more rhythmic vitality. This is true conceptual blending and from that point on, both the saints and sinners come together in song. After the gospel showstopper, everyone sings "Follow the Fold," Sarah and Adelaide sing their one duet, and the show comes to a rousing conclusion with a full-chorus reprise of the show's title song.

The square and nonsquare associative maps reveal that the gamblers are more likely to sing straight (especially when they're in love) than the missionaries are to syncopate or swing, but these two charts are predominantly negative images of one another—until the end, that is. Finally, the

Table 6.1. List of musical works and keys

**ACT I**

| No. | Description/song/[music] | Key |
|---|---|---|
| | Overture | various |
| 1 | Opening: "Runyonland" | various |
| 2 | Trio: "Fugue for Tinhorns" (Nicely, Benny, Rusty) | D♭ |
| 3 | Quintet: "Follow the Fold" (Sarah, Arvide, Agatha, Mission Group) | C |
| 3a | Exit of Sarah and the Mission Band: ["Follow the Fold"] | |
| 4 | Concerted Number: "The Oldest Established" (Nathan, Nicely, Benny . . .) | D♭, C, A♭, C |
| 5 | Entrance of the Mission Group: "Follow the Fold" | C |
| 6 | Duet: "I'll Know" (Sarah and Sky) | A (Sarah), E (Sky) |
| 6a | Interlude: ["I'll Know"] | F, g |
| 6b | Vocal Finish: "I'll Know" | A♭ |
| 6c | Change of Scene (2 to 3): ["I'll Know"] | F |
| 7 | Fanfare | C |
| 7a | Song: "A Bushel and a Peck" (Adelaide and Hot-Box Dolls) | B♭, G, A♭ |
| 7b | The Customers' Exit: ["Home Sweet Home"] | A♭ |
| 8 | Song: "Adelaide's Lament" | G♭, G |
| 8a | Change of Scene (4 to 5): ["Adelaide's Lament"] | C |
| 9 | Opening Scene 5: ["Follow the Fold"] | C |
| 10 | Duet: "Guys and Dolls" (Nicely and Benny) | F |
| 11 | Opening Scene 6: ["Follow the Fold"] | C |
| 12 | Change of Scene (6 to 7): ["Fugue for Tinhorns," unsyncopated] | C |
| 13 | End of Scene 7: ["Follow the Fold"] | C |
| 14 | Havana: ["Cuban Café Shango," "Polite Rhumba," "a la Tango," "Samba," "Rhumba" various] | |
| 15 | Song: "If I Were a Bell" (Sarah) | E♭ |
| 16 | Change of Scene: (9 to 10) ["I'll Know"] | A♭ |
| 17 | Song: "My Time of Day" (Sky) | F, g, A♭, G |
| 17a | Duet: "I've Never Been in Love Before" (Sky and Sarah) | B♭ (Sky), D (Sarah) |
| 18 | The Raid: ["Fugue for Tinhorns," unsyncopated and fast] | F |
| 19 | Curtain Music: ["I've Never Been in Love Before"—Maestoso] | A♭ |
| 20 | Entr'acte | various |

| **ACT II** | | |
|---|---|---|
| 21 | Hot-Box Fanfare | C |
| 21a | Song, Chorus, and Dance: "Take Back Your Mink" (Adelaide and Dolls) | B♭, C, F (dance) |
| 22 | Song: "Adelaide's Second Lament" (Adelaide) | G♭ |
| 22a | Change of Scene (1 to 2): ["I've Never Been in Love Before"] | D♭ |
| 23 | Song: "More I Cannot with You" (Arvide) | D |
| 24 | Change of Scene: (2 to 3) [lead-in to "Luck Be a Lady"] | C |
| 24a | The Crapshooters' Dance: ["Luck Be a Lady"] | C, various |
| 25 | Song and Chorus: "Luck Be a Lady" (Sky and the Crapshooters) | D♭, D, E♭, D♭ |
| 26 | Change of Scene: (3 to 4) ["Luck Be a Lady"] | E♭ |
| 27 | Duet: "Sue Me" (Adelaide and Nathan) | B♭ |
| 27a | Change of Scene: (4 to 5) ["Sue Me . . . Follow the Fold". . . both slow] | B♭ (both) |
| 28 | Song and Chorus: "Sit Down, You're Rockin' the Boat" (Nicely) | F |
| 29 | "The Guys Follow the Fold" | C |
| 29a | Adelaide Meets Sarah [A: Adelaide's Lament/S: I've Never Been in Love Before] | D |
| 30 | Duet: "Marry the Man Today" (Adelaide and Sarah) | c (G bridge) |
| 31 | Opening Scene 7: ["G&D, Luck Be a Lady, Fugue, Luck Be a Lady"] | Various, ends in C |
| 31a | Entrance of the Mission Band: ["Follow the Fold'] | C |
| 32 | The Happy Ending: "Guys and Dolls" (everyone) | E♭ |

Square brackets denote underscored instrumental music and comments. Parentheses show performers.

last part of figure 6.2 combines the previous two charts to show a rough alternation of square and nonsquare numbers and, at least at the beginning, we have a rough alternation of songs by (or instrumental numbers that apply to) gamblers and missionaries. This chart vividly depicts the sort of conceptual blending that happy endings necessitate in love stories involving characters from very different backgrounds and stations in life.[15]

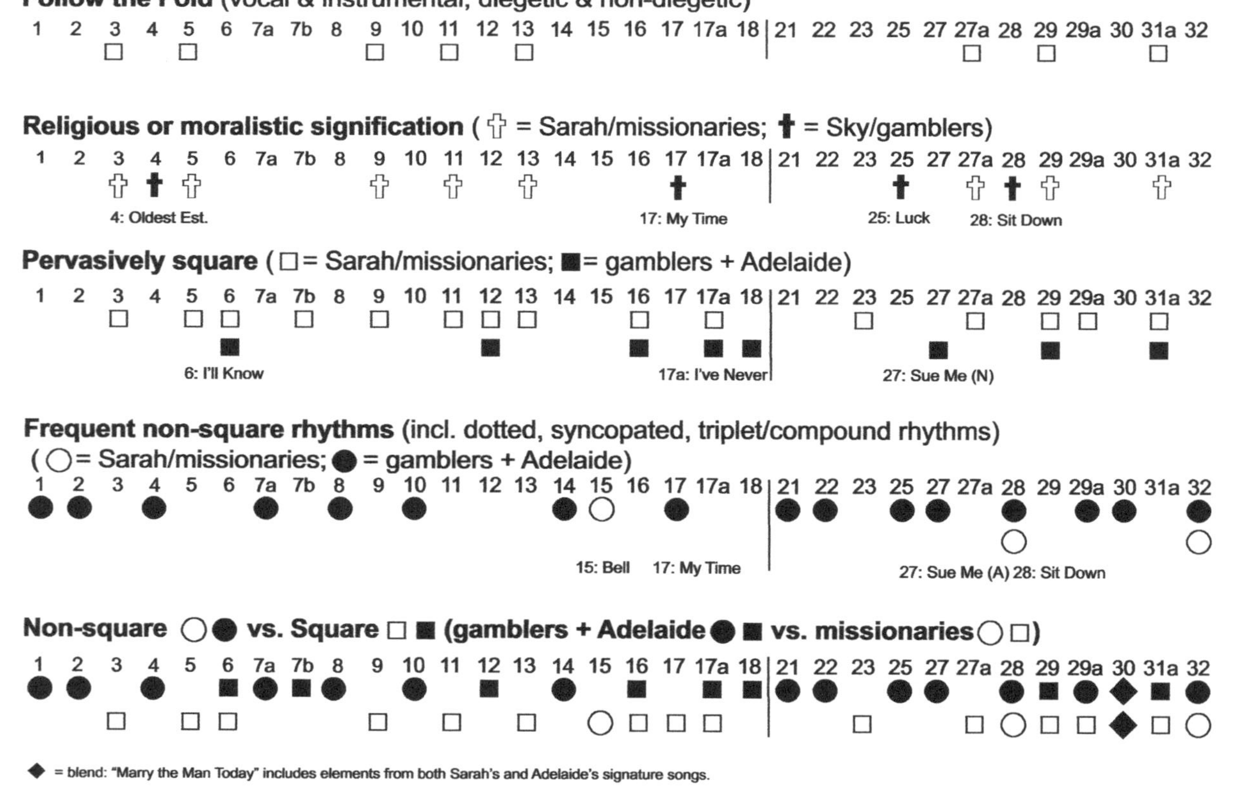


**Figure 6.2.** Associative landscapes in *Guys and Dolls*. Numbers represent the song numbers in the original published vocal score (and also in figure 6.1).

## *DUETS AS FORMAL MARKERS*

While the exposition is dominated by ensemble numbers ("Fugue for Tinhorns," "Follow the Fold," "The Oldest Established," and, a bit later, "Guys and Dolls"), *Guys and Dolls* is principally about relationships among the quartet of central characters, and the show's four duets arguably mark the most important and perhaps the most obvious formal and dramatic junctures. The musically manifest communication problems encountered by the tinhorns and missionaries in act 1 are expressed differently and less directly by the show's two central couples. Whereas religious attributes generally come to the fore in the musical's solo or larger ensemble numbers, duets express relational conflict and accord.

One of Frank Loesser's greatest contributions to musical theater was what I'll call the *argumentative duet*. Rather than the *consecutive duet* discussed below (and heavily favored by Rodgers and Hammerstein), the characters in an argumentative duet trade lyrics, interrupting or overlapping with one another. Loesser deploys this largely comic device in both act 2 duets: "Sue Me" and "Marry the Man Today."[16] In "Sue Me," Miss Adelaide's fast and agitated complaints, "you promise me this, you promise me that, you promise me anything under the sun . . . ," are set in $\frac{6}{8}$ (the same meter as her "Lament") with almost constant eighth notes, rhythmically, if not grammatically running her sentences together even as Nathan attempts to squeeze in a word. Nathan responds to Adelaide's anxious triple divisions in simple $\frac{3}{4}$ time, as he pleads "Call a lawyer and sue me, sue me, what can you do me?" and interjects "Alright already! I'm just a no-good-nick!"

Adelaide's other duet, "Marry the Man Today," sung with Sister Sarah Brown, is led into by "Adelaide Meets Sarah," which directly opposes a slow excerpt of "Adelaide's Lament" (again with triple beat divisions) with Sarah's now-wistful rendition of "I'll know" (unsyncopated and in simple quadruple meter). Both women maintain their own musical markers in "Adelaide Meets Sarah," but "Marry the Man Today" truly is a blended—not an interruptive—number. It reflects neither Sarah's pure diatonicism nor Adelaide's chromatic, anxiety-ridden musical voice, and it places Adelaide's impatient triple divisions into a slow and plodding march—but the only march we've heard since "Follow the Fold."[17]

"Marry the Man Today" sharply differs from the first act's conflicting, but essentially pre-romantic, duet: "I'll Know," a more traditional Broadway duet in which Sarah and Sky sing the same song but with different lyrics.

The two songs sung by the leading couple, Sky and Sarah, are traditional Broadway duets: what I call *consecutive duets* in which one member of the couple sings the verse and chorus, and then the other person sings the verse and chorus, generally with altered lyrics and often in a different key and/or with differently orchestrated backing music. At the very end of a consecutive duet, especially in love duets, the couple unites to sing together, either in octaves or in harmony (often parallel tenths). "I'll Know" is the traditional act 1 I-hate-you-but-I'm-attracted-to-you (conditional) duet (see note 5) that depicts romantic conflict. Sky and Sarah come from different backgrounds and have radically different worldviews, and yet they're both willing to sing the same tune, enumerating what they imagine they're seeking in a partner. The characters might not yet know that they'll fall in love, but we do, especially at the end when they sing "I'll know when my love comes along" in perfect harmony. At the end of act 1, their genuine love duet, "I've Never Been in Love Before," features the same structure, but now the couple are truly on the same page, singing the same lyrics in their consecutive renditions, and again coming together in harmony at the end.

The differences between Sky and Sarah were musically articulated even more strongly in 1976, when *Guys and Dolls* was revived on Broadway in a short-lived (and widely panned) production that featured an all-Black cast. Critical reception notwithstanding, I encourage readers to listen to how James Randolph and Ernestine Jackson handled these roles. Their characters are sharply distinguished: Sister Sarah is voiced traditionally in the first verse and chorus of "I'll Know"; Sky then sings his verse "straight," but moves into a smooth R&B style in the chorus.[18] Sky Masterson vintage 1976 is both racially marked and culturally hip.

In that production, Sister Sarah acclimates to Sky's style at the end of the first act. After Sky pours out his soul in the remarkable "My Time of Day" (which I discuss in detail in Buchler 2008, 49–59), he sings "I've Never Been in Love Before" in disco style and Sarah answers in kind, channeling her inner Donna Summer. That romantic song in its disco incarnation was a symbol not only of Sky and Sarah's love, but of her acquiescence and acceptance of Sky and his lifestyle.

As I mentioned earlier, the duets open a window onto the show's large-scale form, and that form would have been even more tightly connected had the original version that was premiered in Philadelphia in October 1950 lasted until the show's Broadway opening the following month. The act 1 scene in Mindy's Restaurant originally included a wonderful duet called "Traveling Light," which was sung by Sky and Nathan. In it, the guys celebrated living a free-and-easy life, avoiding getting weighted down by marriage and its mundane trappings.

The song's verse is expansive. Rather than the short-short-long (4+4+8 bar) proportional norm of the sentential Broadway phrase, this song opens with a short-short-longer . . . and still longer extension: a phrase that lists so many perceived grievances with marriage that it takes twenty-eight (not the usual sixteen) bars to wind its way to a cadence. Example 6.2 shows the verse's opening melody, lyrics, and harmony; analytical annotations demonstrate that this starts as a normal 4+4+8 sentence—a pair of basic ideas, followed by a continuation—but that continuation's path to the expected cadence gets sidetracked by the musically onomatopoeic (tedious, étudinous arpeggiations!) and hypermetrically disrupting setting of "junior playing the violin." That might have been heard as a weak cadence on a stalled inverted dominant, but then Sky Masterson continues, shifting to minor and interjecting "and they no longer dream about places they'll go, they just brood about places they've been." Neither grammatically nor musically can this be considered a new sentence. The basic ideas ("Most guys buy themselves houses, and promptly box themselves in") are as harmonically basic as the missionaries' song: nothing but an alternation of tonic and dominant; the lengthy continuation then musically models the perceived marital entanglements.[19]

Sadly, Sam Levene, the original Nathan Detroit, couldn't sing this song (or, according to oft-repeated stories by Loesser, Burrows, and Feuer, much of anything else), but its inclusion in the trial runs of *Guys and Dolls* must have made "Marry the Man Today," the complementary concluding duet between Sarah and Adelaide, that much funnier and that much more structurally completing.[20] The cut first-act song mockingly enumerates icons of domesticity (". . . the stove and the wife, a subscription to *Life* . . ."); its surviving second-act companion celebrates them as "the better things, respectable, conservative and clean" ("*Readers Digest*! Guy Lombardo! Rogers Peet! Golf! Galoshes! Ovaltine!").

With "Traveling Light," the pre-Broadway rendition of *Guys and Dolls* featured an unusual symmetry: the guys sang an agreeable duet toward the beginning of act 1 and the "dolls" came together with their agreeable

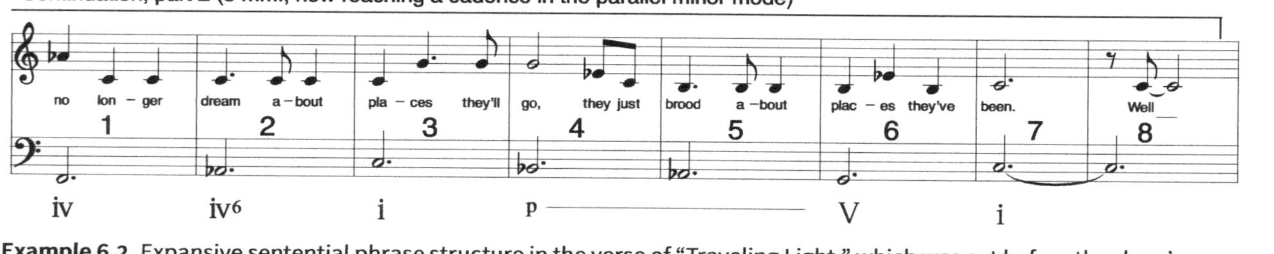

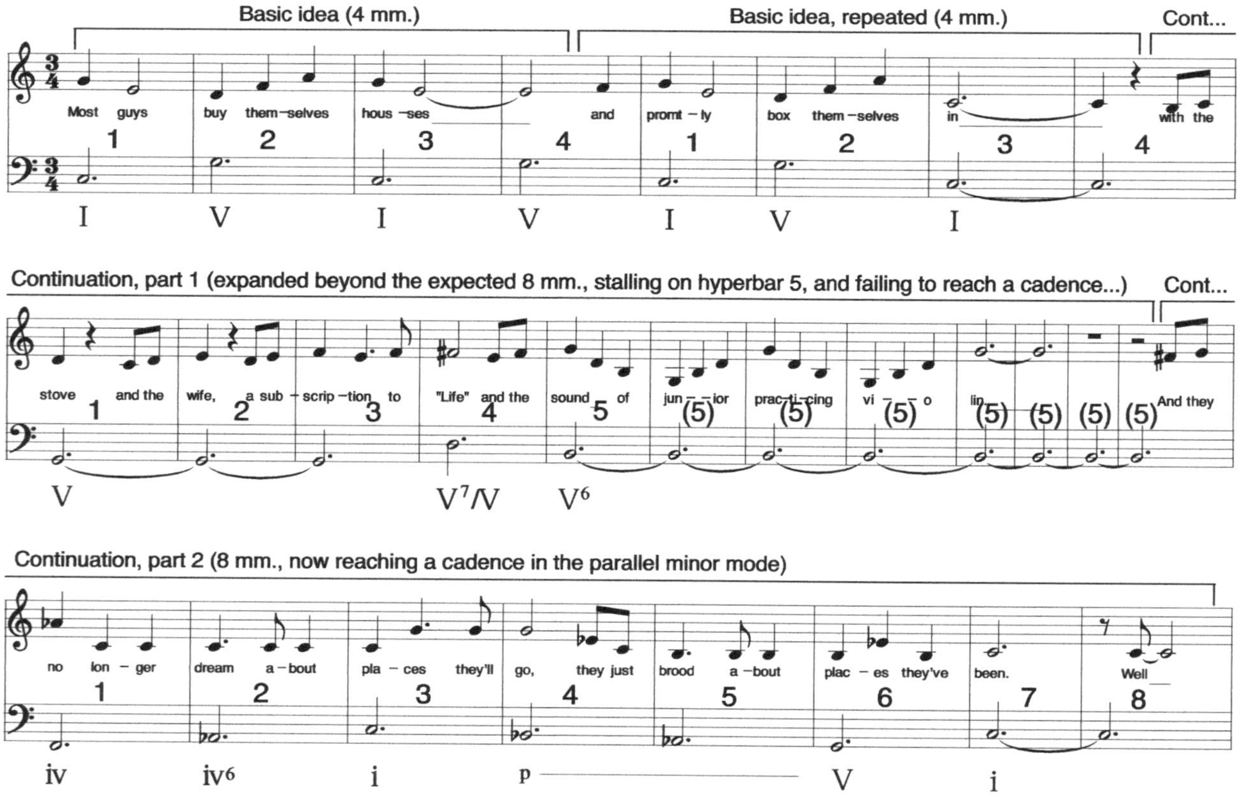

**Example 6.2.** Expansive sentential phrase structure in the verse of "Traveling Light," which was cut before the show's Broadway debut.

duet at the end of act 2; argumentative duets dramatized a central conflict between Sky and Sarah in act 1 and between Nathan and Adelaide in act 2; and Sky and Sarah sang the only love duet in the middle of the show, just before the act 1 curtain.[21]

Frank Loesser's use of readily identifiable musical topics and tropes in the songs and accompanying music helped to establish, and then break down, the central dichotomies of character and plot in *Guys and Dolls*, allowing a narrative that employs but shifts away from caricatures, to focus more on human interaction than on stereotypes. Moreover, Loesser's careful placement of musical markers, especially connoting religion, and his judicious use of duets at key moments, projects a tremendous sense of unity—even symmetry—in a show with several different plot lines and where most of the major characters are balancing different concerns within the drama. Or, as *New York Times* critic Brooks Atkinson succinctly put it a week after the premiere: "Although *Guys and Dolls* is composed of the many bizarre elements essential to every musical show, it seems simple and effortless on the stage. Everything falls into place easily as though the play had been created in one piece, and every song and actor were inevitable."

## NOTES

1. If there were negative reviews, I have not located them. Stacy Wolf also claimed that it was "met with unanimously rave reviews when it opened" (Wolf 2011, 36). Likewise, Thomas Riis, citing Brooks Atkinson's review in the *New York Times* (which concludes this chapter), notes that "rave reviews by such critical arbiters as Atkinson had appeared before in the theatrical press, but seldom if ever can one find the terms 'perfectly-composed' or 'work of art' or the phrase 'as though . . . every song and actor were inevitable' attached to a single musical comedy." . . . "*Guys and Dolls* appealed to everyone, or so it seems" (Riis 2008, 75).

2. By contrast, the famed director and creative mentor, Lehman Engel, hears resonances of John Gay's *The Beggars Opera* and of various Shakespeare plots in *Guys and Dolls* (226–227).

3. Cy Feuer, one of the show's two producers, claims that after they fired Jo Swerling "he [Swerling] insisted that he still receive first billing in the credits for the play and retain some small percentage of the royalties. This in spite of the fact that not one of his words ever appeared in the show" (Feuer 2003, 115; see also Burrows 1980, 142–45).

4. Loesser's previous musical, *Where's Charley?* (1948) was a musical version of a well-known British farce. Not only did he want to avoid repeating that type

of musical, but he and his producers (Feuer and Martin) were deeply aware of the success of Rodgers and Hammerstein's *South Pacific* a year before *Guys and Dolls* opened. That more serious musical married light comedy with more genuine and heartfelt romance.

5. Examples include "People Will Say We're In Love" (*Oklahoma!*), "I'm Gonna Wash That Man Right Out-a My Hair" (*South Pacific*), and "I'm Not At All in Love" (*Pajama Game*). See Magee (2012, 248) for a longer description of "conditional love duet."

6. In the 1955 film, he is her uncle.

7. Indeed, one might wonder why our secondary characters open the show with a song about playing the horses when the plot involves playing the dice. An early version of this song was one of the first numbers Loesser composed on speculation before the script had been written.

8. Riis (2008, 86) reads $ii^7$ chords sandwiched between the $V^7$ chords, but I hear those as mere arpeggiations of the dominant with $\hat{6}$ serving a passing role in every voice.

9. See Buchler 2008 for extensive observations about Loesser's intensifying gestures in *Guys and Dolls* and *How to Succeed in Business without Really Trying*.

10. Knapp makes a similar point, referring to the "gamblers' innate affinities for the religious feelings they overtly shun" (2005, 140).

11. At the end of the film version, we see Nicely-Nicely Johnson (the tinhorn who sings this song) donning a mission uniform. And conversion goes both ways—the 2009 Broadway production has General Cartwright breaking character by belting out a virtuosic coloratura chorus of "Sit Down, You're Rockin' the Boat." That moment seems especially reminiscent of Loesser and Burrows's later show, *How to Succeed in Business without Really Trying*, in which the previously songless uptight head secretary, Miss Jones, has her big solo in the (otherwise male ensemble) gospel showstopper, "Brotherhood of Man."

12. Again, with the sole exception of "Fugue for Tinhorns."

13. According to producer Cy Feuer, Loesser had wanted more song reprises, but the show's director, George Kaufman, prohibited it, insisting that Loesser could reprise a song only if Kaufman and Abe Burrows could reuse jokes (Feuer 2003, 140).

14. 7b is a nondiegetic performance of the "Home Sweet Home," played as nightclub patrons leave at evening's end.

15. Historically, this show follows on the heels of 1949's *South Pacific*, about which one could make very similar observations.

16. Loesser's other overlapping argumentative duets include "Baby, It's Cold Outside," "Make a Miracle," and "It's Been a Long Day."

17. See Wolf (2011, 34–41) for an especially compelling reading of "Marry the Man Today" in the context of the burgeoning female duet in the 1950s.

18. Searching YouTube for "*Guys and Dolls* 1976" currently yields at least two recordings.

19. This example is based on the score draft in the Frank Loesser Collection at the New York Public Library Performing Arts Division. A performance by Gregg Edelman and Tim Flavin with England's National Symphony Orchestra can be found on YouTube.

20. Producer Cy Feuer, librettist Abe Burrows, and the composer's daughter, Susan Loesser, all recount stories about Levene's inability to carry a tune (Feuer, 127–28; Burrows, 153–54; S. Loesser, 105–6)

21. In the 1955 film adaptation of *Guys and Dolls*, "Marry the Man Today" was cut, creating a rather sudden ending, but perhaps creating greater duet symmetry (which I think of more as a wonderfully creative feature rather than a commonplace goal of musical theater).

## WORKS CITED

Atkinson, Brooks. 1950. "'Guys and Dolls': Broadway Rat-Race Based on Some Damon Runyon Characters." *New York Times* (December 3). https://nyti.ms/3aWs4ll

Bordman, Gerald Martin. 2001. *American Musical Theatre: A Chronicle*, 3rd ed. New York: Oxford University Press.

Buchler, Michael. 2008. "Modulation as a Dramatic Agent in Frank Loesser's Broadway Songs." *Music Theory Spectrum* 30 (1): 35–60.

Burrows, Abe. 1980. *Honest, Abe: Is There Really No Business like Show Business?* Boston: Little, Brown.

Chapman, John. 1950. "'Guys and Dolls' Is New York's Musical Comedy." *New York Daily News*. November 25.

Engel, Lehman, and Howard Kissel. 2006. *Words with Music: Creating the Broadway Musical Libretto*. New York: Applause Theatre & Cinema Books.

Ewen, David. 1958. *Complete Book of the American Musical Theater*. New York: Holt.

Feuer, Cy, and Ken Gross. 2003. *I Got the Show Right Here: The Amazing, True Story of How an Obscure Brooklyn Horn Player Became the Last Great Broadway Showman*. New York: Simon & Schuster.

Hanninen, Dora A. 2012. *A Theory of Music Analysis: On Segmentation and Associative Organization*. Eastman Studies in Music. Rochester, NY: University of Rochester Press.

Knapp, Raymond. 2005. *The American Musical and the Formation of National Identity*. Princeton, NJ: Princeton University Press.

Loesser, Frank, Abe Burrows, and Jo Swerling. 1950. *Guys & Dolls; A Musical Fable of Broadway*. New York: Music Theatre International.

Loesser, Susan. 1993. *A Most Remarkable Fella: Frank Loesser and the Guys and Dolls in*

*His Life: A Portrait by His Daughter*. New York: D. I. Fine.

Magee, Jeffrey. 2012. *Irving Berlin's American Musical Theater*. New York: Oxford University Press.

Riis, Thomas Laurence. 2008. *Frank Loesser*. Yale Broadway Masters. New Haven: Yale University Press.

Wolf, Stacy Ellen. 2011. *Changed for Good: A Feminist History of the Broadway Musical*. New York: Oxford University Press.

Zbikowski, Lawrence Michael. 2002. *Conceptualizing Music: Cognitive Structure, Theory, and Analysis*. AMS Studies in Music. New York: Oxford University Press.

# 7 Style, Tonality, and Sexuality in The Rocky Horror Show

NICOLE BIAMONTE

## INTRODUCTION

Tonal relationships and musical style reflect the characters' sexual relationships and transformations in the British camp musical *The Rocky Horror Show* (1973) by Richard O'Brien. A precedent for correlating the tonal plan of a dramatic work with its characters and plot has been well established in opera analysis, mostly in the music of Giuseppe Verdi, in work by David Lawton (1982, 1989), Stephen Huebner (2004), Edward Latham (2008, 2020), and David Easley (2020). In musicals, the association of characters with particular keys or harmonic patterns has been explored by Trudi Wright (2020), Nathan Blustein (this volume), and Michael Buchler (this volume), and the association of characters with particular musical styles has been considered by Paul Laird (2011), Scott McMillin (2006), Nina Penner (2020), and Elizabeth Sallinger (2016). In *The Rocky Horror Show*, flat keys and softer pop-music styles are loosely correlated with the conservative, heteronormative human characters, and sharp keys and hard-rock styles with the sexually open, queer alien characters. The tonal dichotomy also supports the narrative trajectories of the lead characters: Janet's sexual awakening is marked by a significant shift sharpward, from the keys of E♭ major and B♭ major to A major, and Frank's loss of power and control is marked by a shift flatward from his opening key of E major to C major and F major.

The show is set in a dilapidated cinema and parodies the conventions of science-fiction and horror movies as well as those of Broadway musicals. The film version *The Rocky Horror Picture Show* (1975) eclipses the stage musical in popularity, probably because the elaborate tradition of audience participation that developed around the film—involving props, costumes, ritualized shouted commentary, and sometimes a "shadowcast" of amateur performers mirroring the onscreen action—offers a safe space for exploring queer constructions of gender and sexuality.[1] As in many musicals, several main characters are typified by particular styles,[2] such as pop-rock for the wholesome couple Brad and Janet and rockabilly for the biker Eddie. Visually and musically, the show overall is strongly influenced by glam rock, which was prevalent in the UK at the time *Rocky Horror* was composed.[3] Philip Auslander (2006, 63) elucidates this connection: "The association of glam with gothic horror, particularly the Hollywood films of the 1930s satirized by *The Rocky Horror [Picture] Show* that popularized the nineteenth-century novels on which they are based, makes perfect sense. . . . those films, many of them directed by the avowedly gay James Whale, contain multiple, coded references to homosexuality and reflect a covert, queer sensibility based on an identification of the queer and the monster as the Other." Glam artists are known for androgynous self-presentations, flattening the differences between conventionally masculine and feminine gender cues (e.g., David Bowie, Freddie Mercury; see Gregory 2002; Auslander 2006). This association with visual androgyny is particularly apropos to the show's plot, in which a pansexual cross-dressing mad scientist—one of a trio of aliens from the planet Transsexual in the galaxy Transylvania—sexually preys on Earthlings and creates an idealized male lover for himself, evoking both Bernard Shaw's *Pygmalion* and Mary Shelley's *Frankenstein*. The next section of this chapter provides a summary of *Rocky Horror*'s plot and song placement, followed by a discussion of the tonal and stylistic relationships of the songs and the ways they reflect the characters' sexual relationships and narrative trajectories. The chapter concludes with a brief consideration of the different generic conventions the show invokes.

## SYNOPSIS

The show is framed by the Usherette singing "Science Fiction Double Feature," which pays tribute to a variety of classic science-fiction and horror films from the 1930s through the early 1960s.[4] Invoking these films in this opening song also sets audience expectations for possible plot devices, atmosphere, and dramatic register (i.e., camp). As the story begins, the virginal heterosexual couple Brad Majors and Janet Weiss have just attended their friends' wedding, which inspires Brad to declare his love and propose to Janet ("Damn It, Janet"). The lyrics reify their conventionally heteronormative gender roles, and the song's placement early in the show acknowledges the ways in which "the classical . . . musical celebrates heterosexual romance and white patriarchal 'normality'" (Benshoff and Griffin 2006, 147). Such celebrations are typically a narrative goal of musical comedies, so depicting a happy couple at the outset cues the audience to expect an impending reversal and signals that this is not a typical musical comedy. Brad and Janet get engaged and decide to visit the teacher of the science class where they met, Dr. Everett Scott, to share the news. They suffer a flat tire in a rainstorm and seek help at the nearby Frankenstein castle ("Over at the Frankenstein Place"). At the castle they encounter Riff Raff the hunchbacked butler, his sister and apparent incestuous lover Magenta the maid, and the human character Columbia. They dance the show's signature number ("Time Warp") joined by a chorus of four to six phantoms, changed in the movie version to a large number of Transylvanian party guests. Their leader and the star of the show, the mad scientist Frank N. Furter, appears, introduces himself ("Sweet Transvestite"), and invites everyone to the laboratory, where he brings his human creation and intended sexual playmate Rocky to life ("The Sword of Damocles") and admires his physique ("I Can Make You a Man"). The scene is interrupted by Eddie, Columbia's—and possibly Frank's—former lover, who escapes from the freezer where he was stored after Frank harvested half of his brain to use in creating Rocky ("Whatever Happened to Saturday Night/Hot Patootie"). Act 1 ends with Frank, angered by the interruption of his spectacle and his literal and metaphorical loss of center stage, killing Eddie and staging a brief mock wedding to Rocky.

Act 2 begins with the operatic convention of a thinly disguised character seducing other characters: Frank disguised as Brad seduces Janet, and then Frank disguised as Janet seduces Brad, demonstrating that Frank is bisexual as well as nonbinary. Janet sings to Rocky of her newly awakened desire ("Touch-a Touch-a Touch-a Touch Me"; henceforth "Touch-a Touch Me") and seduces him. In the original script, Brad responds to these betrayals with the lament "Once in a While," although this song is often cut. Everyone in the castle is surprised by the arrival of Dr. Scott, who has retired from teaching science and now investigates UFOs for the government; he knows the castle is inhabited by aliens, and he is also, coincidentally, Eddie's uncle ("Eddie's Teddy").[5] Frank prepares to return to the planet Transylvania ("Planet Schmanet"), but first, the characters perform a lingerie-clad floor show ("Rose Tint My World/Don't Dream It/Wild and Untamed Thing"). The floor show is interrupted by Magenta and Riff Raff, who announces that their mission to Earth is a failure, he is now the commander, and Frank is his prisoner. Frank expresses willingness to return with them ("I'm Going Home"), but Riff Raff rejects this idea, kills Columbia, Frank, and Rocky, instructs the others to leave, and, along with Magenta, departs from Earth in the castle. Brad, Janet, and the Narrator lament their situation ("Super Heroes"), and a reprise of the opening song "Science Fiction Double Feature" serves as an epilogue.

## *SEXUAL, TONAL, AND STYLISTIC RELATIONSHIPS*

Figure 7.1 diagrams the characters' sexual relationships and the keys of their songs. Flat keys are loosely correlated with the most important human roles: the main characters Brad and Janet, and the Usherette (also known variously as Miss Strawberry Time, the Belasco Popcorn Girl, and Trixie), a frame narrator who sings the opening and closing song that contextualizes the show as theatrical storytelling in the form of a science-fiction movie.[6] The human characters are also the only ones to sing in minor keys, in the songs that frame act 2: Janet in A minor in the verses of "Touch-a Me," and Brad, Janet, and the Narrator—another external character like the Usherette, who provides spoken introductions to many scenes[7]—in G minor in "Super Heroes." In contrast, sharp keys loosely correlate with the Transylvanians Frank, Riff Raff, and Magenta, and the humans most closely associated with them, Columbia, Eddie, and Rocky. This dichotomy of flat versus sharp keys highlights the difference between the sexually conservative and traditionally gender-conforming human main characters and the sexually open and gender-bending Transylvanian main

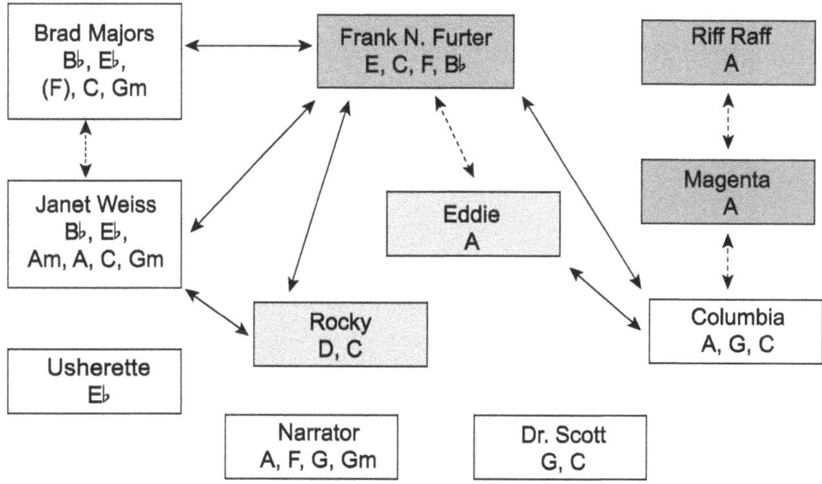


**Figure 7.1.** Tonal and sexual relationships in *The Rocky Horror Show*. Aliens are shaded dark gray, humans modified or created by Frank are light gray, and other humans are unshaded. Listed under each character's name are the keys of their songs and/or verses, in the order in which they occur in the show. Explicit sexual relationships are shown with solid lines and implicit ones with dotted lines.

characters. Along with stylistic differences in these characters' music, this opposition correlates with the central conflict of the narrative as well as with its characters' development. The show's star, Frank, and its female lead, Janet, have the broadest tonal trajectories, spanning half the circle of fifths and reflecting their changing motivations and relationships. Frank's entrance number, "Sweet Transvestite," is in E major, the sharpmost key in the show, but later in act 1 he sings to Rocky in C major and B♭ major, and his songs in act 2 are in C major and F major. This flatward path can be interpreted as reflecting the trajectory from Frank's initial status as the leader of the aliens' mission to his ultimate failure, and possibly also his increasing sexual preoccupation with Earthlings.

Janet's tonal trajectory moves in the opposite direction, from singing in flat keys in act 1 to expressing her sexual awakening in A major at the beginning of act 2, but her music returns to the flat key of G minor for the lament at the end of the show. Brad and Janet sing the same number of songs, but Brad's tonal trajectory is much narrower, spanning half the tonal distance (a quarter of the circle of fifths, from E♭ major to C major), which can be interpreted as suggesting that he is far less changed by his experiences in the castle than Janet. The effect of the tonal distinctions among the characters is enhanced by the stripped-down instrumentation of the show, which is more typical of a rock band than most musicals: piano, synthesizer, guitars, bass, drums, and tenor saxophone. The tonal effect (when no songs are transposed) is subtle but perceptible, especially in the prominent guitar and bass parts, because they have more open strings in sharp keys.[8]

Figure 7.2 is a table of the songs, characters, styles, and keys in the musical, in order of occurrence.[9] The show's first six songs establish a clear tonal contrast between the first three songs and the next three songs (bracketed in the figure), as well as a stylistic contrast between the innocent, conventional humans who are introduced in flat keys, and the sexually aggressive, queer aliens who are introduced in sharp keys. The framing song "Science Fiction Double Feature" is sung by the female usher in E♭ major,[10] and Brad and Janet's pair of scene-setting duets are in B♭ major and E♭ major. All three songs can be characterized as pop or soft rock. "Science Fiction" features doo-wop backing vocals, and the chorus uses the archetypal doo-wop progression I–vi–IV–V, rotated to IV–V–I–vi.[11] Julian Cornell (2008, 49n7) describes both "Damn It, Janet" and "Over at the Frankenstein Place" as a mixture of older rock and roll with Broadway show tunes. "Damn It, Janet" is exaggeratedly repetitive in several domains: the looped progression I–iii–vi under $\hat{8}$–$\hat{7}$–$\hat{6}$, the spoken interjections of "Janet" or "Oh Brad" after nearly every line, and the syntactically similar verse lyrics, which, in Knapp's words, "revel in their own uninspired inadequacies" (2010, 246)—for instance, Brad sings "The river was deep, but I swam it . . . the road was long, but I ran it," and Janet responds "Now we're engaged and I'm so glad / that you've met Mom and you know Dad." The next song, "Over at the Frankenstein Place," is more Broadwayesque, partly because the texture dramatically expands from the opening verse, which consists only of Janet's vocal melody and a bass line played on piano, to the following chorus, which includes the full band, harmonized lead vocals, and choral backing vocals. In conjunction with the repeated lyric "There's a light," the gospel-inflected backing vocals suggest, misleadingly, that the literal light seen by the characters could be a metaphorical means to their salvation.

The next three songs offer both stylistic and tonal contrast to the first three. "Time Warp," in the key of A major—which is almost as remote as possible from the E♭ major of the preceding song—presents the possi-

| No. | Title | Character(s) Singing | Style | Key(s) |
|---|---|---|---|---|
| | | ACT 1 | | |
| 1 | Science Fiction Double Feature | Usherette | soft rock | E♭ major |
| 2 | Damn It, Janet | Brad, Janet | pop-rock | B♭ major |
| 3 | Over at the Frankenstein Place | Brad, Janet, chorus (bridge: Riff Raff) | showtune/ rock | E♭ major |
| 4 | Time Warp* | Riff Raff, Magenta, Columbia, Narrator, chorus | rock | A major |
| 5 | Sweet Transvestite* | Frank | rock | E major |
| 6 | The Sword of Damocles | Rocky, chorus | rock | D major |
| 7 | I Can Make You a Man (Charles Atlas Song)⁺ | Frank | showtune | C major |
| 8 | Whatever Happened to Saturday Night/Hot Patootie | Eddie | rockabilly | A major |
| 9 | I Can Make You a Man reprise⁺ | Frank (interjection by Janet) | showtune | B♭→E♭ major |
| | | ACT 2 | | |
| 1 | Touch-a Touch-a Touch-a Touch Me | Janet | pop-rock | v: A minor c: A major (→ B♭ maj.) |
| 2 | Once in a While (not in all versions) | Brad, Narrator | country rock | F major |
| 3 | Eddie's Teddy⁺ | Dr. Scott, Narrator, Columbia, chorus | pop-rock | G major |
| 4 | Planet Schmanet⁺ | Frank, chorus | rock | F major |
| 5a | Floor Show: Rose Tint My World | Columbia, Rocky, Brad, Janet | showtune/ rock | C major (→ A maj.) |
| 5b | Floor Show: Don't Dream It, Be It | Frank, chorus, Dr. Scott | anthem | C major |
| 5c | Floor Show: Wild and Untamed Thing | Frank, chorus (interjection by Riff Raff) | rock | F major |
| 6 | I'm Going Home | Frank | ballad | F major |
| 7 | Super Heroes | Brad, Janet, Narrator | lament | G minor |
| 8 | Science Fiction Double Feature reprise | Usherette | soft rock | E♭ major |

* In the original version, "Sweet Transvestite" preceded "Time Warp"; this ordering was changed for the movie version in 1975 and in theater versions beginning with the 1990 West End revival.

⁺ These songs were added two months after the premiere, when the show changed venues from the Royal Court Theatre Upstairs to the Chelsea Classic Cinema in mid-August 1973.

**Figure 7.2.** Songs, characters, styles, and keys in *The Rocky Horror Show*.

bly incestuous Transylvanian siblings Riff Raff and Magenta, as well as Frank's discarded (Earthling) lover Columbia. Frank's first song, "Sweet Transvestite" in E major, is equivalent to an entrance aria that establishes him as the show's diva, flaunting both his gender-bending and his sexuality: dramatically and affectively, "Sweet Transvestite" is not very different from Carmen's entrance aria in Bizet's eponymous opera. In the following number, "The Sword of Damocles," Frank's creation Rocky laments his existence in D major. These three songs, which introduce the alien characters and their relationships, are marked musically by the hardest-rocking styles heard so far and visually by the characters' spectacular entrances and costumes. "Time Warp" functions as both a dance song and a parody of a dance song, with instructional lyrics. It features several rock signifiers, including the partly palm-muted strumming in the opening, and two chord progressions characteristic of late 1960s rock: I–II–♭VII–IV–I in the verse and ♭VI–♭III–♭VII–IV–I in the refrain. The verse ends with a double-plagal progression of root motion by descending fourths or ascending fifths, which is extended in the refrain to a quadruple-plagal progression (Biamonte 2010). These plagal progressions mark the song as rock music and, through their extended reversals of the more conventional descending-fifth progression, suggest otherness.[12] The harmonic language of "Sweet Transvestite" is typical of both classic rock and its influential progenitor, the blues: the verse progression, I–♭III–IV–I, is based on a pentatonic motive idiomatic to the guitar that I have called a "reverse axe-fall progression" (Biamonte 2010, 106), and the refrain follows the pattern of a blues cadence, V–IV–I.[13] The insistently rising chromatic motive in octaves that comprises the accompaniment is based on an underlying pentatonic scale that is characteristic of the blues, but the rising chromatic motives also signal desire.[14] "The Sword of Damocles" draws on the simple three-chord patterns and boogie-blues figurations typical of early rock and roll. The accompaniment textures of all three songs foreground the electric guitar, the instrument most representative of rock music, in contrast to the piano-centric accompaniments of "Damn It, Janet" and the beginning of "Over at the Frankenstein Place."

These first six songs establish the characters and their interpersonal, stylistic, and tonal relationships. The rest of act 1 presents a conflict that ultimately results in the show's tragic ending. The next song, "I Can Make You a Man," is a conventional show tune that Frank sings to Rocky in C major. This key can be interpreted as mediating between the flat/sharp–

human/alien dichotomy established by the previous songs, providing a tonally neutral meeting ground for the impending consummation of their relationship and perhaps also signaling Frank's impending loss of power. The ending segues into "Whatever Happened to Saturday Night/ Hot Patootie" in A major, approached from C major via the common tone E. The 1950s rockabilly style evokes Elvis or—as Cornell (2008, 43–44) argues—the UK glam version of Elvis, Gary Glitter, and the lyrics establish Eddie's heteronormative perspective and lament his lost teenage naiveté.[15] Although Eddie is human, Frank has removed half of his brain to use for Rocky, transforming him: as Eddie sings in the first verse, "It don't seem the same since cosmic light came into my life—I thought I was divine." This change, and the fact that he is now (mostly) under Frank's control, offers analytical justification for the setting of his song in the Transylvanians' key of A major. A more direct connection is the strong similarity of the "Hot Patootie" chorus progression, I–II–IV–I, to the "Time Warp" verse progression, I–II–♭VII–IV–I in the same key. At the end of act 1 Frank briefly reprises "I Can Make You a Man," with an enthusiastic interjection by Janet, "I'm a muscle fan!" This contradicts her comment just before the first performance of the song, "I don't like men with too many muscles," and prefigures her sexual liberation at the beginning of act 2. The reprise is in B♭ major, two keys flatward and the same key as Brad and Janet's opening love duet, a tonal relationship that could be interpreted as a vain attempt by Frank to perform heteronormativity. In the movie and later versions of the show, a coda in E♭ major quoting Mendelssohn's wedding march was added. Frank's mock wedding to Rocky parallels the wedding that Brad and Janet attended just before their opening song, the wedding-march quotation suggests a veneer of ironic conventionality, and the return to E♭ major lends tonal coherence to act 1. Like Brad and Janet's engagement, Frank and Rocky's presumed consummation happens too soon: this is only the end of act 1.

In act 2, changes in tonality help to mark the characters' transformations. The most dramatic of these is Janet's sexual awakening, depicted in the opening song "Touch-a Touch Me" by a shift from the weakly defined A minor of the verse to A major in the chorus—a key associated with the Transylvanians, and by extension, with sexual agency. Stylistically, however, this song is closer to the pop-rock of Janet's opening music than the hard rock of the aliens' early songs. This stylistic resemblance signals her humanness and perhaps also that, unlike the aliens, her sexual agency is not yet fully realized. On a more pragmatic level, the comparatively soft style of the song may have been prompted by her gender: female vocalists are more typical in pop styles and male vocalists in rock styles. Figure 7.3 shows a chord chart for the second verse and first chorus of "Touch-a Touch Me." This is the first instance of a minor tonic for a character's song in the show. In combination with Janet's opening lyrics, "I was feeling done in, couldn't win; I'd only ever kissed before," and low register, the minor key represents her emerging discontent with the conventional model of gender and sexuality to which she has heretofore been confined. In contrast, in the heightened "breakout chorus"[16] she owns and flaunts her sexuality, using the same progression as the "Hot Patootie" chorus (I–II–IV–I), a close subset of the "Time Warp" verse progression. All three songs are in the same key: A major, associated with the aliens. In addition to the shift to the parallel major, the music increases in intensity via a higher vocal register, faster surface rhythm, faster harmonic rhythm, and expansion of the accompaniment texture. The song concludes with a pump-up modulation[17] to B♭ major that reflects her increasing excitement and also restores the key of her first song, suggesting that she has internalized this new sexual agency.[18] Millie Taylor (2012, 30) describes a similar transformation from act 1 to act 2: "[Janet's sexual liberation] is represented by her musical development from the pop sounds and clear soprano tones in the refrain of 'Damn It Janet' to her solo 'Touch-a Touch Me' with its rock-rumba rhythm, introduction of a lower vocal register, and a throatier, full-bodied vocal sound."

Janet's act 2 solo was originally balanced by "Once in a While," a ballad for Brad expressing pain, regret, and forgiveness. The song is set in an entirely diatonic F major, reflecting Brad's lack of a liberating transformation, in contrast to Janet's newfound sexuality. In terms of the overall pacing of the show, its slow tempo and soft country-inflected style dissipate all the energy of the opening number, so it is often cut in performances, and was cut from the movie as well. The two songs that follow were added to the show two months after its premiere. Like "Once in a While," both consist of simple diatonic harmonies, but their brisker tempos and denser surface rhythms help to sustain momentum. In "Eddie's Teddy," which is Dr. Scott's only lead vocal, he recounts his nephew's transgressive biker lifestyle and disturbing disappearance. Frank sings "Planet Schmanet" as he harasses Janet and advises her to "wise up," suggesting that her transformation is not yet complete. The song is set in F major, the key of most of

**verse 2:**

Am G C Dm
i VII III iv
"Now all I want to know..."

G C (D) E (D) E
III VII IV V IV V
"I'll put up no resistance..."

**chorus:**

A B D A
I II IV I
"Touch-a touch-a touch-a touch me..."

A B D Am
I II IV i
"Thrill me, chill me, fulfill me"

**Figure 7.3.** Chord chart for "Touch-a Touch Me," verse 2 into first chorus. Only the initial text of each line is shown.

Frank's music in act 2, reflecting his loss of control and thus of his status as leader of the alien mission.

The set piece that follows, the "Floor Show," is the central scene of act 2. It parodies the musical genre conventions of both the song-and-dance spectacle and the ensemble number in which the characters are reconciled and live happily ever after. In the opening song, "Rose Tint My World," four characters sing of the ways in which Frank has changed them: Columbia sings of disillusionment and drugs, Rocky of doubt and lust, Brad of confusion and fear, and Janet of sexual empowerment. Figure 7.4 provides chord charts for each verse. The first two verses are sung by Columbia and Rocky in C major. Their vocal lines are melodically and rhythmically active, oscillating between chord roots and fifths over harmony that prolongs the tonic. In contrast, Brad's verse begins on the subdominant, F major, and is then inflected by the minor subdominant, emphasizing his humanness (only humans sing in minor keys) and his continued trepidation regarding queerness of gender and openness of sexual expression. His melody moves much more slowly than in the preceding verses and is narrowly focused on middle C, expressing a kind of panicked paralysis. Janet's verse follows the same chord progression as Brad's, but it modulates to A major, the key of her sexual liberation. She begins with the same repeated long notes as Brad, but over the course of the verse her rhythmic density increases and her pitch range expands, helping depict her embrace of her newfound sexuality. This is the point of maximal contrast between Brad's and Janet's music, reflecting their different responses to their experiences. At the beginning of the show, they sing together in B♭ major and E♭ major. In the second half, their tonalities are increasingly distantly related: F major versus A minor/major at the beginning of act 2, and C major versus A major in the floor show. They are reunited in the closing lament, when they sing the same music in the same key of G minor. This flat-side tonality reconfirms their humanness, but the minor mode signals that they have been fundamentally changed and even damaged by their experiences in the castle. In the reprise of "Science Fiction" that closes the show, the line "Darkness has conquered Brad and Janet" confirms this interpretation, in a final refusal of the happily-ever-after narrative promised by their opening love duet.

Columbia's and Janet's verses of "Rose Tint My World" both invoke Frank, preparing—even demanding—his entrance. The music returns to C major as Frank makes what is described in the script as "a spectacular entrance" and sings "Don't Dream It, Be It," an ode to self-realization through hedonism. The slow introduction ("Whatever happened to Fay Wray") leads to a verse that begins with music very similar to Brad's verse in "Rose Tint My World." Both melodies consist of a repeated note C over the chord progression IV–iv–I, but with more or less opposite lyrics. Brad sings "It's beyond me, help me Mommy," while Frank urges, "Give yourself over to absolute pleasure." The anthemic chorus that follows, "Don't Dream It, Be It," is widely interpreted as the central message of the show despite Frank's tragic end. The music remains in C major, repeating the title phrase over the doo-wop progression, I–vi–IV–V, which as Knapp (2010, 249) has observed, regularizes the rotated version used in the framing song "Science Fiction." The script calls for the characters to "come together touching and fondling one another, Frank in the centre" (in the movie, this scene takes place in a swimming pool). The floor show concludes with a chorus line danced to the energetic "Wild and Untamed Thing." This song uses the same progression as "Rose Tint My World," now in F major, and repeats the title lyrics from the earlier song as a refrain, creating a symmetrical lyrical and musical frame for the "Floor Show." The keys of the floor-show music, F major and C major, represent a tonal meet-

**verse 1 (Columbia):**

| C | C | F | C | C | C | D | G |
|---|---|---|---|---|---|---|---|
| I | I | IV | I | I | I | V/V | V |

"It was great when it all began…"

| C | C | F | C | C | G | F | C |
|---|---|---|---|---|---|---|---|
| I | I | IV | I | I | V | IV | I |

"Now the only thing that gives me hope…"

**verse 2 (Rocky):**

| C | C | F | C | C | C | D | G |
|---|---|---|---|---|---|---|---|
| I | I | IV | I | I | I | V/V | V |

"I'm just seven hours old…"

| C | C | F | C | C | G | F | C |
|---|---|---|---|---|---|---|---|
| I | I | IV | I | I | V | IV | I |

"Now the only thing I've come to trust…"

**verse 3 (Brad):**

| F | F | Fm | Fm | C | C | C | C (C7) |
|---|---|---|---|---|---|---|---|
| IV | IV | iv | iv | I | I | I | I (V7/IV) |

"It's beyond me, help me, Mommy…"

| F | F | Fm | Fm | C | C | C | G |
|---|---|---|---|---|---|---|---|
| IV | IV | iv | iv | I | I | I | V |

"What's this? Let's see…"

**verse 4 (Janet):**

| D | D | Dm | Dm | A | A | A | A (A7) |
|---|---|---|---|---|---|---|---|
| IV | IV | iv | iv | I | I | I | I (V7/IV) |

"I feel released, bad times deceased…"

| D | D | Dm | Dm | A | A | A | E |
|---|---|---|---|---|---|---|---|
| IV | IV | iv | iv | I | I | I | V |

"The game has been disbanded…"

**Figure 7.4.** Chord chart for "Rose Tint My World," verses 1–4. Only the initial text of each line is shown.

ing ground between the humans and the aliens—Frank sings in a (human) flat key, as he has done since the end of act 1, and the humans sing in the (alien) rock style, in a temporary, dreamlike accord.

The spectacle is dramatically interrupted by the mutiny of Magenta and Riff Raff. Riff Raff asserts: "Frank N. Furter, it's all over, your mission is a failure, your lifestyle's too extreme. I'm your new commander, you now are my prisoner. We return to Transylvania—prepare the transit beam." He sings these lyrics to the same repeated-note melody and IV–iv–I progression that set Brad's plea for help in "Rose Tint My World" and Frank's exhortation to pleasure in "Don't Dream It, Be It." Thus music that first underlays an expression of fear more or less caused by Frank is later used to set Frank's call for self-gratification, and finally to underlay his loss of power and control. His last song, the torchy piano-driven ballad "I'm Going Home" in F major, is his final piece of self-indulgence. Riff Raff kills him for his hubris, then kills Columbia and Rocky, and departs with Magenta.

The final scene comprises the lament "Super Heroes," which was cut from the movie, possibly to avoid two consecutive slow-tempo songs at the end. In the key of G minor, the relative minor of their opening duet, Brad laments his pain and loss ("down inside I'm bleeding"), Janet seems to lament her newly awakened sex drive ("still the beast is feeding"), and the Narrator concludes with a negative outlook on the human race ("lost in time, and lost in space . . . and meaning"). The bleakness of this scene stands in sharp contrast to the spectacle of the "Floor Show." As Kelly Kessler (2010, 119) observes, "a narrative based on communal annihilation and death, [*Rocky Horror*] drives this failed convention [of reality-defying happy endings] home by presenting numbers reminiscent of early Hollywood musicals just prior to the ensemble's ultimate destruction and disillusionment." *The Rocky Horror Show* is a rare and early example of a musical with a tragic ending. The final song, a reprise of "Science Fiction" in E♭ major, re-establishes the external frame for the story, returning the audience to its position as spectators.

Kessler reads *Rocky Horror* as a satirical critique of musicals, symptomatic of the late-twentieth-century destabilization of the genre because its central character dies (2010, 6). She compares it to other contemporaneous musicals that end with the male lead's death: *Hair* (1967), *Godspell* (1971), and *All that Jazz* (1979). These shows are imperfect analogies with *Rocky Horror*, however, because Frank functions as both male and female lead, and also because his death is overdetermined by other generic conventions in play. The oldest of these is the ancient Greek model of tragedy, in which the hero dies as punishment for his hubris. A tragic narrative underlies both *Rocky Horror* and its influential progenitor *Frankenstein*: both mad-scientist characters play God and defy nature by artificially creating human life. Frank additionally maims and kills Eddie and has nonconsensual sex with other characters. Numerous commentators have construed Frank's death as punishment for his hedonistic lifestyle and/or his queerness (Bozelka 2008; Endres 2008; Grant 1991; Kilgore 1986; Kinkade and Katovic 1992; Reale 2012). This interpretation is analogous to the well-established convention that horror-movie characters who have sex—especially female characters—must die, and in some ways Frank is coded as female.[19] Frank's death is also in keeping with his status as an operatic heroine, who like countless divas before him is subject to societal control of his excesses as well as a voyeuristic glamorization of his suffering and death (Clément 1988; McClary 1991). Like Carmen, Frank is contextualized as an exotic, feminine Other, and like her, he sings a rhythmically teasing and insistently chromatic entrance aria—almost a name aria—flaunting his sexuality. (A potential gender-based difference in the musical representation of these characters is that Carmen's chromaticism is in the melody and descends, while Frank's chromaticism is in the bass line and ascends). Like Dido and Butterfly, although unlike Carmen, Frank sings an exit aria; Knapp compares his "diva-farewell" scene to Norma Desmond's in *Sunset Boulevard* (2010, 244). The onstage deaths of the main character in both *Carmen* and *Rocky Horror* were groundbreaking for their time. McClary has described the function of Carmen's death as to "purge all traces of the exotic and chromatic, to restore social and musical order" (1990, 61), which applies equally well to Frank's death in *Rocky Horror*. Thus Frank dies because he is a hubristic male tragic hero, because he is a transgressive queer, and because he is an overly sexual female diva.

These interpretations, however, are dispiritingly at odds with the exuberant celebration of queerness and sexuality that constitutes the core of the show, which is celebrated, in turn, by the unprecedented culture of audience participation that has grown around *Rocky Horror*. The tragic ending is set at a distance by the framing conceit that it is a late-night showing of a science-fiction movie, and the real-life shadowcast performances and other forms of audience participation at cinema screenings of the movie version add an additional layer of creative commentary. The widespread tradition of participation in cinema screenings has inspired performances of the live musical that encourage or incorporate audience participation. The patriarchal, heteronormative moral that the show's ending apparently conveys is rejected by the audience's reception of the movie, and more recently of the live musical, as a safe space for display and experimentation with gender and sexuality.

In this chapter, I have demonstrated various stylistic, tonal, harmonic, and motivic relationships in the music of *The Rocky Horror Show*: the association of humans with flat keys and pop styles versus aliens in sharp keys and rock styles; Frank's tonal trajectory flatward into human territory, signifying his loss of power and control; Janet's tonal trajectory sharpward, signifying her sexual awakening; and Brad's lack of a tonal trajectory, signifying that he is fundamentally unchanged by his experiences. These musical relationships help to define the characters and subtly support the narrative—an important function in light of the convoluted and improbable plot of this groundbreaking satirical musical that bends both genders and genres.

## NOTES

Thanks to Greg Decker, Michael Buchler, and Jerry Cain for helpful comments on this paper.

1. For discussions of constructs of gender and sexuality in the movie version, see Aviram 1992; Kessler 2010, 162–63; Knapp 2010, 240–52; Peraino 2006; Reale 2012; and Weinstock 2008. The tradition of audience participation is analyzed in Austin 1981; Ellis 2020; Kinkade and Katovich 1992; Locke 1999; and Weinstock 2008.

2. In this volume, authors Greg Decker, Michael Buchler, and Robert Komaniecki use this concept as a jumping-off point for their respective analyses.

3. Lloyd Whitesell (2006, 271) argues that the emphasis on carnality and base desires in *Rocky Horror* marks it as burlesque rather than glam.

4. In the order they are mentioned in the song, the movies are: *The Day the Earth Stood Still* (1951), *Flash Gordon* (1936), *The Invisible Man* (1933), *King Kong* (1933), *It Came from Outer Space* (1953), *Doctor X* (1932), *Forbidden Planet* (1956), *Tarantula* (1955), *The Day of the Triffids* (1962), *Night of the Demon* (1957), and *When Worlds Collide* (1951). In the original script, the roles of the Usherette and Magenta are doubled, i.e., played by the same actor.

5. The script calls for the same actor to play Eddie and Dr. Scott.

6. Nina Penner (2020) describes frame narrators as appearing at the beginning and end of a show, inviting the audience to understand the middle section

as storytelling (65–66), and theatrical storytelling as "a nested performance for a fictional audience" (49).

7. The Narrator is a modern version of the Greek chorus: he directly addresses the audience, provides transitions between scenes, and comments on the action. In Penner's model of character-narrator types, he is a choral narrator (Penner 2020, 62–63).

8. The open strings on a bass are E–A–D–G (low to high), which are also the lowest four open strings on a guitar in standard tuning (an octave higher), plus B–E. Thus E is one of the most resonant keys on the guitar, and when played in open positions, E and A chords, and to a lesser extent D chords, have the most resonant bass notes. By contrast, in flat keys, the roots of the primary triads are all stopped notes on the guitar and bass, which sound less reverberant.

9. Instrumental music is excluded from this table: the overture, incidental music during scene changes, the entr'acte, and music for bows. The original score used for productions in the 1970s had no overture. A brief blues-rock overture in C major was added for the UK revival in 1984; it was replaced with a different overture in D major for the Broadway revival in 2000.

10. In the movie version, "Science Fiction Double Feature" is sung by Richard O'Brien.

11. The rotated version of this progression in the "Science Fiction" chorus became common after the doo-wop era; some well-known examples are the choruses of Peter, Paul, and Mary's "Blowin' in the Wind" (1963), the Beatles' "I Want to Hold Your Hand" (1964), and Arlo Guthrie's "City of New Orleans" (1972).

12. The "Time Warp" verse progression I–II–♭VII–IV–I nests its double-plagal progression within the Lydian-inflected I–II–IV–I, which is also fairly common in classic rock: it underlies the verses of several Beatles songs, including "Eight Days a Week" (1964) and "You Won't See Me" (1965), as well as the verses of the Rolling Stones' "As Tears Go By" (1966). The quadruple-plagal progression of the "Time Warp" refrain is the basis of the Leaves' "Hey Joe" (1965) and its better-known cover by Jimi Hendrix (1966), and the chorus of Deep Purple's "Hush" (1968).

13. The "reverse axe fall" I–♭III–IV–I harmonizes the choruses of Sam and Dave's "Hold on I'm Coming" (1966), the verses of Steppenwolf's "Born to Be Wild" (1966), and—as dominant seventh chords—the choruses of the Beatles' "Sgt. Pepper's Lonely Hearts Club Band" (1967).

14. The most famous instance of a rising chromatic motive used to signal desire is the "Desire" motive from Wagner's music drama *Tristan und Isolde*. An example from music that is stylistically closer to "Sweet Transvestite" occurs in the Beatles' "I Want You," which conveys desire through a more concise ascending semitone at the end of the title phrase.

15. The nature of Eddie and Frank's relationship is not made clear, which is why in figure 7.1 I have connected them with a dotted line rather than a solid one. When Brad and Janet first arrive at the castle, other characters describe Frank's

and Eddie's relationship with sexual innuendos: Columbia comments that he was a delivery boy whose delivery wasn't good enough, and Riff Raff explains that Frank wanted to help Eddie find "a new position" (these lines were cut from the movie version). However, shortly after murdering Eddie, Frank comments that "He had a certain naïve charm, but no muscle. We had a mental relationship," which suggests that Frank was not sexually attracted to Eddie and was using him only to harvest part of his brain. Just before the floor show, however, Columbia complains to Frank, "First you ditch me for Eddie, and then you throw him off like an old overcoat for Rocky," implicitly equating Frank's relationship with Eddie to his relationships with her and with Rocky. Frank's response adopts this parallel framing as well: "Rocky's behaving just as Eddie did."

16. Doll (2011, [2]) defines a breakout chorus as "increas[ing] in intensity with respect to various parameters, including loudness, lyrical content, pitch level (both melodic and harmonic), rhythmic and textural activity, and timbral noise" as compared to the preceding verse section. Breakout choruses in the relative major are very common, because verse and chorus share a background diatonic collection. Breakout choruses in the parallel major are much more rare, because the background collection shifts three moves in the sharp direction. One example is Dusty Springfield's "You Don't Have to Say You Love Me" (1966).

17. The very common strategy of modulating up a half or whole step between repeated choruses at the end of a popular song has been given a variety of nicknames; "pump-up modulation" (Doll 2011; Ricci 2017) and "elevating modulation" (Griffiths 2015; Hanenberg 2017) seem to have become the most widespread. See Buchler 2008 for a discussion of this modulation type in songs of Frank Loesser, and Blustein in this volume for an even more germane examination of pump-up modulations as a strategy for tonal return.

18. See Nathan Blustein's chapter in this volume for a detailed consideration of the dramatic implications of pump-up modulations that return to previous keys.

19. The entry "Death by Sex" at the TV Tropes website gives many examples. https://tvtropes.org/pmwiki/pmwiki.php/Main/DeathBySex

## WORKS CITED

Auslander, Philip. 2006. *Performing Glam Rock: Gender and Theatricality in Popular Music.* Ann Arbor: University of Michigan Press.

Austin, Bruce A. 1981. "Portrait of a Cult Film Audience: The Rocky Horror Picture Show." *Journal of Communication* 31 (2): 43–54.

Aviram, Amittai. 1992. "Postmodern Gay Dionysus: Dr. Frank N. Furter." *Journal of Popular Culture* 26 (3): 183–92.

Benshoff, Harry M., and Sean Griffin. 2006. *Queer Images: A History of Gay and Lesbian Film in America.* Lanham, MD: Rowman & Littlefield.

Biamonte, Nicole. 2010. "Triadic Modal and Pentatonic Patterns in Rock Music." *Music Theory Spectrum* 32 (2): 95–110.

Blustein, Nathan. 2023 "'Was It Ever Real?': Tonic Return via Stepwise Modulation in Broadway Songs." In *Here for the Hearing: Analyzing the Music in Musical Theater*, edited by Michael Buchler and Gregory J. Decker. Ann Arbor: University of Michigan Press.

Bozelka, Kevin John. 2008. "'Your Lifestyle's Too Extreme': *Rocky Horror*, Shock Treatment, and Late Capitalism." In *Reading Rocky Horror:* The Rocky Horror Picture Show *and Popular Culture*, edited by Jeffrey Andrew Weinstock, 221–25. London: Palgrave Macmillan.

Buchler, Michael. 2008. "Modulation as a Dramatic Agent in Frank Loesser's Broadway Songs." *Music Theory Spectrum* 30 (1): 35–60.

Buchler, Michael. 2023 "Three Notions of Long-Range Form in *Guys and Dolls*." In *Here for the Hearing: Analyzing the Music in Musical Theater*, edited by Michael Buchler and Gregory J. Decker. Ann Arbor: University of Michigan Press.

Clément, Catherine. 1988. *Opera, or the Undoing of Women*. Translated by Betsy Wing. Minneapolis: University of Minnesota Press.

Cornell, Julian. 2008. "*Rocky Horror* Glam Rock." In *Reading Rocky Horror:* The Rocky Horror Picture Show *and Popular Culture*, edited by Jeffrey Andrew Weinstock, 35–49. London: Palgrave Macmillan.

Doll, Christopher. 2011. "Rockin' Out: Expressive Modulation in Verse-Chorus Form." *Music Theory Online* 17 (3).

Easley, David B. 2020. "Verdi's Dramatic Use of Tonality, Topics, and Recurring Themes." In *Singing in Signs: New Semiotic Explorations of Opera*, edited by Gregory J. Decker and Matthew R. Shaftel, 193–224. New York: Oxford University Press.

Ellis, Sarah Taylor. 2020. "'Let's Do the Time Warp Again': Performing Time, Genre, and Spectatorship." In *The Routledge Companion to the Contemporary Musical*, edited by Jessica Sterman and Elizabeth L. Wollman, 273–82. Milton Park, UK: Routledge.

Endres, Thomas G. 2008. "'Be Just and Fear Not': Warring Visions of Righteous Decadence and Pragmatic Justice in *Rocky Horror*." In *Reading Rocky Horror:* The Rocky Horror Picture Show *and Popular Culture*, edited by Jeffrey Andrew Weinstock, 207–19. London: Palgrave Macmillan.

Grant, Barry K. 1991. "Science Fiction Double Feature: Ideology in the Cult Film." In *The Cult Film Experience: Beyond All Reason*, edited by J. P. Telotte, 122–37. Austin: University of Texas Press.

Gregory, Georgina. 2002. "Masculinity, Sexuality and the Visual Culture of Glam Rock." *Culture and Communication* 5 (2): 35–60.

Griffiths, Dai. 2015. "Elevating Form and Elevating Modulation." *Popular Music* 34 (1): 22–44.

Hanenberg, Scott J. 2017. "Rock Modulation and Narrative." *Music Theory Online* 22 (2).

Huebner, Stephen. 2004. "Structural Coherence." In *The Cambridge Companion to Verdi*, edited by Scott L. Balthazar, 139–53. Cambridge: Cambridge University Press.

Kessler, Kelly. 2010. *Destabilizing the Hollywood Musical: Music, Masculinity, and Mayhem*. London: Palgrave Macmillan.

Kilgore, John. 1986. "Sexuality and Identity in *The Rocky Horror Picture Show*." In *Eros in the Mind's Eye: Sexuality and the Fantastic in Art and Film*, edited by Donald Palumbo, 151–59. Westport, CT: Greenwood Press.

Kinkade, Patrick T., and Michael A. Katovich. 1992. "Toward a Sociology of Cult Films: Reading *Rocky Horror*." *Sociological Quarterly* 33 (2): 191–209.

Knapp, Raymond. 2010. *The American Musical and the Performance of Personal Identity*. Princeton: Princeton University Press.

Laird, Paul. 2011. "Musical Style and Song Conventions." In *The Oxford Handbook of the American Musical*, edited by Raymond Knapp, Mitchell Morris, and Stacy Wolf, 33–44. Oxford: Oxford University Press.

Latham, Edward D. 2008. *Tonality as Drama: Closure and Interruption in Four Twentieth-Century American Operas*. Denton: University of North Texas Press.

Latham, Edward D. 2020. "Sowing the Seeds of Loss: Permanent Interruption in Verdi's *Otello*." In *Singing in Signs: New Semiotic Explorations of Opera*, edited by Gregory J. Decker and Matthew R. Shaftel, 105–27. New York: Oxford University Press.

Lawton, David. 1982. "Tonal Structure and Dramatic Action in *Rigoletto*." *Verdi: Bollettino dell'Istituto di studi verdiani* 9: 1559–81.

Lawton, David. 1989. "Tonal Systems in *Aida*, Act III." In *Analyzing Opera: Verdi and Wagner*, edited by Carolyn Abbatte and Roger Parker, 262–75. Berkeley: University of California Press.

Locke, Liz. 1999. "'Don't Dream It, Be It': *The Rocky Horror Picture Show* as Cultural Performance." *New Directions in Folklore* 3.

McClary, Susan. 1991. *Feminine Endings*. Minneapolis: University of Minnesota Press.

McMillin, Scott. 2006. *The Musical as Drama*. Princeton: Princeton University Press.

Penner, Nina. 2020. *Storytelling in Opera and Musical Theater*. Bloomington: Indiana University Press.

Peraino, Judith. 2006. *Listening to the Sirens: Musical Technologies of Queer Identity from Homer to "Hedwig."* Berkeley: University of California Press.

Reale, Steven Beverburg. 2012. "A Sheep in Wolf's Corset: Timbral and Vocal Signifiers of Masculinity in *The Rocky Horror Picture/Glee Show*." *Music, Sound, and the Moving Image* 6 (2): 137–62.

Ricci, Adam. 2017. "The Pump-Up in Pop Music of the 1970s and 1980s." *Music Analysis* 36 (1): 94–115.

Sallinger, Elizabeth. 2016. "Broadway Starts to Rock: Musical Theater Orchestrations and Character, 1968–1975." PhD diss., University of Kansas.

Taylor, Millie. 2012. *Musical Theatre, Realism, and Entertainment*. Farnham, UK: Ashgate.

Weinstock, Jeffrey Andrew, ed. 2008. *Reading Rocky Horror:* The Rocky Horror Picture Show *and Popular Culture.* London: Palgrave Macmillan.

Whitesell, Lloyd. 2006. "Trans Glam: Gender Magic in the Film Musical." In *Queering the Popular Pitch*, edited by Sheila Whiteley and Jennifer Rycenga, 263–77. Milton Park: Routledge.

Wright, Trudi. 2020. "It's Still *Working*: Collaborating to Perform the Stories of Everyday Americans, Then and Now." In *The Routledge Companion to the Contemporary Musical*, edited by Jessica Sterman and Elizabeth L. Wollman, 152–62. Milton Park, UK : Routledge.

# 8

# *Music, Time, and Memory in Jason Robert Brown's* The Last Five Years

*JONATHAN DE SOUZA*

On a certain level, *The Last Five Years* (2001) presents a typical musical-theater story: an aspiring actress and an aspiring writer meet in New York City, fall in love, and marry. Yet composer-lyricist-author Jason Robert Brown twists this conventional plot in several ways. First, the romantic leads, Cathy and Jamie, are the only characters onstage. The show alternates between their solos, and Brown (2017) describes it as "a song cycle for two people." *The Last Five Years* thus embodies a stripped-down form of the dual-focus narrative structure that Rick Altman (1987, 16–59) identifies in American film musicals—a structure based on the opposition and ultimate union of two thematic poles, which are identified with the two romantic leads.[1] Second, while this narrative structure normally ends with the couple's wedding, *The Last Five Years* keeps going. Here Cathy and Jamie fall out of love and separate, in a precise inversion of the standard plot. Finally—and, for present purposes, most importantly—the show involves a temporal trick: Jamie's scenes move forward through time, while Cathy's go backward. At the end of the show, she has just met her future husband; in the first song, "Still Hurting," she mourns their failed marriage.

Cathy's beginning, then, is also an ending. In a sense, it frames the show, and a close reading of "Still Hurting" can illuminate *The Last Five Years* as a whole. As Cathy sings "Jamie is over and Jamie is gone," her melody descends from $\hat{5}$ to $\hat{3}$ over a tonic harmony that is prolonged by subdominant and subtonic chords (for an analytical reduction, see example 8.1). As Cathy obsessively names her ex, the two-measure musical idea repeats. Her concluding line ("and I'm still hurting"), which recurs throughout the song, comes to rest on $\hat{1}$ but breaks the rhyme scheme. It flips from a third-person to a first-person perspective, as Cathy returns to her own pain. In mm. 25–32, the music strays from the tonic (leading to a half cadence in m. 32), and the lyrical perspective shifts again, with Cathy posing a series of questions to her absent partner. The opening section returns in mm. 33–41, completing an **AABA** song form—but this form's concluding tonic chord features a suspension that refuses to

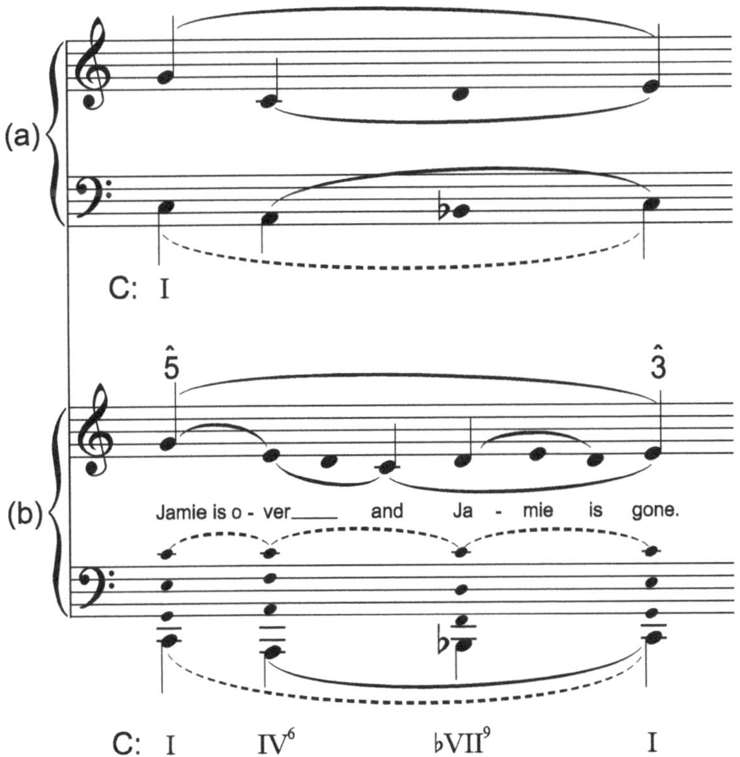


**Example 8.1.** Middleground and foreground sketches for the motif introduced in "Still Hurting," mm. 5–6.

resolve (mm. 40–41). Like Cathy, the harmony cannot yet find closure. The resulting tension launches a new section (mm. 42–57), with chromatic descents above pedal tones (climbing from the tonic C to E♭ in mm. 50–53). Cathy again addresses Jamie, now with imperatives instead of questions, and finally expresses her anger. After an instrumental interlude based on the opening material, she repeats the B section (mm. 67–76), then returns to the opening line, "Jamie is over" (m. 77). At the end of the song, Cathy has gone nowhere. She is stuck in the same mood, the same moment. Still hurting.

This opening sets out an initial temporal level (the end of the relationship) and point of view (Cathy's), as well as a certain musical style. Yet two moments in the number diverge from these established levels. First, the piano's brief prologue. In contrast to Cathy's contemporary musical-theater idiom, the prologue's hesitant waltz hearkens back to an earlier era. (Also, where Cathy's music seems tied down by the tonic, the waltz lacks a root-position I chord, starting on $\text{ii}^{\varnothing 6}_{5}$ and ending on the $V^7$ that sets up the segue into Cathy's song.) Second, the strings' interlude in mm. 58–66 recasts the A material in quasi-baroque counterpoint, with imitation and ornamentation. Both passages involve distinctive shifts in musical discourse, yet their significance is not immediately clear. Both point to something beyond the song itself, and both will recur, transformed, later on.

These moments reveal a network of specific and generic references, a web of musical relationships that generate interpretive questions about Cathy and Jamie. Such analysis, however, requires a more theoretical approach to temporality in musical theater.[2] Drawing on literary theory and music psychology, this approach necessarily goes beyond Brown's work and touches on varied musical theater repertoire. It guides analysis of *The Last Five Years* and ultimately shows how reprise and pastiche—two of musical theater's most maligned features—play with time and memory.

## *TEMPORALITY IN MUSICAL THEATER; OR, STORY TIME, SONG TIME, SHOW TIME*

Though the audience never sees Jamie write, we do see him read his stories aloud. He presents an excerpt from his novel at a public reading.[3] And, more intimately, he tells Cathy a "Christmas story" in "The Schmuel Song." In it, an aged tailor named Schmuel encounters a magic clock that gives him the "unlimited time" that he needs to sew the dress of his dreams. Jamie's readings, like all storytelling, may be understood in terms of a distinction between *story* and *discourse* (Culler 1981, 189).[4] In narratology, story refers to a series of events, while discourse refers to the way these events are presented—from a particular point of view, in a certain order, according to poetic or generic conventions. Jamie might have told Schmuel's story in a different way, without changing any of the events: in present instead of past tense, with the tailor or the clock as a first-person narrator, in iambic pentameter, as a comic strip, and so on. Analytically, the story/discourse distinction suggests two contradictory logics: as Jonathan Culler puts it, "one logic assumes the primacy of events; the other treats the events as the products of meanings" (1981, 198). Schmuel's happily-ever-after ending (in which "a girl in Odessa" promises to love him forevermore) might be "caused" by preceding events in the story, but it might equally be "caused" by the discursive norms of the folktale genre.

The distinction can also illuminate narrative temporality. For example, the time taken by narrated events (*erzählte Zeit*, or "told time") is distinct from the time it takes to narrate them (*Erzählzeit*, "telling time," see Müller 1948; Dowling 2011, 47–48). Schmuel's story involves an "endless night," but Jamie tells it in a few minutes. "The Schmuel Song" also sets up a temporal disjuncture *within* the story. On one level, the clock stops time, delaying the sunrise until the dress is complete; on another, it takes the tailor back forty-one years. World-time stands still while Schmuel-time reverses. The song's metrical shifts reflect this reversal: the halting old-man movement of the opening's $\frac{4}{4}$ + $\frac{7}{8}$ gives way to a sprightly, waltzing $\frac{6}{8}$ in m. 77. While Schmuel magically moves backward in story time, actually recovering his youth, Cathy moves backward only in discursive time.[5] The show's title, along with numerous lyrical references to time and age, emphasizes that the underlying story time is entirely naturalistic.

Of course, tension between story and discourse is not unique to *The Last Five Years*. It is central to musical theater. Though story and discourse align in realistic dialogue or diegetic performance, characters in a musical do not necessarily sing or dance when the actors do (cf. Penner 2013). Lyrics might correspond to story-based speech. But they might also represent inner thoughts or speech that has been transformed via repetition or rhyme. Again, this distinction has temporal implications. Like Jamie's spoken book reading, Cathy's audition piece—the Jerome Kern–like "When You Come Home to Me"—is performed in real time (schematically, story time = song time). Yet a four-minute song might instead correspond to a brief moment of introspection (story time < song time). This would follow a long-standing convention in musical theater and opera, which juxtaposes real-time scenes and temporally static numbers. A single song might also traverse several years in the story (story time > song time). For example, in "Hakuna Matata" from *The Lion King* (1997) and "I Know It's Today" from *Shrek: The Musical* (2008), multiple actors portray a single character at different ages.[6] This relation between story time and song time may also be indeterminate: in "Still Hurting," Cathy's conflicting emotions might play out in a single moment or over several hours.

Such temporal relations also emerge at the level of a show as a whole. In *A Chorus Line* (1975), it is fairly easy to imagine that the duration of the diegetic audition (experienced by the characters in the show) matches the duration of the show (experienced by the performers and audience)—despite the final performance in costume, which functions as a kind of epilogue. By contrast, Rodgers and Hammerstein's *Oklahoma!* (1943) mostly spans a single day of story time (again, with an epilogue), while their *Allegro* (1947) spans thirty-five years, following Joseph Taylor Jr. from birth to professional maturity.[7] Meanwhile, musical revues—such as Brown's *Songs for a New World* (1995)—neutralize any larger sense of temporal progression, presenting a series of disconnected moments.

Unlike many shows, *The Last Five Years* does not present the story in chronological order. Gérard Genette refers to such discursive reorderings as "anachronies" (1980, 35). All anachronies depart from an initial temporal level (what he calls the "first narrative"). Genette not only distinguishes between "analepsis" (flashback) and "prolepsis" (flash-forward), but considers various kinds of each anachrony (1980, 40, 48–49). For example, external analepsis accesses a time before the first narrative—as in *Wicked* (2003), where most of the show is an extended flashback. It reaches beyond the witch's birth and reconnects with the show's opening in the finale.[8] Internal analepsis, by contrast, replays a moment that occurs after the opening time point. This type is represented by "Satisfied" from *Hamilton* (2015), which reenacts the scene where Alexander Hamilton meets the Schuyler sisters, from Angelica's perspective instead of Alexander's.

Musicals such as *Fun Home* (2013) involve other, complex anachronies. Here the cartoonist Alison Bechdel "draw[s] her memories of the past," summoning childhood and college memories that mingle with her present.[9] Each of these interwoven periods involves a different relation between story time and show time. Nineteen-year-old Alison's timeline unfolds chronologically (from her coming out to her father's suicide), whereas the childhood vignettes lack any obvious order. As *Fun Home*'s lyricist/book writer Lisa Kron puts it, "these scenes from the past flow unbidden and on their own terms, as memories do" (2015, 7). Meanwhile, present-day Alison is effectively at a standstill. As Kron emphasizes, Alison is a character, not a narrator. She remains inside the story, even though it is presented from her point of view or "focalized" through her (Genette 1980, 189–90).

If *Fun Home* involves a kind of subjective anachrony, Stephen Sondheim's *Merrily We Roll Along* (1981, revised 1994) might be said to feature objective anachrony. The show begins in 1976, with successful but unhappy composer Franklin Shepard, and ends in 1957, when Frank and his friends are young, idealistic artists. The scenes appear in exact linear order, only reversed. (This temporal structure is already established in the 1934 play by George S. Kaufman and Moss Hart, on which *Merrily We Roll Along* is based.) Furthermore, sung transitions explicitly name the years, situating the story in historical time. In *Merrily We Roll Along*, then, memory does not guide discursive order, and all of the characters are carried along by a single timeline.

*The Last Five Years* blends these approaches. As with *Merrily We Roll Along*, it is not difficult to reconstruct an underlying order of events (see table 8.1). In fact, fans of *The Last Five Years* have created versions of the 2002 cast recording and 2015 film adaptation that put the songs into chronological story order.[10] Yet as in *Fun Home*, the discourse is focalized or character-centered, systematically alternating between Cathy and Jamie's viewpoints.[11] With this alternation, *The Last Five Years* does not offer a nonlinear presentation of the story, but a *bilinear* one. Figure 8.1 represents this graphically.[12] The horizontal axis puts the songs in show order, whereas the vertical axis puts them in story order (with lower positions earlier in time). The two characters' timelines intersect in the duet "The Next Ten Minutes," where Jamie and Cathy get married. Here the temporal crossing plays out in song time as well as show time, as Jamie's introduction and Cathy's coda occur at the same moment in story time.

For Brown, the show's temporal structure represented a solution to a technical problem. In a sense, it added discursive complexity to compensate for a relatively straightforward story:

Table 8.1. Songs in *The Last Five Years*, arranged by show order and hypothetical story order

| Show Order | Story Order |
|---|---|
| 1. Still Hurting (Cathy) | 2. Shiksa Goddess (Jamie) |
| 2. Shiksa Goddess (Jamie) | 14a. Goodbye Until Tomorrow (Cathy) |
| 3. See I'm Smiling (Cathy) | 12. I Can Do Better Than That (Cathy) |
| 4. Moving Too Fast (Jamie) | 4. Moving Too Fast (Jamie) |
| 5. A Part of That (Cathy) | 6. The Schmuel Song (Jamie) |
| 6. The Schmuel Song (Jamie) | 10. Climbing Uphill (Cathy) |
| 7. A Summer in Ohio (Cathy) | 9b. When You Come Home to Me (Cathy) |
| 8. The Next Ten Minutes (duet) | 8. The Next Ten Minutes (duet) |
| 9a. A Miracle Would Happen (Jamie) | 9a. A Miracle Would Happen (Jamie) |
| 9b. When You Come Home to Me (Cathy) | 7. A Summer in Ohio (Cathy) |
| 10. Climbing Uphill (Cathy) | 5. A Part of That (Cathy) |
| 11. If I Didn't Believe in You (Jamie) | 11. If I Didn't Believe in You (Jamie) |
| 12. I Can Do Better than That (Cathy) | 13. Nobody Needs to Know (Jamie) |
| 13. Nobody Needs to Know (Jamie) | 3. See I'm Smiling (Cathy) |
| 14a. Goodbye Until Tomorrow (Cathy) | 14b. I Could Never Rescue You (Jamie) |
| 14b. I Could Never Rescue You (Jamie) | 1. Still Hurting (Cathy) |

> My initial instinct was that I wanted to write a simple piece with two people. But I thought that if it went all song, song, song, song in chronological order I'd have to come up with surprises in the plot. I'd have to keep throwing extra theatrical ideas at them to keep the plot moving forward because otherwise it's just a relationship. And what I realized was that if I had them coming at it in separate directions that on a practical level it solved a lot of the story problem for me because you never really knew what was coming next—except you also *always* knew where the story was. (Brown 2016)

*The Last Five Years*, then, embodies the double temporality of narrative theorized by the philosopher Paul Ricoeur. For Ricoeur, every story is simultaneously told forward and backward (Dowling 2011, 10). That is, narrative combines the viewpoints of the characters, who move through a story without knowing its ending, with that of the narrator, who starts with the ending in mind. As with *Wicked*, *Fun Home*, and *Merrily We Roll Along*, *The Last Five Years* reveals its ending at the beginning, encouraging the audience to toggle between the characters' and narrator's perspectives. Its double orientation toward future and past, toward Jamie and Cathy,

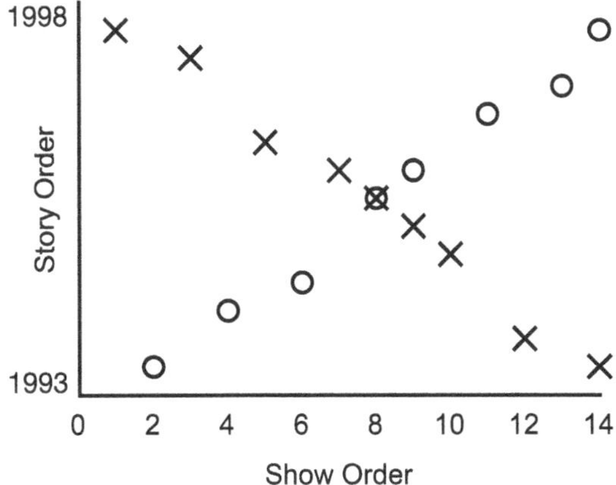


**Figure 8.1.** Temporal chart for *The Last Five Years*. The horizontal axis represents the songs' show order; the vertical axis, their story order. Xs and Os represent Cathy's and Jamie's songs, respectively. (For song titles, see table 8.1.)

affects experiences of the story. But this doubling can also shape interpretation of specific musical details, particularly when it comes to repetitions and references, as in the oblique instrumental passages—that is, the prologue's waltz and the quasi-baroque interlude—in "Still Hurting."

## *REPRISE, REVERSE REPRISE, AND DOUBLE ANACHRONY*

Echoes of "Still Hurting" resound throughout *The Last Five Years*, but the show also includes more localized repetitions. For example, consider Jamie's penultimate song. Like many internal analepses, "Nobody Needs to Know" fills in a gap or discloses a secret (Genette 1980, 50–52). In this case, Cathy's suspicions, voiced early in the show, are finally confirmed: while she is performing summer stock in Ohio, Jamie is having an extramarital affair in New York. His obsessive mood is matched by a looping progression with a chromatically descending inner voice over an A♭ tonic pedal (for a reduction, see example 8.2). The loop creates an increasingly oppressive sense of harmonic stasis, which is relieved when Jamie breaks his train of thought (in mm. 43, 81, and 159). While the progression appears in the song's coda, this section also echoes an earlier song. "Since I need to be in love with someone," Jamie tells his lover, "maybe I could be in love

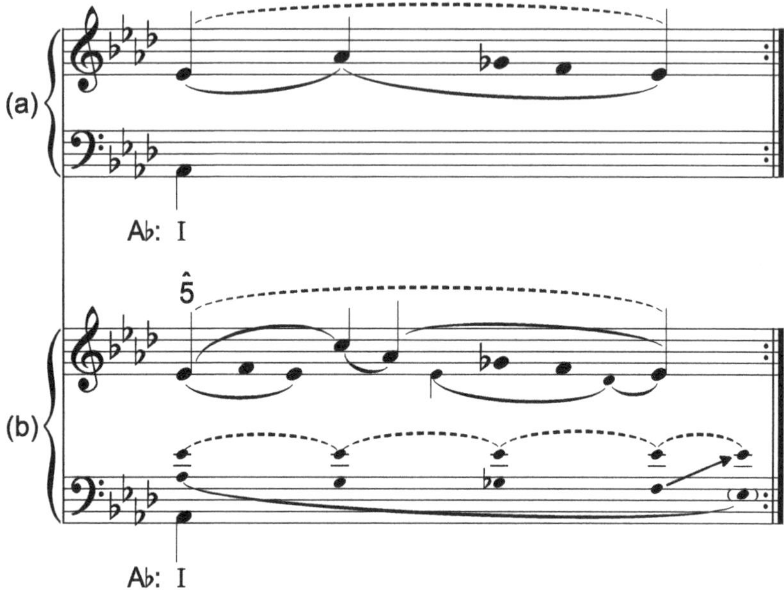


**Example 8.2.** Middleground and foreground sketches for "Nobody Needs to Know," mm. 9–12, illustrating the looping progression.

with someone like you." The lyric "someone like you" recalls the last line of Jamie's first song, where he identifies Cathy as the "Shiksa Goddess" that he's been waiting for. Both numbers close with a sustained high note, over an unexpected off-tonic ending—a direct modulation from A♭ to G in "Nobody Needs to Know" (what might be understood as an unusual "pump-down" modulation), and a deceptive resolution to vi (F♯ minor) in "Shiksa Goddess." The beginning of his affair echoes the beginning of his relationship with Cathy.

This is nearly a minimal instance of reprise, repeating only a few words and a musical gesture. But whether fragmentary or exact, reprises connect distant moments.[13] The past makes itself heard in the present. In the Hammersteinian integrated musical, reprise typically puts familiar music into a new dramatic context. As Stephen Sondheim explains, "The tune, even the lyric, might be the same, but the situation would be changed, lending the reprise poignancy or triumph or, rarely in Hammerstein's case but often in the hands of his followers, irony" (2010, 381). Often this corresponds to a scene of recognition (what Aristotle called *anagnorisis*), where a narrative goal reveals itself within the story, where characters accede to the power of discourse (Dowling 2011, 9). In *Oklahoma!*, for example, the reprise of "People Will Say We're in Love" marks the point when Curly and Laurey give in to their overdetermined pairing, and also when the cowboy realizes that he is destined to become a farmer in the new state. Such recognition embodies a paradox of narrative causality: "no, it was entirely unforeseeable; yes, we now see that it was inevitable all along" (Culler 1981, 194). And reprise can emphasize this tension. The story continues to move forward, while musical discourse looks backward.[14]

Yet anachronies can alter the temporal implications of reprise. "See, I'm Smiling," the third song in *The Last Five Years*, presents Cathy's side of a conversation. Jamie has come to Ohio for her birthday. But when Cathy discovers that he plans to return to New York without seeing her show, her hope turns to disappointment and anger. Lyrically, an essential twist comes at the song's closing, when the eponymous lyric from mm. 8–9 becomes "see I'm crying" (mm. 110–111). Arguably a more significant moment comes out of Cathy's anger. In this section, her declamation speeds up; the music leaves the home key of A major and ascends by minor thirds (from A minor to C minor to E♭ minor). "You can't spend a single day," she tells him, "that's not about you and you and nothing but you" (mm. 94 and 98–99). This passage recurs in Cathy's penultimate song, "I Can Do Better than That" (mm. 111–114 and 119–120). There, however, "you and you and nothing but you . . ." expresses not Jamie's self-adoration but her adoration for him.

Though this example features Hammersteinian recontextualization, the timeline is flipped. "I Can Do Better than That" could be viewed as a proleptic reprise, which refers to a future moment in story time. Or "See, I'm Smiling" could be a reprise that is presented before the original. Sondheim refers to this phenomenon as "reverse reprise," and he uses it throughout *Merrily We Roll Along*:

> The structure of *Merrily We Roll Along* suggested to me that the reprises could come first: the songs that had been important in the lives of the characters when they were younger would have different resonances as they aged; thus, for example, "Not a Day Goes By," a love song sung by a hopeful young couple getting married, becomes a bitter tirade from the wife when they get a divorce, but the bitter version is sung first in the musical's topsy-turvy chronology. This notion also gave rise to an unconventional use of melodic material: what were vocal lines in their early lives

could become accompaniments for other songs in their later lives, undercurrents of memory, but the audience would hear the accompaniments first. (Sondheim 2010, 381)

The reverse reprise in "See, I'm Smiling" closely resembles Sondheim's use of "Not a Day Goes By," both musically and dramatically. Both prospectively echo a love song that occurs earlier in story time but later in show time.[15]

Other repetitions in the show are more temporally ambiguous, especially those involved in "Still Hurting." The piano's waltz reappears with lyrics at the end of the show as Jamie's final goodbye, "I Could Never Rescue You." Here his timeline finally reconnects with the first narrative. As the couple separates, he gives voice to his feelings of resignation and nostalgia. In show time, the vocal version follows the instrumental one; in story time, it either precedes or is simultaneous with it. From this perspective, the introduction to "Still Hurting" is an instrumental double, heard before the original that seems to unlock its meaning. This reading would explain why the prologue distances itself from Cathy's music: it stands in and speaks for the absent Jamie. The concluding lyrics are implicit in the instrumental prologue, so that the show's end is embedded in its beginning.

This reading, however, is complicated by the appearance of the waltz, played by the strings, in "The Next Ten Minutes" (when the two timelines intersect). The waltz introduces what Genette calls a "double anachrony" (1980, 83). If the waltz emerges from the first narrative, its appearance at Cathy and Jamie's wedding would be an "analeptic prolepsis," a retrospective flash-forward. ("As we have already seen, they will fall out of love later.") Yet this can easily be inverted. If the waltz originates at their wedding (an earlier moment in story time), then the prologue would form a "proleptic analepsis," an anticipatory flashback. ("As we will see later, they were in love once.") In one reading, the strings echo the piano and voice; in the other, the piano and voice echo the strings. Of course, the two interpretations are complementary. Both connect the waltz—that quintessential couple's dance—with both characters, not with Jamie alone. The ambiguity of the waltz, temporally and as a signal of both love and loss, is irresolvable.[16]

Similar issues affect the opening of "Still Hurting," which is the most repeated material in the show. Aspects of it recur in three of Cathy's songs:

the distinctive I–IV$^6$–♭VII$^9$–I chord progression closes "A Part of That" (mm. 119–200), and the coda melody is orchestrally reprised in both "A Summer in Ohio" (mm. 128–129) and "I Can Do Better than That" (mm. 183–187). Each of these three songs presents melody or accompaniment (but not both) from "Still Hurting," and each represents a "reprise-as-coda" (Blustein 2016). But there are also notable differences. In "A Part of That," Cathy expresses uncertainty about their relationship. She reflects on both Jamie's eccentricities and his creative powers. The music vacillates between "bouncy" optimism and a more expansive half-time feel. This is musically, temporally, and affectively close to "Still Hurting," and the instrumental quotation might be seen as a tragic answer to her questions about the relationship. While the reprised chord progression is unmistakable, the melodic reprises in "A Summer in Ohio" and "I Can Do Better" are less obvious. Musically, the melody's rhythm is altered; affectively, both songs are exuberant and represent earlier stages in their relationship. In show time, "I Can Do Better than That" presents the last instance of the "Jamie is over" melody. But in story time, it is the first instance, appearing after Cathy asks Jamie to move in with her. This again engages the paradoxes of double anachrony.

Furthermore, Jamie sings this melody at nearly the same moment in story time, when the couple has "found an apartment on 73rd." In "Moving Too Fast," the melodic quotation is rhetorically marked by a modulation to the key of ♭VI in m. 39. The funk-rock reinterpretation of Cathy's music may seem arbitrary or puzzling. After all, Jamie isn't hurting. He's carried away by romantic and literary success, a feeling that is musically emphasized by the pump-up modulations in the song's final section (from A to B♭ in m. 90, then to B in m. 94, and to C in m. 98). Yet Jamie's lyrics parallel Cathy's from "Still Hurting." Recall that Cathy focused on Jamie, with the repeated last line of each stanza ("And I'm still hurting") returning to herself. Similarly, in "Moving Too Fast," Jamie's lyrics criticize "some people," who are emotionally or creatively stuck, with the last line of each stanza returning to himself ("But I keep rollin' on"). Ultimately his desire to move forward will lead him to move away from Cathy, whose personal and professional stasis resembles the "some people" he disdains. Whether entering or exiting a relationship, Jamie keeps moving on.

This interpretation fits with an echo of "Still Hurting" in another of Jamie's songs, "If I Didn't Believe in You." As they fight, he comes to express his love conditionally. If he hadn't believed in her, Jamie says, he

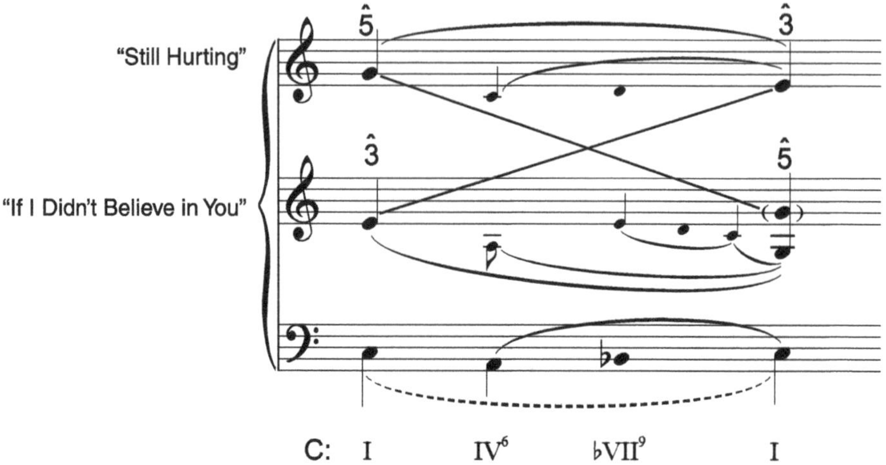


**Example 8.3.** Reduction of melodies with a shared chord progression, from Cathy's song "Still Hurting" (see mm. 5–6) and Jamie's "If I Didn't Believe in You" (see mm. 19–20). To facilitate comparison, the latter has been transposed from F major to C major.

simply wouldn't have fallen in love with her. Here, as in "A Part of That," the I–IV$^{6}$–♭VII$^{9}$–I chord progression recurs without the melody. This progression is most prominent at the end of each stanza, highlighted by a temporary metric shift from $\frac{12}{8}$ to $\frac{9}{8}$ (m. 29). The progression, however, underpins the first main section (m. 19), entering after the parlando introduction. Intriguingly, Jamie's melody here may be understood to reverse Cathy's melody from "Still Hurting." Where her basic idea went from $\hat{5}$ to $\hat{3}$, his goes from $\hat{3}$ to $\hat{5}$. (The analytical reduction in example 8.3 uses crossing lines to highlight this relation between their melodies.) The virtual voice exchange over the show's most iconic progression suggestively mirrors the temporal exchange that happens throughout the show as a whole. This moment is both a standard reprise of "Moving Too Fast" and a reverse reprise of "Still Hurting," simultaneously looking toward the past and the future. The music makes it clear: when Jamie no longer believes in Cathy, he will no longer love her.

These interrelated echoes reflect Brown's commitment to what he calls "the lyric musical theatre," "where songs explore the characters" and where "everything is of a piece and there for a reason" (quoted in Shenton 2015). This musical integration does not lock down meaning, though, and Brown's references are not leitmotifs that represent stable, identifiable signifiers.[17] They instead function as a kind of "prosthetic memory" (Margulis 2014, 22). Musical repetition orients the audience's remembering in an open-ended way. Although at first the material from "Still Hurting" is associated with Cathy's heartbreak, this becomes increasingly ambiguous as the show progresses. In the end, Cathy's pain and Jamie's progress are musically entwined.

## *PASTICHE OR PARODY?*

The strings' quasi-baroque interlude in "Still Hurting" is bound up with this network of musical repetitions, since it elaborates material that recurs in five later songs ("Moving Too Fast," "A Part of That," "A Summer in Ohio," "If I Didn't Believe in You," and "I Can Do Better than That"). Still, the archaic counterpoint sticks out, as the only moment in *The Last Five Years* that explicitly references classical music. Formally, this interlude might be understood as an instrumental substitute for a vocal recapitulation of the A section. After all, when Cathy begins to sing again, she takes up the B section (mm. 67–76). Perhaps developing this material also enhances its memorability, preparing the audience for the callbacks that appear later in the show. According to research in music cognition, recognition memory requires a musical passage to be distinctive and also repeated (Huron 2006, 224). If the ♭VII$^9$ chord contributes to the opening's distinctiveness, the imitative interlude would add varied repetition. These explanations, though, do not yet account for the interlude's learned style.[18]

This stylistic imitation differs from the quotations discussed in the preceding section, and it engages a different kind of memory. Recognizing a tune or progression—a specific sequence of notes or chords—involves veridical expectations and episodic memory (that is, memory for particular events). Recognizing a musical style or genre, on the other hand, involves schematic expectations and semantic memory (Bharucha 1994, 213–39; Huron 2006, 224–25; Margulis 2014, 92). This distinction from music psychology helps to account for deceptive resolutions and related phenomena. In "A Summer in Ohio," for example, there is a moment when the piano accompaniment falls apart (mm. 47–48).[19] This "mistake" is written into the score, and the cast recording preserves a single, fixed version of it, which sounds exactly the same on repeated listening. Because of this consistency, fans of *The Last Five Years* will develop veridical expectations and episodic memories for that "mistake." But it still sounds funny, because it violates the schematic expectations that correspond to stylistic norms. This distinction may also explain why the interlude in "Still Hurting" can seem jarring: despite my veridical knowledge of the piece, the stylistic shift remains schematically surprising.

Though Brown does not use this psychological terminology, the composer consciously tries to manage musical expectations. He made extended comments on this phenomenon in a 2014 interview:

> There are things that just sound like "this is what's supposed to happen" and "this chord goes to that one." And I think most pop music sort of does that. And for me musically, it's . . . If you *know* it's supposed to do that, then my job is to ask the question, "Why do we know that? What else could it be?" And I find that when you ask those questions—I find that when *I* ask those questions—the emotional life sort of blossoms. You know, I start to feel things that I can't articulate. That's the whole point of writing music, is to be able to write things that you can't articulate. But I think that the essential ambivalence, the essential ambiguousness, of our lives is able to come out in the music that I write, if I'm doing it right. (Laufer Krebs 2014)

Challenging expectations, then, is not just a compositional game. It has dramatic and affective implications. For Brown, this is essential to "real art." He wants to inhabit a place "between what is definite and what is unsure," rather than "the land of the certain" (Laufer Krebs 2014). And this illuminates many of Brown's compositional choices. For example, it helps explain his reliance on deceptive resolutions and unexpected modulations, or his rare augmented-sixth chords, which invariably correspond to moments of emotional revelation.[20]

But imitating a conventional style would seem to contradict Brown's aesthetic goals. Doesn't this imitation move away from so-called "real art" toward the certainty that he attributes to "most pop music"? Arguably, musical predictability and ambiguity are mutually implicated, and schematic or generic passages offer a range of dramatic effects.

Style's function in musical theater can be approached via Frederic Jameson's distinction between parody and pastiche. For Jameson (1991, 17), both involve "the imitation of a peculiar . . . style, the wearing of a linguistic mask." But whereas parody sets the borrowed style against a normal stylistic register, pastiche flattens stylistic hierarchies and neutralizes any sense of a privileged, natural style. Pastiche, then, is "blank parody" (Jameson 1991, 17). In musical theater, pastiche can be found in the free stylistic play of Andrew Lloyd Webber and Tim Rice's *Joseph and the Amazing Technicolor Dream Coat* (1968), whose score ranges from vaudeville to country to calypso to Elvis impersonation and so on. But in their *Jesus Christ Superstar* (1970), King Herod's vaudeville style stands out from the prevailing rock-opera idiom, an instance of parody that marks him as inauthentic.[21] Similarly, in Lynn Ahrens and Stephen Flaherty's *Seussical* (2000), vaudeville and rag-influenced music functions as merely one element in a stylistic potpourri; in the same team's *Ragtime* (1996), by contrast, the titular style is established as a normal musical register, a historical vernacular.

The parody/pastiche distinction seems less helpful with diegetic songs like Cathy's audition piece, which imitates early-twentieth-century musical theater within the world of the story. The distinction is more relevant to Cathy's nondiegetic songs. For example, "A Summer in Ohio" adopts a swing style, complete with light cocktail piano and a clear **AABA** form (mm. 9–57). Writing to Jamie from her summer stock gig, the newlywed Cathy presents a series of fantasies—involving wealth, travel, beauty, and so on—that "wouldn't be as nice" as her underwhelming circumstances in Ohio, far from her new husband. After the written-in "mistake" at the end of the B-section bridge (mm. 47–48), her sarcasm intensifies, with fantasies transformed into nightmares (eating rotten fish, chewing tinfoil, demonic dental work). The irony in the lyrics is enhanced by the too-sunny music, whose style diverges from Cathy's normal voice. Just as "Still Hurting" established the temporality of the first narrative, it also established Cathy's "natural" mode of expression. That normal voice comes out in the middle section of "A Summer in Ohio," when Cathy speaks of their relationship as the one thing she's done right. In the rest of the song, she is joking, to be sure, but also struggling to make the best of a frustrating situation. Musical parody, then, reflects emotional subtext.

Cathy takes on a similar musical mask in "A Part of That," which opens with a "bouncy" swing feel and jazz-violin fills. Here she tries to put a positive spin on her marital frustrations. She wants to convince herself that everything is okay, but her optimism is difficult to sustain. Unlike "A Summer in Ohio" with its "Tempo di Stripper" finish, "A Part of That" drifts away from the opening style and ends subdued and bittersweet. The song goes from parody to sincerity, in a version of the process that Ronald Rodman calls a "stylistic dissolve" (2000, 98).

What about Jamie? His various styles in "The Schmuel Song," represent different characters. Though this is not a diegetic song, its musical masks are tied up with performative narration rather than self-expression. But conventional styles are also central to songs in Jamie's own voice. His opening, "Shiksa Goddess," comes just after their first meeting. Jamie is thrilled. He's been waiting, he says, for a non-Jewish girl: not for this particular woman, but for a type. The music is full of generic types too, alternating between Latin-feel verses and a rock 'n' roll chorus, with the occasional dash of klezmer (mm. 58–59). (The klezmer insertions are an obvious musical topic, a sign of Jewishness.)[22] Jamie's "natural" voice, then, is initially hard to pin down, but mid-song, he starts to let his guard down. As he acknowledges his fear, the harmonic language opens up: a French $\frac{4}{3}$ resolves to $V^6_4$ in the home key of A, initiating a passage with a stepwise, chromatic bass line (mm. 70–83). Later, a deceptive resolution to ♭VI (F major) launches a section, marked "dreamy," where Jamie's stylistic masks recede further (mm. 105–124).

Jamie's stylistic code-switching involves the same keys in "Moving Too Fast" and "A Miracle Would Happen." In the latter, bluesy A major supports Jamie's half-joking complaints about his attraction to other women. After Cathy's audition interlude, though, the song is suddenly in F major, and he addresses his wife directly (see m. 107). In "Moving Too Fast," the prevailing A-major "funky rock" gives way to F major when Jamie sings the melody from "Still Hurting." Some generic inflections remain here (for example, the R&B–flavored dominant ♭9/13 in mm. 44 and 53). Still, given the larger pattern, it seems that F (as ♭VI of A) is marked as a zone of sincerity for Jamie. The juxtaposition of conventional and "natural" styles would again make this parody, not pastiche.

That said, the generic is not necessarily ironic, and in Jamie's songs, conventions in music often converge with conventions of life. As Lauren Berlant argues, "genres provide an affective expectation of the experience of watching something unfold, whether that thing is in life or in art" (2011, 6). "Moving Too Fast" makes it clear that Jamie's vision of the good life combines romantic and literary fantasies. Both are more or less generic. He wants to get the All-American Girl and to write the Great American Novel. These fantasies reflect Jamie's self-understanding, though they also require partners ("a woman I love" and "an agent who loves me"). "All genres," Berlant notes, "produce drama from their moments of potential failure" (2011, 148). The couple might not come together, the hero might not win, or a tonal composition might not find its way back to the home key. Yet Berlant is centrally concerned with "the waning of genre," with what happens when the fantasies that inform a life cannot be sustained, opening up an "impasse" whose ambiguities produce new anxieties but also new possibilities and pleasures (Berlant 2011, 6, 199–200). *The Last Five Years* features a certain waning of genre too. As Jamie becomes more ambivalent about his personal and professional life, stylistic tropes in his music fade away. They are absent in the raw moments when the marriage is falling apart ("If I Didn't Believe in You" and "Nobody Needs to Know"). Jamie, it seems, is only able to recapture the generic, to regain a coherent personal narrative, in the final waltz.

Nonetheless, "The Next Ten Minutes" lacks this association of musical style and lifestyle. In their desire to marry and have children, Jamie and Cathy are arguably at their most normative, yet the duet resists generic markers. It features gently rolling quartal harmonies, evoking the movement of the water in Central Park. This antiparodic quality suggests complete sincerity, true love. But it also heightens the contrast with the strings' waltz, whose entrance engages both veridical and schematic recognition. Again, then, Brown's music juxtaposes the predictable and the ambiguous, the specific and the generic, playing with multiple modes of expectation and memory.

## *CONCLUSION*

*The Last Five Years* stages a gap between story time and show time. Like other pieces that feature anachronies, it brings time to the audience's attention. Yet this idiosyncratic structure reveals temporal aspects of musical theater in general. Spoken scenes and songs, for example, imply different relations to the presumed real time of the story, and moving between these modes of performance is also moving between temporalities. From this perspective, reprise and parody/pastiche have temporal implications too. Reprise refers to moments inside the show; parody/pastiche, to styles outside of it. Both engage distinctive modes of musical memory and can foster a sense of irony or authenticity. As it takes apart a love story, *The Last Five Years* reveals music-theatrical conventions that are often taken for granted.

Though all of this informs interpretation, *The Last Five Years* also shows how musical relationships can orient listeners without determining meaning. As Berlant puts it, "A musical phrase is powerful because it repeats: as we become attached to it, it helps us find a place before the plot tells us what it means and where that place is" (2011, 157). Of course, *The Last Five Years* never provides complete answers. In the end, the audience's relationship to Cathy and Jamie might parallel the couple's relationship to each other—a mix of attachment and ambivalence.

The ambiguities in the show—its musical and temporal puzzles—encourage a particular kind of spectatorship. They call for active, repeated listening, and conversation. Fans of *The Last Five Years*, like so many musical theater fans, form an interpretive community; their connection to the show is productive (Kuhn 2002, 196–212; Wolf 2011, chap. 7). They create reordered versions of the soundtrack and film, blog posts, performances uploaded to YouTube. Music analysis is simply a more formal, academic contribution to this discussion. The activity is retrospective, sustained by memories of a show. But analysis might truly involve a kind of double temporality, recalling past experiences while anticipating future ones, looking for new ways to hear music we love.

## NOTES

1. Elsewhere, I have discussed some limits of Altman's account (see De Souza 2012, 80).

2. To be clear, "temporality" refers not to time itself but to our relationships with time (e.g., lived experiences, concepts, or aesthetic representations of time). On time and temporality in music, see Hatten (2006, 62–63).

3. In the show, Jamie's reading is a spoken monologue. In the liner notes to the original cast recording, the excerpt is printed with formatting that recalls the *New Yorker.*

4. The story/discourse opposition takes many forms, from the Russian formalists' *fabula/syuzhet* to Tzvetan Todorov's *histoire/discours* to Gérard Genette's *histoire/récit*. This narratological distinction also underpins the opposition of diegetic/nondiegetic in film music scholarship (Gorbman 1987; Winters 2010). Finally, Byron Almén (2008) offers a more general approach to music and narratology.

5. This parallel does not seem coincidental. As the song's epilogue reveals, Schmuel and the clock represent Cathy and Jamie, respectively, and he is encouraging her to pursue her own dreams.

6. It is perhaps no coincidence that both of these shows are based on films, since cinematic montage has long been used to depict the passage of time.

7. *Les Misérables* (1980) nicely demonstrates how the relation between story time and show time may involve variable pacing. Its first act goes from 1815 to 1832, whereas its second act remains within 1832, with discourse time slowing considerably to focus on the ill-fated Paris uprising.

8. In Genette's terms, *Wicked*'s analepsis is also "complete," because it rejoins the first narrative. Partial analepsis, by contrast, remains separated from the opening temporal level (Genette 1980, 62).

9. In this volume, Rachel Lumsden considers these anachronies through the lens of "queer temporalities."

10. At the time of writing, several chronological versions were available on YouTube (e.g., https://youtube.com/playlist?list=PL_dQnq0Chp4MBnWlaPhjti6RhKEVa_bdw, based on the 2002 recording, and https://youtu.be/LKVlQJ0b3q4, based on the 2015 recording).

11. Genette refers to this as "variable focalization" (1980, 189).

12. According to Brown (2015), the musical spans from 1993 to 1998. As such, I have indicated these dates in figure 8.1.

13. A general theory of reprise types has been offered by Nathan Beary Blustein (2016).

14. Of course, reprise might stay within the world of story—as in Cathy's diegetic auditions in *The Last Five Years* or the von Trapps' repeated performances in *The Sound of Music* (1959). Yet since the same music can be attached to different dramatic situations, reprise is predicated on the potential divergence of story and discourse. In a revue, reprise may lack narrative grounding, fostering the musical pleasure that typically results from "relistenings" (see Margulis 2014, 95–102). Something similar happens in overtures that proleptically introduce tunes without narrative context, tunes whose dramatic significance emerges only later.

15. Musical foreshadowing is similar to reverse reprise. For example, in Frank Loesser's *The Most Happy Fella* (1956), Rosabella receives a love note from Tony, and she sings Tony's tune before he does (even before he appears onstage). Thanks to Michael Buchler for bringing this example to my attention.

16. See also Greg Decker's and Rachel Lumsden's essays in this volume, both of which discuss the waltz as a musical signifier for love and romance.

17. Carolyn Abbate (1989) critiques leitmotivic-semiotic interpretation (and ideas of musical narrative, more generally).

18. The interlude might also be a demonstration of learnedness per se, a marker of compositional skill and musical seriousness.

19. In the score, this written-in mistake is marked "very Jonathan Edwards," referring to the comedic lounge-pianist alter ego of arranger and composer Paul Weston.

20. See "Shiksa Goddess," mm. 70–71; "The Next Ten Minutes," mm. 58–59; and "If I Didn't Believe in You," m. 53. In each case, the augmented-sixth chord resolves to a cadential $^6_4$.

21. Lin-Manuel Miranda uses a similar parodic strategy in *Hamilton*, with King George III's light pop style diverging from the main character's hip-hop vernacular. The Wizard's "Wonderful" in *Wicked* follows the same pattern. In each case, the music emphasizes a powerful character's shallowness.

22. Michael Buchler (2019) discusses a similar instance of code-switching between klezmer and contemporary popular vocal styles in *I Can Get It for You Wholesale* (1962).

## WORKS CITED


Abbate, Carolyn. 1989. "What the Sorcerer Said." *19th-Century Music* 12: 221–30.

Almén, Byron. 2008. *A Theory of Musical Narrative*. Bloomington: Indiana University Press.

Altman, Rick. 1987. *The American Film Musical*. Bloomington: Indiana University Press.

Berlant, Lauren. 2011. *Cruel Optimism*. Durham, NC: Duke University Press.

Bharucha, Jamshed J. 1994. "Tonality and Expectation." In *Musical Perceptions*, edited by Rita Aiello and John A. Sloboda, 213–39. New York: Oxford University Press.

Blustein, Nathan Beary. 2016. "Playwriting in Song: 'Reprise Types' in Stephen Sondheim's *Sweeney Todd*." Paper presented at the Annual Meeting of the American Musicological Society and the Society for Music Theory, Vancouver, November 6.

Brown, Jason Robert. 2015. "Jason Robert Brown Q&A The Last Five Years (NYC)." YouTube video. February 20, 2015. https://youtu.be/ofnb9xEAjOQ

Brown, Jason Robert. 2016. "The Last 5 Years—Jason Robert Brown on Bringing the Show to London." YouTube video. October 28, 2016. https://youtu.be/1GSLYaUgGVs

Brown, Jason Robert. 2017. "Go Behind 'If I Didn't Believe in You' with Jason Robert Brown." YouTube video. January 18, 2017. https://youtu.be/O7bGcERnXA8

Buchler, Michael. 2019. "'Sing Me a Song with Social Significance': Battling Industrialist Oppressors on the Broadway Stage." Keynote presented at the Music Theory Midwest Conference, University of Cincinnati.

Culler, Jonathan. 1981. *The Pursuit of Signs: Semiotics, Literature, Deconstruction*. Ithaca, NY: Cornell University Press.

De Souza, Jonathan. 2012. "Film Musicals as Cinema of Attractions." In *From Stage to Screen: Musical Films in Europe and United States (1927–1961)*, edited by Massimiliano Sala, 71–91. Speculum Musicae 19. Turnhout, Belgium: Brepols.

Dowling, William C. 2011. *Ricoeur on Time and Narrative: An Introduction to Temps et Récit*. Notre Dame, IN: University of Notre Dame Press.

Genette, Gérard. 1980. *Narrative Discourse: An Essay in Method*. Translated by Jane E. Lewin. Ithaca, NY: Cornell University Press.

Gorbman, Claudia. 1987. *Unheard Melodies: Narrative Film Music*. Bloomington: Indiana University Press.

Hatten, Robert S. 2006. "The Troping of Temporality in Music." In *Approaches to Meaning in Music*, edited by Byron Almén and Edward R. Pearsall, 62–75. Bloomington: Indiana University Press.

Huron, David. 2006. *Sweet Anticipation: Music and the Psychology of Expectation*. Cambridge, MA: MIT Press.

Jameson, Frederic. 1991. *Postmodernism, or, The Cultural Logic of Late Capitalism*. Durham, NC: Duke University Press.

Kron, Lisa. 2015. "Foreword." In *Fun Home*, by Jeanine Tesori and Lisa Kron. New York: Samuel French.

Kuhn, Annette. 2002. *Dreaming of Fred and Ginger: Cinema and Cultural Memory*. New York: New York University Press.

Laufer Krebs, Bonnie. 2014. "Jason Robert Brown Exclusive Interview—The Last Five Years." YouTube video. September 7, 2014. https://youtu.be/eo_3feEG4D0

Margulis, Elizabeth Hellmuth. 2014. *On Repeat: How Music Plays the Mind*. New York: Oxford University Press.

Müller, Günther. 1948. "Erzählzeit und erzählte Zeit." In *Festschrift Paul Kluckhorn und Hermann Schneider*, 195–212. Tübingen: J. C. B. Mohr.

Penner, Nina. 2013. "Opera Singing and Fictional Truth." *Journal of Aesthetics and Art Criticism* 71: 81–90.

Rodman, Ronald. 2000. "Tonal Design and the Aesthetic of Pastiche in Herbert Stothart's *Maytime*." In *Music and Cinema*, edited by James Buhler, Caryl Flinn, and David Neumeyer, 187–205. Hanover, NH: Wesleyan University Press; University Press of New England.

Shenton, Mark. 2015. "The Big Interview: Jason Robert Brown." *The Stage*, May 24, 2015. https://www.thestage.co.uk/features/interviews/2015/big-interview-jason-robert-brown

Sondheim, Stephen. 2010. *Finishing the Hat: Collected Lyrics (1954–1981) with Attendant Comments, Principles, Heresies, Grudges, Whines, and Anecdotes*. New York: Alfred A. Knopf.

Winters, Ben. 2010. "The Nondiegetic Fallacy: Film, Music, and Narrative Space." *Music & Letters* 91: 224–44.

Wolf, Stacy. 2011. *Changed for Good: A Feminist History of the Broadway Musical*. New York: Oxford University Press.

# 9 *Lesbian Desire in* Fun Home

RACHEL LUMSDEN

The Tony Award–winning musical *Fun Home* (2015) offers a distinctive, innovative perspective on queer sexuality. As Stacy Wolf (2011) notes, musicals traditionally exude a "heterosexual imperative" (214) where "heterosexual relationships, romance, and marriage provide the narrative spine" (213). When gay characters do appear, Wolf emphasizes that they are usually secondary characters who ultimately "bolster heteronormativity" by providing a contrast (often humorous) to the primary heterosexual relationship that drives most musicals (216).[1]

*Fun Home* upends these conventions. The heart of the musical is the complex relationship between a father (Bruce Bechdel) and daughter (Alison Bechdel), which is further complicated by their respective sexualities. The musical chronicles Alison's emerging awareness of her lesbian identity and contrasts her eventual acceptance of her own sexuality with that of her closeted gay father, who commits suicide.

In this essay, I examine how *Fun Home* represents Alison's queerness. I begin with a short overview that describes how the plot and dramatic structure intersect with processes frequently discussed in queer scholarship, such as "slippage" and "queer temporality." Next, I analyze the two songs that focus on Alison's sexual identity—"Ring of Keys" and "Changing My Major"—to explore what happens when a musical foregrounds lesbian identity and takes it seriously. *Fun Home* deserves in-depth scholarly consideration not just because it features a lesbian as a central character, but for the extraordinary ways that its music envisions and envoices lesbian sexuality.

## *SLIPPAGES, QUEER TEMPORALITIES, AND THE STRUCTURE OF* FUN HOME

*Fun Home* is based on the eponymous graphic memoir by cartoonist Alison Bechdel (2006). Feminist and queer scholars have praised its innovative visual and narrative style.[2] In a 2009 interview, Bechdel notes that her work draws on processes of "slippage" that exploit the fractures "between appearance and reality . . . between the expected and unexpected" (12:36–59).[3] The memoir slips back and forth in time and lacks a conventional linear structure; Bechdel has described its form as a labyrinthine spiral (Chute 2010, 183). Ann Cvetkovich (2008) and Valerie Rohy (2010) both characterize *Fun Home* as a "queer archive" that problematizes traditional (heterosexual) life narratives and simplistic distinctions between past and present. Rohy explains how Bechdel's memoir, like other forms of queer historiography, purposefully "resist[s] teleology, linearity, causality, and the pose of epistemological mastery in favor of nonidentity, plurality, circularity, and the nonsequential narrative" (2010, 343).

The musical also has an unusual structure that flirts with the bounds of past and present, fact and memory. The musical eschews a traditional multi-act form and chronological narrative. Three different actresses depict Alison's character in three different life stages: "Small Alison" (young child), "Medium Alison" (college freshman), and "Alison" (forty-three-year-old).[4] Presented in a single ninety-minute act, the story skips unpredictably back and forth between the three different time periods of the three Alisons. For example, the two songs discussed in this chapter appear in reverse chronological order: the audience hears Medium Alison's triumphant solo, "Changing My Major" approximately thirty minutes before Small Alison's solo, "Ring of Keys." Lisa Kron, who wrote the musical's book and lyrics, emphasizes that "the scenes flow unbidden and on their own terms, as memories do" (2016, vii).

The large-scale design of the musical and memoir also resonates with scholarship on "queer temporality," which explores how queer lives and artistic works can work as transgressive forces that rupture conventional (and dominant) chronologies typically associated with heterosexual lives (childhood, marriage, childbearing, etc.). Jack Halberstam stresses that queer temporality "disrupts the normative narratives of time that form the base of nearly every definition of the human" (2005, 152). In her study of the musical *Rent*, Sarah Taylor Ellis describes how its "queering" of a traditional linear timeline provides "a lifeline of identification that is particularly resonant for socially marginalized subjects and communities" (2011, 197). *Fun Home* has obvious intersections with these ideas. As Cvetkovich emphasizes, *Fun Home* "embraces a queer temporality, one that refuses narratives of progress," in which there is "no self-congratulatory separation of past and present" (2008, 124).

## *"RING OF KEYS"*

I begin with "Ring of Keys," Small Alison's only solo number, which occurs approximately two-thirds of the way through the musical. The inspiration for this song is a sequence of panels midway through the memoir, in which, as young child, Alison sees a "truck-driving bulldyke" (described in the musical as an "old-school butch") while eating in a diner with her father. In the panel that features the "ring of keys" of the song's title, young Alison stares from afar, wide-eyed, at a heavyset butch delivery woman[5] in the foreground. The butch woman sports a button-down plaid shirt and work pants; the eponymous "ring of keys" dangles from her right hip, prominently affixed to a wide black belt by a hardy leather loop with a snap. Bechdel's captions for this sequence emphasize its transformative impact on Alison: "I didn't know there were women who wore men's clothes and had men's haircuts. . . . The vision of the truck-driving bulldyke sustained me through the years" (Bechdel 2006, 118–19).

Bechdel contrasts young Alison's admiration and fascination with her father's disdain, as he glares at the butch woman through narrowed, suspicious eyes. This sequence encapsulates the tensions between young Alison and her father, who frequently regulates her appearance; earlier in the memoir, Bechdel writes that "he was attempting to express something feminine through me" (2006, 98). These panels call to mind other moments in which Alison's father attempts to feminize her by insisting that she wear a velvet dress (35), barrette (96–97), pearl necklace (99), ponytail (116), or even that her dress have a proper neckline (15). (Indeed, Alison even has a barrette in her hair in these particular panels.) The sequence foregrounds the butch woman as young Alison gawks in wonder at her short hair, flannel shirt, and key ring. In contrast to the butch woman's confident, hands-on-hips pose, Alison quivers with excitement, her hands clutched in her lap, eyes wide, eyebrows raised in astonishment. Finally, young Alison sees a real-life example of the kind of woman she could be.

In a 2015 interview, composer Jeanine Tesori describes "Ring of Keys" as an existential touchstone for Small Alison, explaining that it "is not a love song. It's a song of identification because for girls you have to see it to be it" (Clement 2015). Like the memoir, the musical frames "Ring of Keys" with other scenes in which Alison's father controls her appearance. The song is preceded by a terse exchange of dialogue (Bruce: "Where's your barrette? It keeps the hair out of your eyes." Alison: "So would a crewcut." Bruce: "If I see you without it again, I'll wale you.").[6] Adult Alison then interrupts to shift the scene, describing the moment the butch woman enters the diner just before Small Alison begins to sing. The staging also helps stress the significance of this encounter for Small Alison, since she sings this number while her father and Adult Alison (two queer adults living very different kinds of queer lives) surround her from opposite points of the stage. In a gripping performance by Sydney Lucas at the 2015 Tony Awards ceremony, Small Alison turns and faces Adult Alison while she sings the second verse and chorus, creating an emotional link between past and present, child and adult.[7] Another important difference between the memoir and musical is that the butch woman is not shown onstage in the musical, which highlights how the moment is not really about the butch woman per se, but her transformative impact on Alison and her identity.

Scholarship on Bechdel's memoir typically discusses this scene and its implications in a strictly visual context, examining how Alison "sees" the butch woman, and how Bechdel offers a queer, lesbian rebuttal to a traditional "masculine gaze" (Lemberg 2008, 134–37; McBean 2013, 109–11). I will return to these ideas later in this essay, but in this section I want to explore how Tesori's sonic choices, combined with Lisa Kron's lyrics (which do not appear in Bechdel's memoir), offer an alternative interpretation of the scene. In the original panel Small Alison has no words for what she sees—she simply sits in astonished silence. But the musical flips this on its head, since Small Alison's seeing the butch woman propels her into song. In the musical, seeing not only helps Alison clarify her identity and desires, it (quite literally) helps her begin to find her own voice.

One of the most noticeable features of this song is the halting, fragmented phrases that begin each verse. Here Small Alison's song disintegrates, for she cannot find the words to adequately express how she feels. The lyrics break off at just the moment when she tries to make sense of what she sees: "Someone just came in the door / Like no one I ever saw before / I feel— / I feel—." (The second verse contains similar ruptures, such as "I want—," "You're so—," and "I, um—.") Kron's textual lapses intersect with contemporary queer scholarship on the use of ellipses to express the unspeakable. (Following traditional notational practices for lyrics, dashes are used to show the breaking off of the text, not ellipses, but the effect is similar.) Martha Vicinus notes that a textual lapse like an ellipsis "begs for interpretation, yet resists it" (2004, 234). Halberstam describes how the textual breaks in "Ring of Keys" reflect "the unspeakability of affectionate regard," explaining that "there are no words for such affect, no precedents for generations of butches past who may also have seen strong, genderqueer, female-bodied women and who may have wanted to claim them" ([1998] 2018, xx).

But in these passages, it is both the music and the lyrics that combine to depict Small Alison's initial bewilderment. The opening phrase (shown in example 9.1) illustrates her inability to fully express her feelings; her halting, fractured lyrics create a complicated nexus of allure, fascination, and self-identification. Measures 5–8 begin as a characteristic sentence (2+2+4 measures).[8] But after a presentation with two basic ideas (2+2 measures) that establish a clear expectation for continuation cadence, the phrase continues circling through a static I–IV progression and no cadence materializes, reflecting her inability to fully comprehend or articulate what she sees. (The same passage returns in the second verse in mm. 35–42, with the words "I thought it was s'posed to be wrong / But you seem okay with being strong / I want— / You're so—.")

The second phrase of the verse (mm. 13–18, also shown in example 9.1) begins identically to the first, with the same set of two-measure basic ideas. Either of these phrases easily could have been written as a traditional 2+2+4 sentence; a hypothetical version is shown in example 9.2. (This example, which I have composed, illustrates how utterly *un*interesting such a "normal" phrase would be.) But instead, the second phrase is even more deviant than the first: it's shorter (six measures instead of eight), and unravels even further. After gasping, "I feel—" Small Alison completely stops singing, and the phrase ends not with a balanced four measures (as

**Example 9.1.** "Ring of Keys," first verse. (Similar music appears in the second verse, mm. 35–48.)

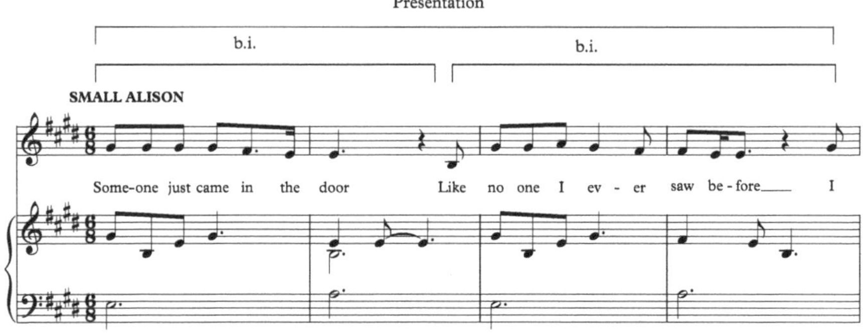


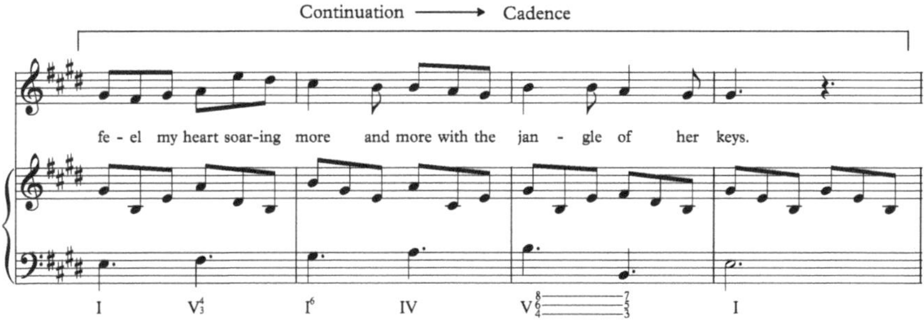


**Example 9.2.** Hypothetical recomposition of the first phrase of "Ring of Keys" as a paradigmatic (but much more boring) sentence.

it did before) but a two-measure instrumental break that leads into the chorus. Notably, at the same point in the second verse, she is so overcome that she can only utter single syllables ("I, um—").

Although Small Alison's verses are faltering and fragmented, her conviction builds during the choruses. This shift hinges on the lyrics, which suddenly swerve from her initial emotional shock into a detailed list of the butch woman's physical characteristics ("Your swagger and your bearing and the just-right clothes you're wearing / Your short hair and your dungarees and your lace-up boots"). Small Alison's focus on these "just right" qualities contrasts sharply with the very *wrong* types of clothing and accessories that her father has adorned her with in an attempt to make her conform to traditional standards of female beauty. The phrase structure of the chorus also becomes more regular and tight-knit, changing to a simple, regular 4+4+4 pattern that differs from the unpredictable verse.

Alison's thoughts and emotions gain new clarity during the chorus, when she focuses more intensely on the butch woman's appearance.

Alison's confidence continues to build during the bridge (mm. 63–73), as she begins to articulate affections of camaraderie with the butch woman ("Do you feel my heart saying hi? / In this whole luncheonette why am I / The only one who sees you're beautiful? / No. I mean . . . Handsome."). The stripped-down texture shown in Example 9.3 lends a sense of clarity to Alison's inner ruminations. Sustained chords appear in the accompaniment (mm. 63–64), instead of the rollicking, swaying eighth-notes heard throughout the other sections. A new ascending bassline appears for the first time in mm. 63–65 and 67–69 (C♯–D♯–E or $\hat{6}$, $\hat{7}$, $\hat{8}$ in the home key). This rising bassline (coupled with parallel tenths in the vocal line) gives these measures a feeling of emboldened optimism. The ascending stepwise bassline in this passage contrasts with the static I–IV motion throughout the verses and descending basslines in the choruses (mm. 19–21 and mm. 49–51). The hopeful $\hat{6}$, $\hat{7}$, $\hat{8}$ bassline is also echoed in

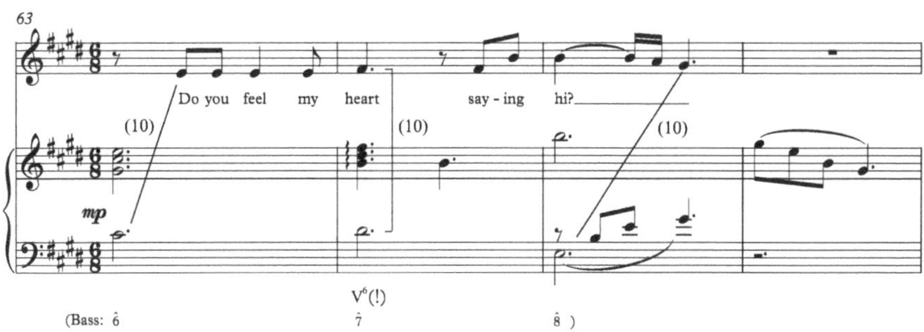


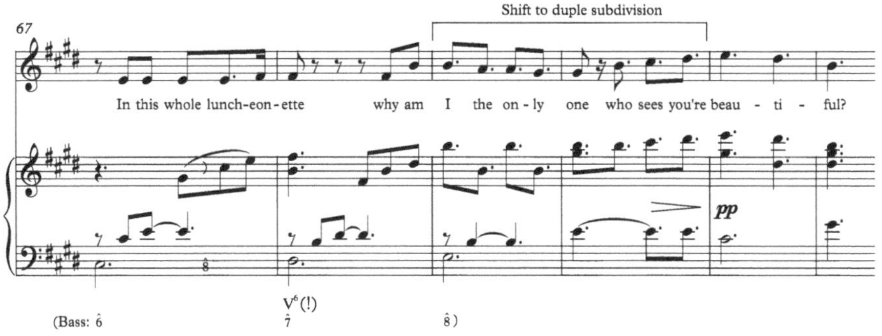


**Example 9.3.** "Ring of Keys," mm. 63–72.

the vocal line in mm. 70–71, where Alison ascends $\hat{5}$, $\hat{6}$, $\hat{7}$, $\hat{8}$ (with the text "who sees you're beautiful") up to E5, the highest note of the song.

Text-painting also helps depict her increasing self-awareness and "outsider" status in this section. In mm. 69–70, the music suddenly shifts from the triple division of the notated $\frac{6}{8}$ meter to a duple division with the words "Why am **I the only one who sees you're**" (the shift to a duple pulse occurs on the bolded text). This tension reflects Small Alison's unique perspective—in the entire diner, only she appreciates and admires the butch woman—and her increasing awareness of her own identity outside of heterosexual norms. Remarkably, the only other shift to a duple pulse in the vocal part occurs during the chorus, where Alison sings "and the **just right** clothes you're wearing" (m. 21, m. 51, and m. 78). Even more remarkably, the pitches Alison sings during the "just right" duple shift are identical to the ones that occur in m. 69 (the linear descent B–A–G♯), lending a subtle connection between the "just right" clothes and Alison's ability to see the woman for who she really is. These momentary shifts to duple meter depict how the butch woman's appearance pushes against dominant heterosexual gender norms (just as a shift to a duple division disrupts the established compound meter), but it is "just right" for her—and, ultimately, for Alison too.

The harmonic plan of the song also reflects her reactions to the butch woman. One noticeable feature of "Ring of Keys" is its lack of cadences. Remarkably, there is no root-position V–I cadence in the primary key (E major) during the entire song. The first sixteen measures simply sway between I and IV harmonies, gently rocking between E and A in the bass. The first clear dominant in the main key does not even appear until m. 64, during the song's bridge, but it is a passing chord in first inversion (refer back to example 9.3). Definitive V–I motion occurs only during the end of the chorus, which modulates to G major and rocks between I and $V^{(7)}$ in the new key as Small Alison sings "And your keys, oh / Your ring of keys."

I hear these harmonic choices in a few different (and intersecting) ways. First, the meandering effect of so much I–IV–I motion evokes a noticeable circularity that mirrors the "ring" of keys of the song's title. At the same time, the heavy emphasis on I and IV, plagal motion frequently associated with religious works (especially the final "Amen" in Christian hymns), lends a feeling of transcendence—perhaps even spirituality—to the song. Indeed, "Ring of Keys" even concludes with its own "Amen" moment in mm. 92–95, where the music again alternates between I and IV as Small

Alison quietly sings "I know you" in the song's final measures. Finally, the lack of cadences in the main key helps depict Small Alison's present situation. As a child (who lives with an overbearing and sometimes abusive father), she cannot fully understand or become the butch woman she sees. The definitive V–I cadences in the secondary key, during the music about the butch woman and her appearance, represent a yearning for an identity that has not yet been fully actualized. The chorus provides a vision of the future—the "ring of keys" (of course, an obvious metaphor for power) that Alison herself will hold one day.

In his essay for the cast album of *Fun Home*, theater critic Jesse Green explains how "Ring of Keys" reflects Small Alison's character, noting that "it's as if the song itself, like Alison, were thinking its way into coherence" (2015, 5). But I hear "Ring of Keys" as much more than a subtle reflection of Small Alison's nascent identity. To me, it directly articulates an overt resistance to her father's attempts at control, as well as to prevailing heterosexual norms. "I know you," Alison sings to the butch woman. In *Female Masculinity*, Halberstam describes how tomboyhood can serve as a "politics of refusal" that (for some butches) is sustained into adulthood (2005, 177). Halberstam emphasizes how tomboys like Small Alison "offer a set of opportunities for theorizing gender, sexuality, race, and social rebellion . . . the desires, the play, and the anguish they access allow us to theorize other relations to identity" (2005, 175). Halberstam's work resonates with McBean's discussion of this scene in Bechdel's memoir. McBean argues that in this moment, Alison (even as a child) "is able to articulate a particular kind of resistance. It is consistently drawn in *Fun Home* as constraining as well as opening up to alternative possibilities" (2013, 110). In "Ring of Keys," Small Alison does much more than slowly develop a "coherent" perspective: she recognizes—and feels solidarity with—the kind of woman she will eventually become. As a tomboy child she can't quite grasp the butch woman's ring of keys yet, but she will. In fact, the musical shows that in some sense, she already has.

## *"CHANGING MY MAJOR"*

This ecstatic number is the other solo that focuses on Alison's sexual identity, and it provides an important counterpoint to "Ring of Keys" since it occurs approximately thirty minutes earlier in the musical. (When Small

Alison admires the butch woman and feels a kinship with her, the audience has already seen that eventually she will fully embrace her own sexuality.) Medium Alison sings "Changing My Major" in her college dorm room just after having sex with a woman for the first time. Kron (2016) describes this song as Alison's "coming-out scene" (vii) and "a joyful opening into a world of wondrous possibility" (vii–viii).

Although superficially these songs seem to have little in common, they share some important similarities. Both songs are dramatic solos, and the only solo numbers that these two characters sing. Both songs involve important "firsts" for Alison regarding her sexual identity: the first time she sees a butch woman and the first time she has sex with another woman. The staging of these songs is similarly provocative. In both songs Alison sings alone, but she is surrounded by other silent characters onstage, who provide a visual frame of reference for her thoughts. In "Ring of Keys," Small Alison is framed by the two adult characters that represent her own conflicts with her identity: her father (the closeted gay man who tries to regulate and control her) and adult Alison (the lesbian she will eventually become). In "Changing My Major," Medium Alison sings while her first lover, Joan, sleeps onstage in her bed.

Both songs also rely on the bodies of other lesbian women to clarify Alison's thoughts and emotions. Small Alison idolizes the butch woman's physical presence and appearance (her "swagger," "short hair," and more). Medium Alison enumerates specific features of Joan's body (her "inner thighs," "ass," and "well-made outline"). But these embodied characteristics transcend mere objectification: both songs offer a lesbian perspective that deconstructs a traditional "male gaze," famously discussed by film theorist Laura Mulvey.[9] Numerous scholars and artists have explored the ramifications of the "male gaze" and the potential for an alternative, feminist "female gaze" to transform it. For example, in a 2016 keynote address, director Joey Soloway describes how a "female gaze" can work as a transgressive "empathy generator" (39:39–40). Soloway's female gaze draws on empathetic processes of "feeling/seeing" and "attempts to get inside of the protagonist, particularly when the protagonist is not a cis male" (17:36–53). Soloway emphasizes how this creates "a feeling of being *in feeling* rather than looking at the character . . . I'm not just showing you this thing, I really want you to feel it with me" (17:58–18:10).

Soloway's comments explain how empathy, emotion, and self-identification can offer an alternative to the objectification of the female body that is typically associated with the male gaze. Both Alison characters perceive the female bodies that inspire their songs with a spirit of egalitarianism, not conquest. For example, Medium Alison humorously emphasizes how she will "Familiarize myself with her [Joan's] well-made outline / While she researches mine." Both Alison characters are imbued with empathy and emotions traditionally associated with fear and weakness (rather than strength and domination). In "Ring of Keys," Small Alison wonders, "Why am I the only one who sees / You're beautiful . . . no, I mean, handsome," and even concludes the song by singing "I know you." In "Changing My Major," Medium Alison frequently undercuts her lusty outbursts with self-deprecating rejoinders, such as: "I feel like Hercules! / Oh god, that sounds ridiculous" (mm. 54–55), "I have to trust that you don't think I'm an idiot or some kind of animal" (mm. 20–21), or an extended passage where Alison nervously stammers, "And I'll work on calming down / So by the time you've woken up / I'll be cool, I'll be collected / And I'll have found some dignity / But who needs dignity? / 'Cause this is so much better" (mm. 56–62). She even expresses how vulnerable she feels after having sex with Joan, "Overnight everything changed / I am not prepared / I'm dizzy, I'm nauseous / I'm shaky, I'm scared" (mm. 107–12). *Fun Home* thus deconstructs a traditional male gaze on several different levels. The Alison characters view the butch woman and Joan with admiration and egalitarianism, rather than uncontrolled lust or domination: both Alisons seem to see these women as who they really are, rather than as superficial objects of desire. Further, Small Alison and Medium Alison are presented with a vulnerability that also cultivates empathy from the audience. They are—to quote Soloway—"empathy generators" who subvert traditional (male) paradigms.

The music of "Changing My Major" also charts Medium Alison's emotional reactions to her first sexual experience. Clever manipulations of standard phrase-structure types help to communicate the song's erotic implications. The recitative-like introduction (mm. 1–11) and subsequent verses (mm. 12–25 and 54–69) have a stammering, halting feel because of Alison's quick, nervous lines, which cram rapid-fire lyrics (such as "Oh my God, last night / Oh my God, oh my God, oh my God, oh my God, last night") into consistent two- and four-measure subphrases. The expression marking for the first verse explains the feeling as "Neurotic, a little too fast."

But the mood quickly changes during the choruses of the song, which unexpectedly shift from $\frac{4}{4}$ to a $\frac{3}{4}$ waltz. As Gregory Decker suggests in his chapter in this volume, waltzes in musicals are unequivocally associated with love and romance, so Tesori draws on the waltz topic to connect Alison and Joan's relationship to this enduring legacy in musical theater. Wolf characterizes the waltz as "the dance of romance" that unites couples and "signifies their attachment" (2002, 30). However, the waltz chorus in "Changing My Major" also refutes traditional phrase-structure expectations. Each chorus begins with what seems like a paradigmatic sixteen-measure sentence (4+4+8 measures) with two (4+4) basic ideas (see example 9.4). Yet as the phrase continues, it revels in ambiguity. The continuation differs from a traditional sentence because it begins not with new material, but with a third repetition of the basic idea: the text in mm.

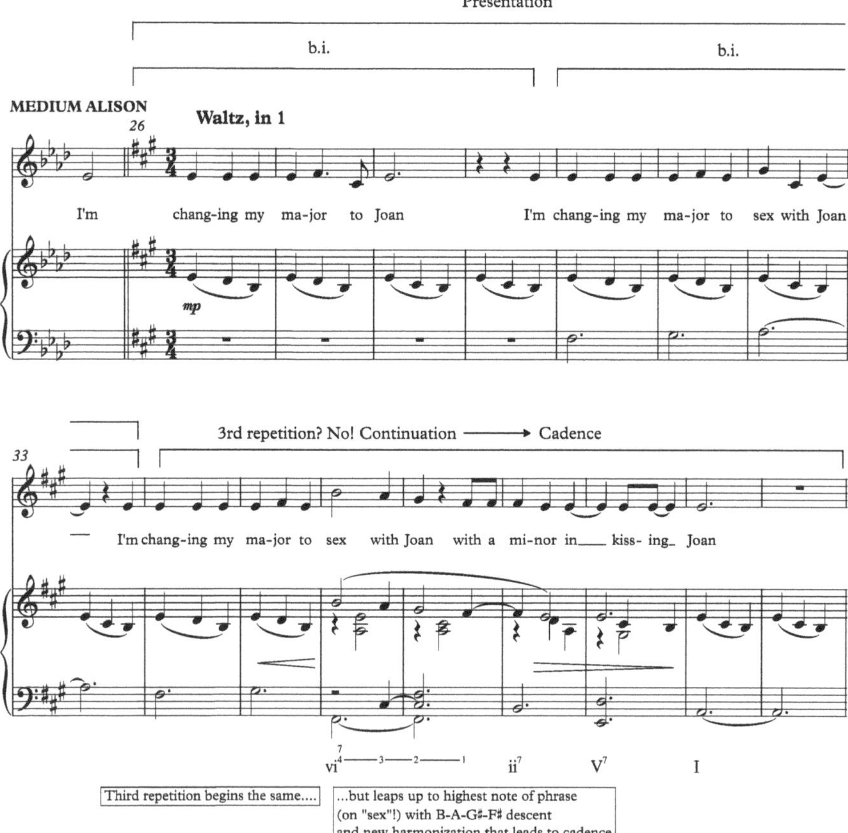


**Example 9.4.** "Changing My Major," mm. 26–41 (first phrase of chorus).

34–37 repeats what was just heard in mm. 30–33, and the music in mm. 34–35 is identical to that in mm. 30–31 (and almost identical to mm. 26–27).

This phrase calls to mind Michael Callahan's (2013) "*SLT3b*" [*n*+*n*+(*n*+*n*)2*n*], a sentence type he identifies in his work on the Great American Songbook.[10] Callahan emphasizes the inherent ambiguity of this sentence type, because its third line of text (set to a third repetition of the basic idea) "complicates the separation between lyrical presentation, continuation, and cadence" (2013, [5.9]). Callahan's "*SLT3b*" loosely intersects with Matthew BaileyShea's sentence with "dissolving third statement," where the continuation begins with a third statement of the basic idea, but eventually "break[s] through toward cadence" (2004, 11). Callahan explains that the tension and ambiguity of this sentence type "is brought about by a passage that, musically or lyrically or both, (1) does what the first two did for the first time (at least initially) and (2) simultaneously gains enough momentum to initiate a continuation that somehow exceeds a mere third like iteration" (2013, [5.7]). Callahan characterizes this sentence type as a complex "sleight-of-hand" [7.2] that relishes "ambivalence" [5.7] and "ambiguity" [5.9].

Subtle details of the phrase help morph the initially ambiguous third statement into a continuation → cadence. The shift hinges on the word "sex," which was just heard in the second basic idea (mm. 30–33), but in m. 36 now suddenly soars up to a B4, the highest note of the chorus so far. From B4, the melodic line glides down in an unbroken stepwise stream (B–A–G♯–F♯) over the new vi$^7$ harmony in mm. 36–37, and the phrase spins to its conclusion (a clear-cut IAC in m. 40). Retrospectively, because of Alison's gradual textual accrual, it becomes clear that what initially seemed like a third textual repetition is actually the first complete sentence of text in the chorus ("I'm changing my major to sex with Joan, with a minor in kissing Joan.").

The chorus continues to defy expectations as it progresses. The second phrase (mm. 42–53) begins with material similar to the first phrase, and easily could have been written as another sixteen-measure (4+4+8) sentence to answer the first, in a large-scale antecedent-consequent structure (thirty-two measures, two sixteen-measure sentences). However, the second subphrase of the second phrase (mm. 46–49) begins to chart a new course. The harmonic rhythm slows to two measures and new, colorful harmonies appear (such as the F♯$^9$ in mm. 48–49). And instead of concluding with a balanced eight-measure continuation → cadence, the second phrase maintains a steady two-measure harmonic rhythm (rather than the usual harmonic acceleration found in a continuation), and ends with a truncated four-measure subphrase that lacks a decisive cadence, and this abridged phrase (4+4+4) slips into the second verse.[11]

I like to think of the ambiguities in these phrases through a queer lens. The choruses draw on traditional ideas (waltz topic, sentence structure) to validate (or possibly legitimize) Alison's feelings for Joan, which are just as authentic as those of other well-known heterosexual lovers in musical theater. However, Alison's music also pushes back against these conventions. I hear these waltz choruses as having moments of "slippage," where Alison borrows from traditional paradigms (waltz, sentence structure), but also refuses to be contained by them.

But for me, the most remarkable aspects of this song involve moments of "slippage" in the harmonic realm. On the surface, "Changing My Major" seems more harmonically stable than "Ring of Keys": dominant harmonies appear frequently, and many phrases feature clear cadences and conclusive ii–V$^{(7)}$–I progressions (such as mm. 38–41 and mm. 42–45, to give just two examples). However, the large-scale structure of this song is much more complex and unpredictable. "Changing My Major" features several "pump up" modulations by ascending half step: over the course of the song, Alison propels the music from A♭ major, to A major, finally ending triumphantly in B♭ major. Walter Everett has described ascending half-step modulations as creating a sudden and "transcendent effect of hyper-arrival" (2008, 283). Part of the song's powerful impact thus rests on these unexpected shifts of key, which drive the music optimistically higher and higher.

Examining the voice-leading details in the passages that launch these half-step modulations provides some insight into why they sound so seamless, even slippery. As discussed above, the song abruptly shifts from the A♭ verse in $\frac{4}{4}$ into a $\frac{3}{4}$ waltz chorus in A major. The verse could have easily ended with a prolonged dominant in A♭ that elides with the chorus and plods along in the same key, as shown in the (extremely unsatisfactory) hypothetical recomposition in example 9.5a. Instead, the closing measures of the verse (mm. 24–25, shown in example 9.5b) are peppered with dissonant fourths, and the music suddenly, and quite literally, slips upward by half step to the dominant of the new key, A major. Similar "slippery" voice leading returns the music to A♭ major for the second verse (see example 9.5c). Now the bass slides up by half step (from E to F), and the

**Example 9.5a.** Hypothetical recomposition of the chorus, staying in A♭ major.

**Example 9.5b.** Tesori's (much more interesting) version of this passage, with dissonant chords in mm. 24–25 and sudden modulation to A major through "slippery" voice leading.

**Example 9.5c.** More "slippery" voice leading returns the music to A♭ major for the second verse.

other chord tones slither down by half step (D to D♭, A to A♭). (The voice descends by an augmented second, a dissonant interval typically avoided in traditional voice leading, because it returns to the same E♭ pitch Alison sang in the previous verse so that the melodic material will remain the same.) Just as the phrase structure slips between the expected and unexpected, so too does the slithery voice leading enact surprising shifts that veer the music into new and unpredictable harmonic realms.

The passage that leads into the final chorus serves as an important musical moment in Alison's character development. In mm. 112–123, Alison drives the music upwards by half step from A to B♭ (the key in which the song concludes) as she sings, "Am I falling into nothingness / Or flying into something so sublime? / I don't know, but I'm / Changing my major to Joan." The reference to "falling" and "flying" reflects one of the central themes of the musical, which begins and ends with Alison playing a game of "airplane" with her father (Bruce) as he hoists her weightless above him.[12] "Falling" and "flying" serve as obvious metaphors for Alison and Bruce's differing views of their sexualities: she eventually embraces her lesbian identity, but he remains closeted and dies when he walks in front of a delivery truck. Notably, in his final song in the musical, Bruce sings the exact same pair of lyrics about "falling" and "flying," but with a much different outcome. The musical differences between these two identical textual moments depict the different character trajectories of Alison and Bruce.

Example 9.6 provides a summary of these two passages. With the word "falling," Alison's music begins to shift from A major to B♭ major: the three sharps of the A-major key signature are removed (G♯4 and C♯4 even "fall" to G4 and C4 in the accompaniment in mm. 112–113), and the phrase ends with a half-diminished seventh chord on A (mm. 119–20). On a very deep structural level, the A-major tonality of the previous chorus and beginning of the bridge (mm. 70–112) has shifted down to the A half-diminished chord that ends the passage. But this A half-diminished seventh chord, sustained over the word "I'm," ultimately functions as a pivot chord that heaves the music upward to B♭ major. The subsequent lyrics "(I'm) changing my major to Joan"—marked fortissimo and "Definite, sure ('to the world!')"—appear with a definitive $IV^6$–$V^7$–I progression in B♭ major, the key in which the song concludes. (Measures 121–122 even stretch out the first part of the phrase to two expansive measures in $\frac{4}{4}$ time, instead of the brisk $\frac{3}{4}$ waltz used for previous appearances of these lyrics.) Other melodic details also give this passage a feeling of triumphant arrival.

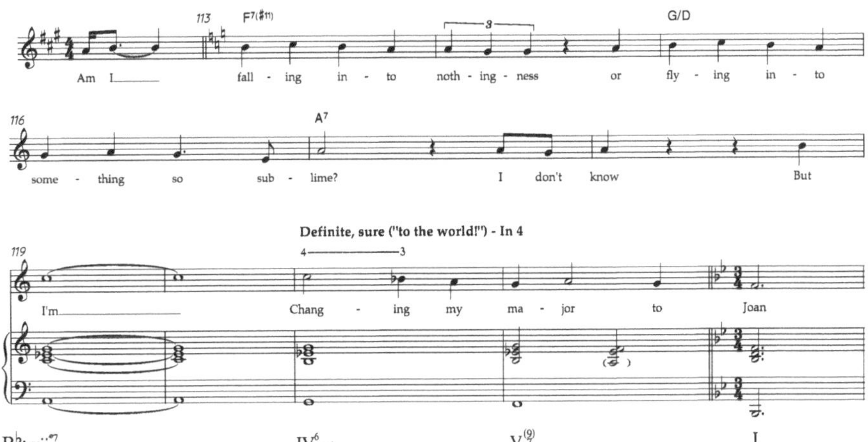


Example 9.6a. "Changing My Major," mm. 112–123.

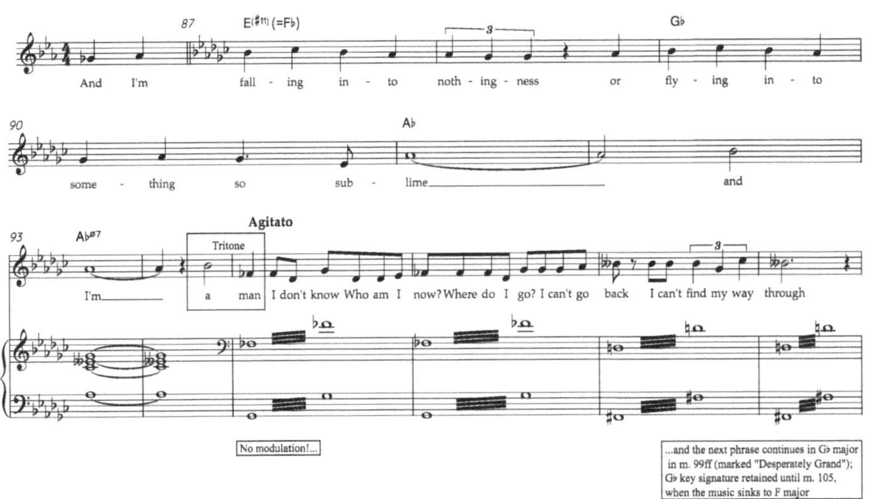


Example 9.6b. "Edges of the World," mm. 87–98.

Alison's climactic C5 ("I'm"), sustained for two full measures (her longest note in the song so far), is restated in m. 121, and precisely over the word "changing," it morphs into a 4–3 suspension that resolves over IV$^{6}$. I hear this "I'm changing" moment as a sonic representation of Alison's evolution: unlike her father, Alison decides to fully affirm her sexuality and soars into her lesbian identity.

The music Bruce sings to the same text, which appears in his unconventional eleven o'clock number "Edges of the World," differs from Alison's and reflects the very different arc of his character. Instead of joyful ascent, Bruce's music remains static, stuck—and ultimately spirals down into desperate, frenetic anguish. Indeed, the expression markings after his version of this passage are "agitato" (m. 95), "desperately grand" (m. 99), and even "crazy" (m. 105). Bruce's reference to Alison's earlier lyrics appears in mm. 87–98. Instead of her celebratory resolution, Bruce despairs, "And I'm falling into nothingness / Or flying into something so sublime / And I'm a man I don't know / Who am I now? Where do I go? / I can't go back / I can't find my way through." Bruce's melodic material in mm. 87–91 (during their shared lyrics "I'm falling into nothingness / Or flying into something so sublime / And I'm") is virtually identical to Alison's, except that it is transposed down by half step (see Example 9.6b).[13] But the path that Bruce's music takes is dramatically different from Alison's. The bass in mm. 87–94 ascends stepwise through F♭, G♭, and A♭, a last-ditch effort at hope. Bruce's phrase ends with the same half-diminished chord Alison sang (transposed down a half step), sustained for two measures over the same word, "I'm." But instead of the triumphant sense of arrival in Alison's song, Bruce's music sinks despondently down. His vocal line collapses into a dissonant descending tritone with the words "a man" (B♭ to F♭, mm. 94–95). Instead of the optimistic half-step pump-up modulation in Alison's song (from A to B♭), Bruce's music—like his character—remains paralyzed, stuck. In m. 95, the bass shifts down from A♭ to G♭, and the six-flat key signature that first appeared at the beginning of this passage (m. 87) is retained. After four measures of trembling tremolo chords over the same bass note, Bruce continues in G♭ major in m. 99 ("I might still break a heart or two"), but this passage ultimately shifts the music downward yet again, to F major (m. 105ff.). Instead of "flying" triumphantly into his sexuality, as his daughter Alison does, Bruce cannot fully come to grips with who he is; his version of these same lyrics reflects his "falling" into frustration, fear—and eventually, death.

## *CONCLUSION*

Wolf (2002) has described musicals as an "aggressively heteronormative genre" (40), emphasizing that "celebration of heterosexuality is the raison d'être of the musical . . . we hum heterosexuality on our way out the theater's doors" (30–31). But twenty-first century musicals have begun to depict a wider range of sexualities and sexual relationships, and detailed analysis of these characters—and the music that they sing—yields important insights into artistic depictions of queerness. Alison's journey into understanding her own sexual identity is a turbulent one, tinged by her fraught relationship with her father and his own sexuality. As Cvetkovich explains, "central to *Fun Home*'s moral and political complexity is its willingness to engage with sexual desire as a messy and unpredictable force" (2008, 118).

But *Fun Home* (both the musical and memoir) also offers a vision of queer sexuality that reveals its potential power for shaping alternative historical legacies. Cvetkovich argues that Bechdel "reminds us of other temporalities and histories that pervade the national consciousness even as they remain largely invisible within it" (2008, 123). Ultimately, *Fun Home* shows the transformative things that can happen when a musical dares to speak—and sing—lesbian sexuality. No mere childhood lark, Alison eventually transcends the metaphor of the "airplane" game she plays with her father. By having the courage to embrace her sexuality, she is finally flying . . . soaring . . . free.

## NOTES

1. Wolf cites *Rent*, *Spring Awakening*, and *Avenue Q* as examples of musicals that feature secondary gay characters who "effectively re-center the straight couple as the norm" (2011, 217). She also notes that most gay (and overtly "gay-seeming") characters in musicals are men (2011, 212–13).

2. Bechdel's memoir has been discussed by a wide array of scholars; space does not permit me to list all of these important sources. In addition to the work cited throughout the essay, see especially Barounis 2016 and Gardiner 2018.

3. Bechdel explains how "disjunctures" and "slippages" between text and image in the cartoons of Charles Adams inspired her own work: "What I found out as I went along is that nothing matches up, that this slippage is everywhere. Even when you try to tell the truth, you can't because language itself has a slippery relationship to reality (13:09–22). . . . the space between the image and words was a very powerful thing if you could figure out how to work with it" (16:10–20).

4. The design of the musical also differs in some ways from the memoir. For example, adult Alison is not a character in the memoir.

5. Throughout this essay, I refer to the butch character as a woman (and use she/her pronouns) because that is how she is described in Bechdel's memoir (2006, 118). Similar gendering occurs in the musical. For example, in the dialogue

that precedes "Ring of Keys," Adult Alison says, "You didn't notice her at first but I saw her the moment she walked in. She was a delivery woman" (Kron 2015, 56).

6. This dialogue appears in Bechdel (2006, 96–97), twenty pages before the "bulldyke" panel sequence. In the musical, another lengthy argument between Bruce and Small Alison about a dress and barrette unfolds in "Party Dress" (which occurs earlier in the musical, just before "Changing My Major").

7. See https://www.youtube.com/watch?v=pMAuesRJm1E (accessed 1 July 2020).

8. For a detailed explanation of the various types of sentences (including characteristic sentences and hybrid types), see Caplin (1998).

9. In her well-known essay "Visual Pleasure and Narrative Cinema," Mulvey argues that "the image of woman as (passive) raw material for the (active) gaze of man" is taken a step further in film, since "cinema builds the way she is to be looked at into the spectacle itself" ([1975] 2005, 301). She also describes a multilayered process of "looking" that involves the relationships between the characters within the film, the camera as it's filming, and the audience "as it watches the final product" (301).

10. Callahan uses "n" to denote "the musical duration of one basic idea" (2013, [1.2]). A standard eight-measure sentence of 2+2+4 measures would be designated *n+n+2n*.

11. Some listeners may hear a half cadence at the end of this phrase because of the strong $\hat{4}$–$\hat{5}$ bass motion in mm. 50–53. However, the chord in mm. 52–53 (shown in example 9.5c) is not a true dominant: it is a D-major triad with E in the bass. This chord could possibly function as an altered dominant, but it lacks the chordal third (G♯) and fifth (B). In addition, half cadences traditionally involve dominant triads, not dominant sevenths (or ninths, or elevenths). The harmonic implications of this moment will be discussed in more detail below.

12. Bechdel's memoir also draws on metaphors of "falling" and "flying": it begins with a multipanel sequence where Alison and her father play "airplane," and concludes with Alison leaping off a swimming pool diving board into her father's arms. Bechdel's memoir also emphasizes the "falling vs. flying" metaphor through its numerous references to the well-known myth of Icarus and Daedalus; these passages are discussed in Freedman (2009, 131–32 and 137–38), Lemberg (2008, 138–39), Pearl (2008, 287–88), and Rohy (2010, 357).

13. One could interpret a possible narrative significance in the choice of keys for these two passages: perhaps the decision to write Bruce's phrase a half-step lower than Alison's is another subtle way of depicting his character's downward course. Of course, this could also be a total coincidence, a natural result of the different keys in which the two songs start and the different keys that they move through. But since Bruce's song contains so many sudden and extreme changes of key, Tesori could have easily set this melody in the same key as Alison's. In any case, the two passages are almost identical transpositions of one another, except

that Bruce's chord in mm. 89–90 is in root position (Alison's was in second inversion), and his chord in mm. 91–92 is a triad (Alison's has an added seventh).

## WORKS CITED


BaileyShea, Matthew. 2004. "Beyond the Beethoven Model: Sentence Types and Limits." *Current Musicology* 77: 5–33.

Barounis, Cynthia. 2016. "Alison Bechdel and Crip-Feminist Autobiography." *Journal of Modern Literature* 39 (4): 139–61.

Bechdel, Alison. 2006. *Fun Home: A Family Tragicomic*. Boston: Mariner/Houghton Mifflin Harcourt.

Bechdel, Alison. 2009. "Reading and Discussion by Graphic Artist Alison Bechdel." Cornell University lecture, April 16. https://www.youtube.com/watch?v=kKyOyJ_Owi4 (accessed 7 January 2020).

Callahan, Michael R. 2013. "Sentential Lyric-Types in the Great American Songbook." *Music Theory Online* 19 (3).

Caplin, William E. 1998. *Classical Form: A Theory of Formal Functions for the Instrumental Music of Haydn, Mozart, and Beethoven*. New York: Oxford University Press.

Chute, Hillary L. 2010. *Graphic Women: Life Narrative and Contemporary Comics*. New York: Columbia University Press.

Clement, Olivia. 2015. "Jeanine Tesori Identifies Her Own 'Ring of Keys' Moment." *Playbill* (June 7). https://www.playbill.com/article/jeanine-tesori-identifies-her-own-ring-of-keys-moment-com-350790 (accessed 9 June 2020).

Cvetkovich, Ann. 2008. "Drawing the Archive in Alison Bechdel's 'Fun Home.'" *Women's Studies Quarterly* 36 (1/2): 111–28.

Ellis, Sarah Taylor. 2011. "'No Day But Today': Queer Temporality in *Rent*." *Studies in Musical Theatre* 5 (2): 195–207.

Everett, Walter. 2008. *The Foundations of Rock: From "Blue Suede Shoes" to "Suite: Judy Blue Eyes."* New York: Oxford University Press.

Freedman, Ariela. 2009. "Drawing on Modernism in Alison Bechdel's *Fun Home*." *Journal of Modern Literature* 32 (4): 125–40.

Gardiner, Judith Kegan, ed. 2018. *Approaches to Teaching Bechdel's* Fun Home. New York: Modern Language Association of America.

Green, Jesse. 2015. "So Beautiful, So Fine." Liner notes for *Fun Home* Broadway Cast Recording, pp. 3–6. PS Classics (PS-1529).

Halberstam, J. [1998] 2018. *Female Masculinity*. Twentieth anniversary edition with a new preface. Durham, NC: Duke University Press.

Halberstam, J. 2005. *In a Queer Time and Place: Transgender Bodies, Subcultural Lives*. New York: New York University Press.

Kron, Lisa. 2015. *Fun Home* (libretto). New York: Samuel French.

Kron, Lisa. 2016. "Foreword." *Fun Home: Vocal Selections*. Music by Jeanine Tesori, book and lyrics by Lisa Kron, vii–viii. New York: Samuel French.

Kron, Lisa, and Jeanine Tesori. 2016. *Fun Home: Vocal Selections*. New York: Samuel French.

Lemberg, Jennifer. 2008. "Closing the Gap in Alison Bechdel's *Fun Home*." *Women's Studies Quarterly* 36 (1/2): 129–40.

McBean, Sam. 2013. "Seeing in Alison Bechdel's *Fun Home*." *Camera Obscura* 84 (28/3): 102–23.

Mulvey, Laura. [1975] 2005. "Visual Pleasure and Narrative Cinema." Reprinted in *Feminist Theory: A Reader*, 2nd ed., edited by Wendy K. Kolmar and Frances Bartkowski: 296–302. Boston: McGraw Hill.

Rohy, Valerie. 2010. "In the Queer Archive: *Fun Home*." *GLQ* 16 (3): 341–61.

Soloway, J. 2016. "J. Soloway on the Female Gaze." *TIFF Masterclass*, September 11. https://www.youtube.com/watch?v=pnBvppooD9I (accessed 5 June 2020).

Tony Awards. "Fun Home Performance Tony Awards 2015." YouTube video, 3:59. July 18, 2015. https://www.youtube.com/watch?v=pMAuesRJm1E

Vicinus, Martha. 2004. *Intimate Friends: Women Who Loved Women, 1778–1928*. Chicago: University of Chicago Press.

Wolf, Stacy. 2002. *A Problem Like Maria: Gender and Sexuality in the American Musical*. Ann Arbor: University of Michigan Press.

Wolf, Stacy. 2011. "Gender and Sexuality." In *The Oxford Handbook of the American Musical*, edited by Raymond Knapp, Mitchell Morris, and Stacy Wolf, 210–24. New York: Oxford University Press.

# 10 *The Hip-Hop History of* Hamilton

*ROBERT KOMANIECKI*

## *INTRODUCTION*

It would be difficult to overstate the influence of hip-hop on American culture over the past nearly five decades. The genre that began in 1973 at a humble Bronx apartment party hosted by DJ Kool Herc has since exploded into a nationwide—and eventually, worldwide—phenomenon. I would even argue that hip-hop exemplifies the great American success story, with successful rappers casting themselves as what Kajikawa calls "the embodiment of American enterprise" (Kajikawa 2018, 474). The giants of American hip-hop, such as Jay-Z, the Notorious B.I.G., and Eminem, have embraced an image of the underdog hustler, obtaining fame and wealth through raw talent and sheer will.

Hip-hop was thus an ideal medium for Lin-Manuel Miranda's depiction of the "young, scrappy, and hungry" American revolutionary Alexander Hamilton, who starts his life with little more than his wit and tenacity, and achieves greatness before his death at the hands of Aaron Burr. *Hamilton*'s characters often rap their lines in a rapid hip-hop style, creating substantially greater lyrical density than in any previous musical. FiveThirtyEight's Leah Libresco details just how fast-paced the lyrics in *Hamilton* really are, stating that the musical's 20,520 words are delivered at an average pace of 144 words per minute, a pace nearly twice as fast as that of the next-fastest musical, *Spring Awakening* (Libresco 2015).

In an interview, cast member Daveed Diggs confessed that he was surprised when listening to demos during the show's original casting. Diggs, an accomplished hip-hop artist well before his successful run in *Hamilton*, was caught off guard to discover that, despite being written for a musical set in the eighteenth century, the rapping is excellent (Binelli 2016). This echoes the experience of hearing the flows in *Hamilton* for the first time for many other rap music lovers, myself included. The show is a jarring juxtaposition of Broadway choreography, acting, and singing with surprisingly authentic hip-hop deliveries. The rapping in *Hamilton* includes many markers of rap flows by the genre's canonic "greats": inventive polysyllabic rhymes, rhythmic precision and variation, and purposeful use of vocal pitch combine with a clearly articulated story in *Hamilton*, making it clear that Miranda was no casual hip-hop fan, but a serious proponent of the genre. Miranda explicitly draws on his knowledge of hip-hop, with regular quotations of and references to a wide variety of rappers (Wickman 2018). Miranda said, "my thesis is that *Hamilton* is this hip-hop story, and he's just that good, so the lyrics also have to be *that* good. So I'd labor over every couplet. . . . It wasn't enough to rhyme at the end of the line, every line had to have musical theatre references, it had to have other hip-hop references, it had to do what my favorite rappers do, which is packing lyrics with so much density, and so much intricate double entendre, and alliteration, and onomatopoeia, and all the things that I love about language" (Fessler 2018).

*Hamilton* may be unusual in its incorporation of hip-hop, but it is certainly not the only "history musical." Elissa Harbert places such musicals on a spectrum between realism and fictionalization, noting that true historical realism is a misnomer in a genre in which characters spontaneously burst into song. Harbert points to *Titanic* and *1600 Pennsylvania Avenue* as examples of musicals that cover historical events but add fictionalized characters or elements, contrasting these with period pieces, such as *Cabaret* and *Miss Saigon*, that are "set in the context of real events but make no claims of historical accuracy" (Harbert 2018, 414). Herbert Lindenberger discusses the contradiction inherent in historical drama, stating that "the very term 'historical drama' suggests the nature of this engagement, with the first word qualifying the fictiveness of the second, the second questioning the reality of the first" (1975, x). Nonetheless, *Hamilton* eagerly flaunts its historical credentials, quoting real writings and aspects of real events that would normally be relegated to historical trivia (such as whether Hamilton wore glasses in his final duel). In its sporadic inclusion of historical detail, *Hamilton* creates a theatrical space in which characters and stories of the American Revolution are seemingly reconciled with modern-day musical aesthetics and politics.

In this chapter, I delve into the various ways the music of *Hamilton* is shaped by the historical events and characters being portrayed. I focus specifically on the characters' delivery of lyrics, or "flow." In the analyses that follow, I will demonstrate that while *Hamilton* is first and foremost a Broadway musical, it is tied intimately to the musical idioms of rap flow, which Miranda uses to achieve specific dramatic goals in telling his story and realizing historical narratives.[1] As discussed in Komaniecki (2019), traditional English-language rap flows are inflected by three parameters: rhythm, rhyme, and vocal pitch. What follows is a description of how Miranda and the performers of *Hamilton* manipulate two of these parameters—rhythm and rhyme—to create a unique work of theater that blends the idioms of both hip-hop and Broadway musicals to convey real historical events and characters.

## *RHYTHM AND METER*

Rap music typically sidelines harmony and melody to a great extent, arguably making rhythm hip-hop's defining musical feature. Indeed, rhythm is sometimes the only thing preventing us from hearing rapping as simply amusical speech. As Condit-Schultz (2016) says, "rap is made musical, as opposed to poetic, by its rhythm." Miranda's rhythmic settings of lyrics in *Hamilton* demonstrate a knowledge of how this parameter can shape an audience's perception of a character's fluency and confidence.

One of numerous examples of rhythm as drama in *Hamilton* appears in the early number "Aaron Burr, Sir." After an exchange between main characters Hamilton and Burr, the audience is introduced to secondary characters John Laurens, Marquis de Lafayette, and Hercules Mulligan. Compared to the relatively refined dialogue between Hamilton and Burr, these secondary characters get a bawdy introduction, beginning with the cry of "What time is it? Showtime!" often used by modern-day street performers in the New York City subway system, and shouting their lines while swinging pints of ale. That these characters are less refined is conveyed rhythmically as well: John Laurens raps in a distinctly old-school flow as he delivers his lines "I'm John Laurens in the place to be / Two pints of Sam Adams, but I'm workin' on three!"

The musical factors that contribute to the old-school aesthetic of these lines include metrically strong beats that are consistently emphasized, eighth notes are swung, syncopation is minimal, and a limited range of rhythmic durations is used.[2] Compared to much of *Hamilton*, the rhyming is also quite basic, with a simple quatrain, monosyllabic rhymes, and rhymed syllables generally falling in the same metric locations. Miranda acknowledges this explicitly old-school flow in interviews, calling it a "love letter to old school hip-hop" (Miranda and McCarter 2016, 25). In an interview, Miranda has called Laurens's style "super-beginner," written that way in order to contrast the character Hamilton, who uses "six rhymes on a line, it's insane polysyllabic internal assonance. He needs to be like from the future" (Rose 2016). Later in this chapter, we see the extent to which Miranda conveys this distinction.

Immediately following Laurens's lines, the audience is introduced to Lafayette, whose dramatic portrayal is inextricably tied to rhythm. At this early point in the show, Lafayette is presented comically, struggling with heavily accented English and frequently interjecting French phrases, as he delivers his first couplets, beginning with his self-introduction *en français*, "*Oui oui, mon ami, je m'appelle Lafayette!*" and ending with the polyglot brag, "Tell the King '*Casse toi!*' Who's the best? *C'est moi!*" Lafayette's lines are delivered in the same rhythmic style as those of John Laurens: laid-back, swung eighth notes, emphasis on strong beats, and with little rhythmic diversity or syncopation. This rhythmic character, when combined with Lafayette's teasing lyrics and over-the-top, Pepé Le Pew accent, contributes to the audience's perception of the Frenchmen as more comedic than threatening.

Historically informed audiences of *Hamilton* may have been surprised to hear such a comedic interpretation of the historical figure of Gilbert du Motier, Marquis de Lafayette. Indeed, as *Le Héros des Deux Mondes* (The Hero of the Two Worlds), Lafayette is known for his tactical brilliance and relentless devotion to not only the American Revolutionary War, but the French Revolution of 1789. Born in 1757 to a distinguished family in Auvergne, Lafayette sympathized with the American cause from a young age. He sailed to the American colonies, learning English en route, and was commissioned to serve as a major general in 1777, at the age of twenty. Lafayette's accomplishments in battle were numerous, and he displayed both tenacity (by quickly recovering from a gunshot wound to the leg) and cleverness (by tricking British troops into believing they were outnumbered by ordering them to appear at strategic locations and fire on the redcoats).

Later in act 1, in one of Lafayette's final appearances onstage, his character's evolution is demonstrated musically. In "Guns and Ships," Lafayette has grown from a young upstart to a bona fide commander, diplomat, and insurgent. Historically speaking, at this point Lafayette has returned from a brief trip back home to France, during which he has conscripted additional military support, supplies, and personnel. Miranda demonstrates the character's prowess and aggression in an extremely efficient fashion by writing him the fastest couplet in Broadway history (Libresco 2015). This narrative decision is made explicit by Miranda in *Hamilton: The Revolution*, a collection of lyrics, essays, and reminiscences about the show's creation:

> The speed at which Lafayette rhymes here was always meant to be a punchline: Here's Lafayette, the Frenchman, who struggles with the word *anarchy* in "My Shot," and he's a speed demon. It's also meant to demonstrate how Lafayette flourished once he was put in command. He goes from being one of Hamilton's friends to a rap god/military superhero. Doesn't hurt that [actor] Daveed [Diggs] is one of the most technically gifted rappers I've ever met, so I knew I could build him tapestries. (Miranda and McCarter 2016, 118.)

Consider the first four measures from "Guns and Ships," which shows the degree to which Lafayette's rapping has matured rhythmically. This excerpt begins with the line "Lafayette, I'm takin' this horse by the reins, makin' redcoats redder with blood stains" and ends with "Lafayette, I go to France for more funds. Lafayette, I come back with more guns." Lafayette's name is called out by the full company and the rest of the lyrics are recited by Lafayette himself. Speed aside, there is a greater diversity of rhythmic values, with rhymes being placed in less predictable locations, as well as more fluent, multisyllabic rhyming with none of Lafayette's native French.[3] As Miranda mentions in the quote above, original Lafayette actor Daveed Diggs is an exceptionally proficient rapper, and his performances with his avant-garde

**Example 10.1.** The evolution of Lafayette's character is demonstrated rhythmically in "Guns and Ships."

hip-hop group clipping often features blinding speed and even complex asymmetrical meters. See example 10.1 for a sample of Lafayette's rhythms.

Rhythm, rhyme, and vocal emphasis interact to add a tricky bit of syncopation in Lafayette's moment in the spotlight. In m. 3 of the above transcription, there is scarcely a wasted syllable, as Miranda crams three instances of a four-syllable rhyme in a single measure.[4] Performer Daveed Diggs emphasizes the second syllable of each four-syllable grouping, each of which occurs in a slightly different metrical position. It's as if Miranda is taking a measure to impress upon the audience that not only can Lafayette rap quickly, he can handle complex rhythmic dissonance with ease.

In addition to rhythm, it seems clear that Miranda also considered meter (at least occasionally) when shaping narratives. Unsurprisingly, duple/quadruple meters reign supreme in *Hamilton*, as is true for most contemporary musicals and most rap music. However, at a crucial moment in the narrative of the musical's first act, this tacit metrical expectation is subverted.

"Meet Me Inside" occurs immediately following a duel between Lieutenant Colonel John Laurens and Major General Charles Lee. Alexander Hamilton served as second for Laurens in this duel, which took place in 1778. According to Hamilton's own description, Laurens insisted on the duel after Lee cast aspersions on George Washington. Accounts of the circumstances surrounding the duel are marred by uncertainty, due in part to Lee's later denial that he had said anything overtly offensive about George Washington, and that doing so would be "incompatible with the character he would ever wish to sustain as a Gentleman" (Syrett 1961, 602–4). The duel itself was a bit of a mess, even by duel standards. Laurens shot Lee in the side; Lee exclaimed that he was injured, and then later seemed to

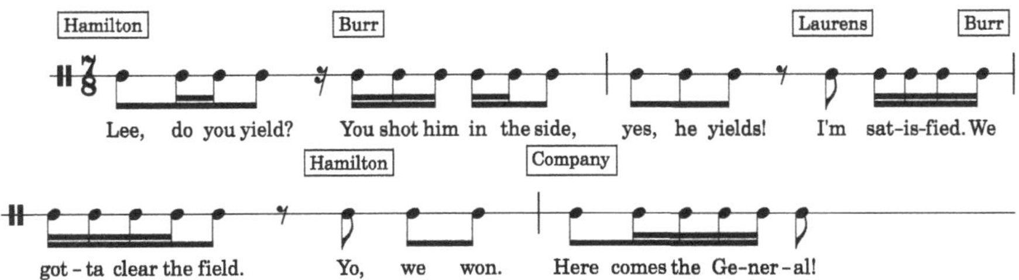


**Example 10.2.** The off-kilter nature of the septuple meter at the beginning of "Meet Me Inside" underscores the chaotic nature of the scene.

retract this declaration by suggesting that the two fire a second time. John Laurens, who had walked forward to assist Lee after shooting him, was nevertheless amenable to the idea of shooting him a second time, but both duelers were persuaded to end the affair by their seconds, Colonel Alexander Hamilton and Major Evan Edwards.

Unsurprisingly, many of the details of the duel between Laurens and Lee are lost in the musical staging, but Miranda still musically portrays much of the confusion and panic of the moment. Following the shot, the music shifts to $\frac{7}{8}$ for the first and only time in the show, marking for the audience how discombobulated the characters onstage must feel. See example 10.2.

Miranda himself has commented on this moment, remarking that it is hard to sustain and "feels chaotic, [and] messy." (Miranda and McCarter 2016, 104.) While asymmetrical meters could be considered "marked" in nearly any genre of music, they are especially so in hip-hop, a genre that is nearly always irremovable from dancing, clapping, and characteristic snare hits on the second and fourth beats of a given bar in duple meter. Oskar Eustis, artistic director for the Public Theater, where *Hamilton* premiered, compared Miranda to Shakespeare in the way that "he takes the language of the people, and heightens it by making it verse. It both ennobles the language, and the people saying the language." The jagged meter underscoring the lyrics at the beginning of "Meet Me Inside" undermines the so-called "language of the people," underscoring the chaos and uncertainty central to the musical's plot at this point.

## *RHYME*

Miranda frequently turns to rhyme when musically portraying the title character of *Hamilton* as an intellectual, virtuoso, and a force to be reckoned with. More specifically, as I demonstrate in this section, Miranda's writing for the character Alexander Hamilton involves especially generous use of internal rhymes, and a lyrical texture that is densely scattered with rhyme syllables. Miranda talks often of rhyme in his interviews and writings, and cites many examples from hip-hop and musical theater that he considers to be inspirations. One can learn quite a lot about the type of writing Miranda aspires to from a rhyme-dense couplet cited by Miranda as one of his favorites from Puerto Rican rapper Big Pun:

> Dead in the middle of Little Italy little did we know
> That we riddled some middlemen who didn't do diddly.[5]

In *Hamilton: The Revolution*, Miranda discusses this specific couplet as a moment of bonding between him and director Tommy Kail back in 2002, when the two were laying the groundwork for Miranda's earlier musical *In the Heights* (Miranda and McCarter 2016, 22). The density of rhymes in this couplet speaks to the type of writing that Miranda views as virtuosic—scarcely a syllable is used that doesn't have multiple rhymes elsewhere in the couplet.

Another rhyme that Miranda considers a favorite comes from the 1960 musical *Bye Bye Birdie*, which he mentions on his Twitter account (@Lin_Manuel, October 2, 2018):

> Take off the gloomy mask of *tragedy*, it's not your style.
> You'll look so good that you'll be *glad ya de*cided to smile.[6]

This couplet contains an inventive internal rhyme, another technique that Miranda highly prizes in his own writing. These examples from disparate sources can help us to understand Miranda's lyrical inspirations in *Hamilton*.

While *Hamilton* contains instances of history stated rather plainly and accurately, Miranda also faced the challenge of conveying complex historical attitudes, personalities, debates, and events in a matter of minutes.[7] With respect to the character of Alexander Hamilton, Miranda often turns specifically to rhyme when endeavoring to succinctly convey a character who was ambitious, contentious, brave, confident, and a virtuoso with the written word. The number "My Shot" contains some of Hamilton's extended rap soliloquies, each a depiction of the show's protagonist as the finest lyricist onstage: someone who effortlessly strings together multisyllabic rhymes and internal assonance, all while furthering the plot. The lyric transcription below demonstrates the extent of Miranda's rhyming in this section.

> Scratch that, this is not a moment, it's the movement
> Where all the hungriest brothers with something to prove went.
> Foes oppose us, we take an honest stand,
> We roll like Moses, claimin' our promised land.
> And? If we win our independence?
> 'Zat a guarantee of freedom for our descendants?
> Or will the blood we shed begin an endless
> Cycle of vengeance and death with no defendants?
> I know the action in the street is excitin' but Jesus,
> Between all the bleedin' and fightin' I've been readin' and writin'
> We need to handle our financial situation
> Are we a nation of states? What's the state of our nation?
> I'm past patiently waiting I'm passionately smashin'
> Every expectation, every action's an act of creation
> I'm laughin' in the face of casualties and sorrow,
> For the first time I'm thinking past tomorrow.

While rhymed couplets and quatrains remain supreme in the transcribed section of "My Shot," this is one of the only "basic" features of Hamilton's verse. There is not a single monosyllabic rhyme in the entire section that is not a fragment of a larger rhyme chain—instead, Miranda pieces together series of multisyllabic rhymes and word combinations—sometimes chaining together rhymes that are as long as five syllables, such as "streets is exciting," "bleeding and fighting," and "reading and writing." The following couplet offers another example of the dense writing in this section.

> Foes oppose us, we take an honest stand,
> We roll like Moses, claimin' our promised land.

Miranda's writing here is much more complex than rhyming the final syllable of each line, as we saw in the old school–style rapping of John Laurens in "Aaron Burr, Sir." While there is indeed an end rhyme in "stand/land," on closer inspection, one can see that nearly the entirety of both lines rhyme with one another:

> "Foes oppose us"/"roll like Moses,"
> "take an"/"claimin'," and
> "honest stand"/"promised land."

Finally, Miranda allows the rhyme scheme to spill into the following measure with the lyric "and," creating a moment of poetic enjambment that he specifically points out in *Hamilton: The Revolution*, once again citing rapper Big Pun as his inspiration. "Continuing the rhyme at the top of the next line—this is what Big Pun does *so* well. It knits all his rhymes together. I play with it a lot in this show, and this is my favorite one" (Miranda and McCarter 2016, 29).

Two important expository scenes in *Hamilton*'s second act come in the form of cabinet debates, presented as rap battles. Each of these scenes is dramatized in such a way as to convey a rap "cypher," or gathering, in which emcees occasionally square off against one another in battles of lyrical prowess. In both "Cabinet Battle #1" and "Cabinet Battle #2," Hamilton faces an antagonistic Thomas Jefferson, portrayed in the original cast recording by Daveed Diggs, the same artist who assumed the role of the swashbuckling Lafayette in the show's first act. (Lafayette does not appear in act 2 and Jefferson does not appear in act 1.)

These scenes are not only dense in historical and dramatic exposition, but also in musical information about each of the characters. Through the use of rhyme, Miranda weaves together scenes that successfully portray Jefferson as the "man of the people" that he was, while also honoring the intellectual capabilities of his rival, Hamilton (Miranda and McCarter 2016, 161). Below is the first volley by Jefferson in "Cabinet Battle #1"—a deluge of pointed barbs and sympathetic debate points regarding his disapproval of Hamilton's proposal to assume all state debts and form a national bank (all rhymed syllables are italicized).

> Life, liberty, and the pursuit of happi*ness*,
> We fought for these ideals; we shouldn't settle for *less*.

These are wise words, enterprising men *quote 'em*.
Don't act surprised, you guys, cuz I *wrote 'em*.
But Hamilton for*gets*
His plan would have the government assume states' *debts*.
Now place your *bets* as to who that bene*fits*,
The very seat of government where Hamilton *sits*.

The above excerpt from Jefferson's rapping demonstrates several things, namely the ability of the character to endear himself to those watching ("we fought for these ideals") and his tactic of presenting his argument plainly. The uncomplicated nature of his argument is reflected in the construction of the flow, which is not densely packed with multisyllabic rhymes. Instead, the majority of rhymes in Jefferson's argument are single-syllable rhymes that arrive predictably at the end of a line, with very little internal rhyme.

Miranda made a purposeful decision to contrast Hamilton's rhyming strategy with Jefferson's. In *Hamilton: The Revolution*, Miranda states that he wanted to portray Hamilton as a cold and efficient lyrical assassin, saying "he rhymes the craziest when he is backed into a corner" (Miranda and McCarter 2016, 162). The excerpt from Hamilton's retort below (again with rhymes italicized) demonstrates this—the lyrics are riddled with multisyllabic, partial, and internal rhymes. This serves two purposes: to show that Hamilton is Jefferson's intellectual superior, but also to demonstrate Hamilton's difficulty in endearing himself to his audience and portraying his arguments in an accessible manner.

And another thing, Mr. Age of *Enlightenment*,
Don't lecture me about the war, you did*n't fight in it*.
You think I'm *frighten*ed of you, man? We almost *died in a trench*,
While you were off getting *high with the French*.
Thomas *Jefferson*, always *hesitant* with the *President*
*Reticent*—there isn't a plan he doesn't *jettison*.
*Madison*, you're as *mad* as a *hatter, son*, take your *medicine*.
*Damn*, you're in worse shape than the national *debt is in*.
Sittin' there useless as *two shits*,
Hey, turn around, bend over, I'll show you where my *shoe fits*.

Perhaps the best musical representation of Alexander Hamilton's tireless nature and tendency to use prose to overwhelm his enemies comes in

"Farmer Refuted," the sixth song in *Hamilton*'s act 1. This moment, like many in the musical, is an over-the-top dramatization of a real interaction—in this case, of Hamilton's refutation of Bishop Samuel Seabury, a farmer.

The real history behind "Farmer Refuted" begins with Seabury writing an open letter to New York farmers, under the pen name "A. W. Farmer" ("A Westchester Farmer").[8] Seabury's letter was a plea for stability and compliance with British rule. Apparently distressed by a recent Congressional agreement to halt trading of key goods with Great Britain and some of her colonies, Seabury's quarrel can be summarized in his own words:

> The manufacturers of Great-Britain, the inhabitants of Ireland, and of the West-Indies, have done us no injury. They have been no ways instrumental in bringing our distresses upon us. Shall we then revenge ourselves upon them? Shall we endeavour to starve them into a compliance with our humours? Shall we, without any provocation, tempt or force them into riots and insurrections which must be attended with the ruin of many—probably with the death of some of them? Shall we attempt to unsettle the whole British Government—to throw all into confusion, because our self-will is not complied with? Because the ill-projected, ill-conducted, abominable scheme of some of the colonists, to form a republican government independent of Great-Britain, cannot otherwise succeed?—Good God! can we look forward to the ruin, destruction, and desolation of the whole British Empire, without one relenting thought? Can we contemplate it with pleasure; and promote it with all our might and vigour, and at the same time call ourselves *his Majesty's most dutiful and loyal subjects*? Whatever the Gentlemen of the Congress may think of the matter, the spirit that dictated such a measure, was not the spirit of humanity. (Seabury 1774)

In total, Seabury's complaint was around 9,000 words in length. This made Hamilton's response all the more noteworthy: a whopping 31,000-word essay abbreviated simply as "The Farmer Refuted," published in February of 1775. To say that Hamilton spoke forcefully is an understatement. His opening paragraphs speak for themselves:

> Sir,
>
> I resume my pen, in reply to the curious epistle, you have been pleased to favour me with; and can assure you, that, notwithstanding, I am naturally of a grave and phlegmatic disposition, it has been the source of abun-

> dant merriment to me. The spirit that breathes throughout is so rancorous, illiberal and imperious: The argumentative part of it so puerile and fallacious: The misrepresentations of facts so palpable and flagrant: The criticisms so illiterate, trifling and absurd: The conceits so low, sterile and splenetic, that I will venture to pronounce it one of the most ludicrous performances, which has been exhibited to public view, during all the present controversy.
>
> You have not even imposed the laborious task of pursuing you through a labyrinth of *subtilty*. You have not had ability sufficient, however violent your efforts, to try the *depths* of *sophistry*; but have barely skimmed along its *surface*. I should, almost, deem the animadversions, I am going to make, unnecessary, were it not, that, without them, you might exult in a fancied victory, and arrogate to yourself imaginary trophies. (Hamilton 1775)

Hamilton goes on to exhaustively refute each of Seabury's points in turn in paragraph after overwhelming paragraph. While the written exchange is remarkable, a protracted debate over the merits of exporting certain crops is not exactly tailor-made for the stage. One can imagine, then, that Miranda approached his depiction of this exchange in *Hamilton* with the principal goals of depicting the exchange quickly, clearly, and in an entertaining manner. In figure 10.1, we can see the extraordinary steps taken by Miranda in setting the lyrics of this scene to convey the character Hamilton's prowess with a pen.

The scene is set as a disjunct duet, in which Seabury croons his lyrics in a posh British accent over a heavily embellished harpsichord accompaniment in a style and meter ($\frac{6}{8}$) clearly meant to invoke an eighteenth-century dance. Contrasting the farmer's sung delivery, Hamilton raps nearly all his lyrics, delivering them in Lin-Manuel Miranda's native New York accent after being urged to "tear this dude apart" by Hercules Mulligan. The rhymes in either vocal part alone might seem relatively unimpressive, at least compared to other excerpts from the show. However, "Farmer Refuted" features extraordinary interplay between Hamilton and Seabury, which often includes simultaneous rhymes rather than normally spaced couplets or quatrains.

In the first measure of the section diagrammed in figure 10.1, the character Hamilton begins speaking over Seabury by rhyming (via homophone) the word "he'd" with Seabury's "heed," delivered at the same time. Doubling Seabury's pace, Hamilton rushes forward to do this once more

| Seabury | Hamilton |
|---|---|
| **Heed** | **He'd** |
| **Scream** | **Screams** |
| **Have not** | **Have-nots** |
| **Heart** | **Hard** |
| **Chaos** | **Chaos** |
| **Not** | **Haunt** |
| Don't | Talk |
| Stray | Cost |
| **Congress** | **Congress** |
| Me | Dog |
| Playing | Thee |
| **Game** | **Strange**(ly) |
| **Pray** | **same** |

**Figure 10.1.** This table shows lyrics excerpted from "Farmer Refuted." Each column shows a series of words delivered on the downbeat of subsequent measures, simultaneously by the characters of Hamilton and Seabury as they argue with each other. Bolded lyrics indicate words that rhyme, either via conventional vowel rhyming, homonym, or simply being the same word.

in the same measure, rhyming "(un)ravel" with Seabury's "rabble." In this short dialogue, Hamilton achieves this effect numerous times—sometimes using the same word (e.g., "scream[s]" and "revolution" in m. 2), but also occasionally using different lyrics that match Seabury's vowel sounds. These simultaneous, approximate vowel rhymes occur between "haunt/not" (m. 6), "(sol)ution" and "you should(n't)" (m. 6), and "strange(ly)" and "game" (m. 12). Miranda's musical setting of the exchange between Seabury and Hamilton conveys the nature of the historical event on which it is based—Hamilton refutes each of Seabury's points in turn, inserts arguments of his own, and manages to insert several personal insults as well.

*Hamilton: The Revolution* acknowledges previous hip-hop artists for the inspiration behind musical technique of vowel matching in "Farmer Refuted."

> Lin had been listening to an ingenious tribute that Joell Ortiz had recorded for the greatest Puerto Rican MC, Big Pun. Ortiz had kept all of the rhyming syllables from a classic Pun song, but he incorporated them into new lyrics that paid homage to the late rapper. "It was a weirdly casually brilliant way of doing a tribute," Lin says. In "Farmer Refuted," Lin weaponized the idea . . . (Miranda and McCarter 2016, 47)

There is perhaps no better microcosm of the concept of *Hamilton* than the confluence of inspirations and techniques used in "Farmer Refuted." Harbert states that in this scene, "Hamilton's driving interjections disrupt the simple galant-sounding music and bring the quasi-eighteenth-century minuet into an unmistakably twenty-first-century idiom, a musical demonstration of Hamilton's forward-thinking brilliance" (Harbert 2018, 424). Miranda draws inspiration from hip-hop in order to stage a dramatic scene based on real historical events—all while using specific rapping techniques to convey the relationships of the characters onstage.

## *CONCLUSION*

When considering how characters in musicals are portrayed onstage, some of the first things we think of are their lines, movements, costumes, props, and most vitally, their song lyrics. However, *Hamilton*, with its lyrically dense hip-hop delivery, invites analysts to consider more. As I have shown in this chapter, the very construction and delivery of rhythmic lyrics—or more simply, the flow—of vocal performances in Miranda's megahit musical point toward characters' motivations, talents, flaws, and personality traits. Ancillary characters demonstrate their uncomplicated involvement in the show's plot through simple, old-school rap flows. Thomas Jefferson often delivers his lyrics in an accessible, charismatic flow, endearing himself to his audiences. Lafayette's rapping increases in rhythmic sophistication over time as he grows increasingly confident in his station. Finally, the title character of *Hamilton* demonstrates his remarkable intellectual prowess through rapped verses that are a notch above those of his castmates in terms of rhythm, rhyme density, and rhyme complexity.

*Hamilton* belongs to a long line of history musicals that depict and dramatize past events. What sets it apart is its reliance on idioms and techniques taken directly from hip-hop. In setting his interpretation of Chernow's biography of Alexander Hamilton (2004) to rap, Lin-Manuel Miranda invites audiences to engage with distant history using a medium that is immediately present and heard everywhere. *Hamilton* takes a historical narrative driven by the activities of white men in the eighteenth century and allows it to be told using nonwhite performers and musical idioms that are more representative of America at the time of the musical's composition in 2015. Through the compositional choices made by Miranda in writing each character's rap flows, he shows that this contemporary genre is not just a novelty, but a cultural and musical force that can be used to realign our perception of historical events, allowing past and present to share the stage.

## NOTES

1. Conspicuously absent from this chapter are extended discussions of the racial, political, and cultural dynamics of *Hamilton*. These discussions are omitted not only due to space, but because several more-qualified voices have raised such issues elsewhere. Lyra D. Monteiro's 2016 review essay details much of what is racially problematic with the show, including the fact that actual Black and Indigenous characters from the late eighteenth century are absent, and that *Hamilton*'s diversity comes from BIPOC actors playing white characters. Philip Gentry wrote one of the early musicological treatments of *Hamilton* in 2017, considering issues of race, gender, and sexuality. Elissa Harbert (2018) writes about the ways in which *Hamilton* can be contextualized in the lineage of history musicals, and treads the line between "historical credibility and fictionalization." Justin Williams (2018) frames the musical and ensuing *Hamilton Mixtape* in the broader context of immigration discourse. Donatella Galella (2018) writes of the kind of "national neoliberal multicultural inclusion" in *Hamilton* that has contributed to the musical being lauded by not only the likes of Barack Obama and Hillary Clinton, but also Dick Cheney and Mike Pence. I highly recommend that readers of this chapter seek out these sources to better understand the remarkable, problematic, and potentially confusing dynamics that have contributed to *Hamilton*'s creation and reception.

2. For all references to the rhythm and full text of songs from *Hamilton*, please see the vocal selections score (2016). The publisher, Alfred Music, demanded prohibitive fees to print the examples in this volume.

3. Miranda notes that the decision to use triplets later in this verse (not shown) was suggested by actor Daveed Diggs himself (Miranda and McCarter 2016, 118).

4. Rhyme is a surprisingly subjective parameter of music. My designation of this series of rhymes as four-syllable rhymes is thus a subjective one, and a sound

argument could be made for the exclusion of the final two syllables ("-in' 'em") in each rhymed group due to repetition.

5. This couplet is from "Twinz" by Big Pun (1998).

6. The referenced number is "Put on a Happy Face" from *Bye Bye Birdie*, by Charles Strouse and Lee Adams.

7. For an example of plainly and mostly accurately stated history in *Hamilton*, consider Burr's monologue on *The Federalist Papers* in "Non-Stop": "Alexander joins forces with James Madison and John Jay to write a series of essays defending the new United States Constitution, entitled *The Federalist Papers*. The plan was to write a total of twenty-five essays, the work divided evenly among the three men. In the end, they wrote eighty-five essays, in the span of six months. John Jay got sick after writing five. James Madison wrote twenty-nine. Hamilton wrote the other fifty-one!"

8. Seabury's letter has a characteristically protracted eighteenth-century title, but is typically abbreviated as "Free Thoughts, on the Proceedings of the Congress at Philadelphia, &c."

## WORKS CITED

Binelli, Mark. 2016. "'Hamilton' Creator Lin-Manuel Miranda: The Rolling Stone Interview." *Rolling Stone* (June 1). https://www.rollingstone.com/culture/culture-news/hamilton-creator-lin-manuel-miranda-the-rolling-stone-interview-42607/

Chernow, Ron. 2004. *Alexander Hamilton*. New York: Penguin Press.

Condit-Schultz, Nathaniel. 2016. "MCFlow: A Digital Corpus of Rap Transcriptions." *Empirical Musicology Review* 11 (2): 124–47.

Fessler, Leah. 2018. "A Tweet Lin-Manuel Miranda Wrote in 2009 Shows the Struggle Behind His Genius." *Quartz* (November 18). https://qz.com/work/1467163/hamilton-creator-lin-manuel-miranda-shared-the-struggle-behind-his-genius/

Galella, Donatella. 2018. "Being in 'The Room Where It Happens': Hamilton, Obama, and Nationalist Neoliberal Multicultural Inclusion." *Theatre Survey* 59 (3): 363–85.

Gentry, Philip. 2017. "Hamilton's Ghosts." *American Music* 35 (2): 271–80.

Hamilton, Alexander. 1775. "The Farmer Refuted: Or, A More Impartial and Comprehensive View of the Dispute between Great-Britain and the Colonies, Intended as a Further Vindication of the Congress: In Answer to a Letter from A. W. Farmer, Intitled A View of the Controversy between Great-Britain and Her Colonies: Including, a Mode of Determining the Present Disputes Finally and Effectually, &c." New York: James Rivington. http://hdl.handle.net/2027/osu.32435018260331

Harbert, Elissa. 2018. "Hamilton and History Musicals." *American Music* 36 (4): 412–28.

Kajikawa, Loren. 2018. "'Young, Scrappy, and Hungry': Hamilton, Hip Hop, and Race." *American Music* 36 (4): 467–86.

Komaniecki, Robert. 2019. "Analyzing the Parameters of Flow in Rap Music." PhD diss., Indiana University.

Libresco, Leah. 2015. "'Hamilton' Would Last 4 to 6 Hours If It Were Sung at the Pace of Other Broadway Shows." *FiveThirtyEight*, October 5, 2015. https://fivethirtyeight.com/features/hamilton-is-the-very-model-of-a-modern-fast-paced-musical/

Lindenberger, Herbert. 1975. *Historical Drama: The Relation of Literature and Reality*. Chicago: University of Chicago Press.

Miranda, Lin Manuel, and Jeremy McCarter. 2016. *Hamilton: The Revolution*. New York: Grand Central Publishing.

Monteiro, Lyra D. 2016. "Review Essay: Race-Conscious Casting and the Erasure of the Black Past in Lin-Manuel Miranda's Hamilton." *Public Historian* 38 (1): 89–98. https://doi.org/10.1525/tph.2016.38.1.89

Rose, Pete. 2016. "Hamilton." *60 Minutes*. Aired June 12, 2016, on CBS. https://www.cbsnews.com/news/hamilton-encore-60-minutes-charlie-rose/

Seabury, Samuel. [1774] 1775. "Free Thoughts on the Proceedings of the Continental Congress, Held at Philadelphia, Sept. 5, 1774 Wherein Their Errors Are Exhibited, Their Reasonings Confuted, and the Fatal Tendency of Their Non-Importation, Non-Exportation, and Non-Consumption Measures, Are Laid Open to the Plainest Understandings; and the Only Means Pointed out for Preserving and Securing Our Present Happy Constitution: In a Letter to the Farmers, and Other Inhabitants of North America in General, and to Those of the Province of New-York in Particular." London: reprinted for Richardson and Urquhart. http://hdl.handle.net/2027/aeu.ark:/13960/t1ng5785k

Syrett, Harold C., ed. 1961. *The Papers of Alexander Hamilton*. Vol. 1, 1768–1778. New York: Columbia University Press.

Wickman, Forrest. 2018. "All the Hip-Hop References in *Hamilton*: A Track-by-Track Guide." *Slate*, September 24, 2015. http://www.slate.com/blogs/browbeat/2015/09/24/hamilton_s_hip_hop_references_all_the_rap_and_r_b_allusions_in_lin_manuel.html

Williams, Justin A. 2018. "'We Get the Job Done': Immigrant Discourse and Mixtape Authenticity in The Hamilton Mixtape." *American Music* 36 (4): 487–506.

# 11

# "Isn't It Queer?"
## The Kinsey Sicks and the Art of Broadway Parody

*J. DANIEL JENKINS*

### *INTRODUCTION*

The Kinsey Sicks, four men who perform in drag, self-styled as "America's Favorite Dragapella Beauty Shop Quartet®," have been harmonizing together and making queer art for over twenty-five years.[1] The formation of the group dates to 1993 when five friends dressed in drag to attend a Bette Midler concert in San Francisco. When implored by other concert goers to sing them something, the men laughed it off, but later that evening, after the concert, they found that in fact they could sing. From this group of five, a quartet was formed, and they began performing as an a cappella group in 1994. In their countless performances around the world, on their multiple albums, and in their concert films, the Kinseys perform both original compositions and parodies of everything from light opera to jazz standards to Top 40 pop from a variety of eras. Parodies of songs written for or adapted to the musical theater stage make up no small part of their output.

In this chapter, I lay out the hallmarks of the Kinseys' typical parody practice. I adopt methodologies from Kurt Mosser (2008), Lawrence Zbikowski (2002), and Linda Hutcheon (1985) to create an analytical framework for discussing particular examples. After applying the framework to a couple of Kinsey Broadway parodies to demonstrate its utility, I provide a close reading of "Send in the Clones," the Kinseys' parody of Stephen Sondheim's "Send in the Clowns" from *A Little Night Music* (1973)—one of very few examples in which the Kinseys completely reimagine the *musical* components of a song in their parody process. This analysis will show that by diverging from their typical process and changing musical parameters usually associated with the number, the Kinseys create distance from the original in multiple ways, turning their parody into a satire and simultaneously evoking a musical-performance style and era that bolsters and shades their critique.

## *KINSEY PARODY PRACTICE*

Many reviewers have commented on the Kinseys' ability to write "dead-on song parodies" (Lamble 2007), "right on the money, striking a balance between humor and homage" (Shapiro 2003, 24). To achieve this effect, the Kinseys rely quite explicitly on a listener's familiarity with the original song being parodied. "The goal is to see how little we can change the original words to make the biggest and most disturbing change in meaning," quipped Ben Schatz, a founding member who performed with the group for many years and remains its lyricist (*Boyz* 2013, 12). Examples of these clever turns of phrase are littered throughout the Kinsey Sicks oeuvre. For example, Barbra Streisand's "The Way We Were" becomes a song about herpes "in the corners of my mouth" (Kinsey Sicks 2004, track 9). A ballad from *Showboat* becomes a song about masturbation: "Can't help loving that *hand* of mine" (Kinsey Sicks 2004, track 6). The chorus of "Mamma Mia" from the ABBA-inspired jukebox musical of the same name turns into . . . "Gonorrhea / Here I go again" (Kinsey Sicks 2010, track 8). Schatz says, "We have ruined many favorite songs for people, and when we hear that complaint, we know our work is done" (*Boyz* 2013, 12).

Schatz's propensity to change the words of a song as little as possible extends to the vocal arrangements as well, which also rarely diverge from the source material. Melismatic alterations of the melody, commonplace in a cappella arrangements, are sometimes present, but they are not a frequent part of the Kinseys' practice. In fact, pitch fidelity seems to be very important to Irwin Keller, a former member of the group and erstwhile arranger. Keller's sister, Lynn, used to play bass for Diana Ross. When writing a parody of a Supremes song, Keller, who sings bass, asked his sister what notes she played, just to make sure his vocal part was right (Woods 2003, 28).

Of course, there are limitations. Only so much verisimilitude is possible when arranging for four singers a composition for full orchestra, or a piece of electronic dance music. But within these confines, it is striking how close to the original the Kinseys often come. In "MCI," the Kinseys' parody of "Bali Hai," for example, the final strain of the chorus includes background vocals that call to mind the frilly turns and runs that Robert Russell Bennett wrote for flute, strings, and harp in his original orchestration. Commentators seem to react to the effectiveness of the Kinseys' arrangements; Fertig (1997) wrote "their vocal harmonies make instruments extraneous" (23).

Sometimes the Kinseys also use mimicry to try to replicate the vocal timbre of the original singer. This approach is most clearly heard in their parody of "We Are the World" called "We Arm the World," in which the Kinseys attempt their best vocal impressions of everyone from Bob Dylan and Cyndi Lauper to Michael Jackson, Willie Nelson, and Bruce Springsteen. In some arrangements, particularly those for which electronic and synthesized sounds are essential to the original, the Kinseys take advantage of vocal percussion and other sounds. On the track "Can You Believe I've Lasted This Long?," a parody of Cher's "Believe," they make swooshing sounds to replicate the song's ethereal opening, and on "Botoxic," a parody of Britney Spears's "Toxic," they sing through their noses to imitate electronic sounds. Even sounds from the original tracks that some might not consider part of the music can become fodder for a Kinsey parody. In "The Day We Were," a parody of Streisand's "The Way We Were," a purposeful, loud gasp can be heard in the wordless vocal introduction—an exaggeration of the audible breath that was preserved in Streisand's original recording.

This practice of musical mimicry is a function of how the Kinseys communicate with their audience. When Schatz says that his intention is to change the lyrics as little as possible, he is assuming that his audience will *know* the original lyrics. The effect of his parody depends, to some extent, on the listeners' expectations from having heard the original song and realizing how the parody lyrics subvert or recontextualize the source material. Providing a musical arrangement that also matches listeners' expectations increases the chances that the new lyrics will stick out, making the parody more effective. Analyzing a parody, then, would entail discussing the process of "encoding" (on the part of the Kinseys) and "decoding" (on the part of the listener) to better understand and interpret its intended effect (Hutcheon 1985, chapter 5).

## *ANALYZING PARODY*

The Kinseys insist: "we don't do any covers, but we love doing parody" (*Boyz* 2013, 12). Nonetheless, song covers provide a good starting point for discussing how the Kinseys approach parody. Kurt Mosser (2008) divides cover songs into two categories: reduplication covers and interpretative covers. He lists four subtypes of interpretative covers: (a) minor interpretations (the homage), (b) major interpretations, (c) send-up (ironic) covers, and (d) parody covers.

Mosser uses the term "base song" to refer to a song "that, due to its status, popularity, or possibly other reasons, is taken to be paradigmatic" (2008, I, paragraph 2). For Mosser, the relationship between this referent and the cover version, and how faithfully the base song is preserved in the cover song, places a cover on a continuum, with reduplication and minor interpretations on one end and send-up and parody covers on the other. An example of a reduplication cover would be one performed by a tribute band, in which the musicians try to reproduce the sound of the original in every way: same lyrics, same melodies, same rhythms, same harmonies, same instrumentation, same vocal delivery. In contrast, the parody cover "simply uses the base song as a reference, in order to produce a distinct version that may have little, if anything, to do with the lyrical or general musical content of its base" (Mosser 2008, II d, paragraph 3).

According to Mosser, Weird Al Yankovich's parodies, including titles such as "Eat It" (a parody of Michael Jackson's "Beat It"), "Amish Paradise" (a parody of Coolio's "Gangster's Paradise"), and "Girls Just Want to Have Lunch" (a parody of Cyndi Lauper's "Girls Just Want to Have Fun"), are examples of parody covers (2008, II d, paragraph 4). Just like Kinsey lyricist Schatz, Yankovich often writes parody lyrics that hew closely to the rhyme scheme of the original song, preserving the original words when possible. In keeping with Mosser's definition of parody cover, the content of the *lyrics* has nothing to do with the original song. *Musically*, however, Yankovich and his band often work hard to reproduce the songs they are parodying (Crouch 2014). For example, when working on "Inactive," his parody of "Radioactive" by the band Imagine Dragons, Yankovich accepted the band's help in making his parody version of their song sound as authentic as possible (Graff 2014).

With four a cappella voices, the Kinseys can never come close to the timbral similarity that Yankovich and his band often achieve. However, the Kinseys' usual approach, attempting to match the overall sound of the original musical material they are parodying, is very similar to Yankovich's. They often retain the meter, rhythmic character, pitch content, tempo, and form of the original songs they are parodying, and have consulted performers who recorded the original songs (as when Keller called his sister). If, as Mosser argues, covers fall on a continuum between reproductions and parodies, Yankovich's (and the Kinseys') lyrics are clearly parody, but the *music* is often more in the spirit of a reproduction cover or minor interpretation.

In regard to the Kinseys' Broadway parodies specifically, a base song is often quite easy to identify. It is often the version heard as part of the original cast album, the soundtrack of the film adaptation, or, in the case of a jukebox musical, a version of the song by the recording artist whose version is being referenced within the musical. These are often iconic performances, so identified with one performer that the referent is quite specific. But sometimes a single, paradigmatic referent can be difficult to determine. In such cases, we can turn to what Zbikowski (2002) calls a conceptual model. Conceptual models rest on the principle that humans categorize items from most to least typical. Zbikowski calls those items that are "securely inside the category" Type-1 examples, while those that are "in danger of being excluded" are called Type-2. Consider birds as a category: Type-1 examples would include robins and sparrows, while emus and penguins would be Type-2 examples (2002, 39). These types represent opposing poles on a continuum rather than clear points of demarcation, and the line between Type-1 and Type-2 might be different for each listener.

The analysis of parodies of songs composed before Broadway's golden age (roughly 1940 to 1960) often requires a conceptual model rather than a base song. Before the golden age, original cast recordings were uncommon and the distinction between popular music and Broadway show tune was not as clear as it would later become. "I Got Rhythm" by George Gershwin is a case in point. When writing about "I've Got Rhythm," Zbikowski analyzes a number of different recordings, showing how the very idea of a performance of "I Got Rhythm" changed over time, as the song went from show tune to jazz standard to a basis of improvisation. Zbikowski's analysis strongly suggests that listening to and categorizing a performance of "I Got Rhythm" relies not on a reference to a single, base performance, but much more on the comparison to conceptual models of the song. "When people share the conceptual model for a song (realizing that all such sharing is approximate), they will tend to make similar judgments about what counts as a typical or an atypical rendering of the song (or whether a succession of sound should even be counted as an instance of the song)" (Zbikowksi 2002, 216). "I've Got Rhythm," and the eponymous "rhythm changes" it spurred, is an extreme case to be sure, but the general principle holds that for many songs of that era the referent is not a single, base performance, but rather a conceptual model of what is "typical," probably informed by a number of performances.

Linda Hutcheon's (1985) work further informs the analysis and interpretation of parody. Hutcheon defines parody "as a formal synthesis, an incorporation of a backgrounded text into itself" (1985, 53). Hutcheon notes that with respect to music, parody has sometimes been defined "as repetition, but repetition with difference: . . . there is a distance between the model and the parody" (1985, 65–67). As the discussion of the Kinseys' general parody practice showed, they, too, see parody as repetition—for example, changing words as little as possible and insisting on the same bass line as the original recording—as a way to accentuate and bring greater attention to the moments of difference.

In Hutcheon's theory, parody does not necessarily connote ridicule. Rather, parody has an unmarked ethos. It can, at times, be respectful or even reverential, as when "Prokofiev paid tribute to the wit and urbanity of Haydn and others in his 'Classical' Symphony" (Hutcheon 1985, 67). This unmarked ethos distinguishes parody from satire, a genre with which it is often confused. The difference between the two is that "the aim of parody is intramural and that of satire is extramural" (Hutcheon 1985, 62). In other words, the targets of parody are the original artworks themselves, while the targets of satire are "the vices and follies of mankind" (Hutcheon 1985, 43). "Modern parody . . . rarely has . . . an evaluative or intentional limitation," while satire is specifically oriented "toward a negative evaluation and a corrective intent" (Hutcheon 1985, 54). Satire is marked by a "scornful or disdainful ethos" that is a "kind of encoded anger, communicated to the decoder through invective. . . . Satire should not be confused with simple invective, however, for the corrective aim of satire's scornful ridicule is central to its identity" (Hutcheon, 1985, 56). Both the genres of parody and satire can employ irony, which is marked by a mocking ethos (Hutcheon 1985, 63). Ironic parody evokes a "knowing smile," ironic satire a "disdainful laugh" (Hutcheon 1985, 61). Additionally, in Hutcheon's model, satire may be used in the service of parody, and vice versa. The former is called satiric parody, "whose target is still another form of coded discourse," and the latter parodic satire, "which aims at something outside the text" (Hutcheon 1985, 62). Finally, Hutcheon's work is particularly helpful in this context because her discussions of texted music, including *Orpheus in the Underworld* (1985, 60) and *The Rise and Fall of the City of Mahagonny* (1985, 62–63), elucidate how parody can function and contribute differently in the musical and textual domains within a single artwork.

## *THE KINSEY SICKS ON (AND OFF-)BROADWAY*

Kinsey parodies of songs that have been performed as part of Broadway musicals include examples from the Great American Songbook by Jerome Kern and George Gershwin; golden-age musicals such as *West Side Story* and *The Sound of Music*; later hits such as *Hair* and *Chicago*; and jukebox or "screen-to-stage" musicals including *Mamma Mia*, *Beautiful: The Carole King Musical*, and *Aladdin*. Since the release of their first CD, *Dragapella!*, in 1997, each of their eleven albums has included at least one Broadway song parody, and Broadway parodies were part of their cabaret show, *Dragapella!*, which opened Off-Broadway on October 17, 2001, as the inaugural offering of Upstairs at Studio 54, a smaller venue above the famous Studio 54.[2]

Two Kinsey Broadway parodies, "Anal Warts: A Sing-Along" and "When You're Good to Dubya," are representative of their parody practice. "Anal Warts: A Sing-Along" is a parody of "Edelweiss" from *The Sound of Music*, released on their album *Boyz to Girlz* (1999). The original song has been covered numerous times, not to mention the countless amateur and professional productions of the musical that are produced each year. Of all these performances, the one by Christopher Plummer and Julie Andrews near the end of the 1965 film has perhaps become the paradigmatic, base song, which is certainly better known than the performance by Theodore Bickel and Mary Martin on the original Broadway cast recording.

The musical arrangement of "Anal Warts" is in keeping with the conventions of tempo (moderately slow), meter ($\frac{3}{4}$), harmony, and melody that listeners have come to expect from watching the film. During much of the recording the music sounds "unmarked," even respectful. This is not, however, one of those Kinsey arrangements that seeks to observe every nuance of the original: overwrought changes in dynamics and tempo (particularly ritardando), an exaggerated fermata, and pretending to cry while singing give the performance the mocking ethos of irony. This ironic musical tone supports an even more pronounced irony in the lyrics, which recast Oscar Hammerstein's sentimental song of nostalgia as a ballad about anal warts: "soft and pink" "blossoms of cauliflower" that "bloom and grow."

The Kinseys intensify the distance between the original song and ironic parody by willfully misreading the original context. The recorded track begins with a monologue by the character Trixie, who has just seen a fictitious movie starring "radical feminist actress . . . Julie Andrews" in which she plays a "Nazi spy who disguised herself as a nun so she could get this hunky Australian [not Austrian] sea captain into bed." As the others begin humming the melody, Trixie says that the captain sang about justice, freedom, and love, and that that there was one song that "must have been an aboriginal song that they have been singing in Salzburg for thousands of years because they all knew it" and because it was "so beautiful" that she wants to sing it for the audience (Kinsey Sicks 1999, track 19).

With this ironic monologue to set the context, Trixie sings the opening melodic phrase to "anal warts" rather than the expected "edelweiss." The others eventually provide accompaniment, and after completing the thirty-two-bar song form once, they beckon the audience to sing it with them the second time. As the audience complies, Schatz, in character as Rachel, shouts over them: "fight the Nazis," "sing for freedom," "stop the *Anschluss*," mocking the parallel moment in the film (Kinsey Sicks 1999, track 19). The performance yields an ironic parody that uses the "knowing smile" of ironic distance to lampoon the sentimentality of the original song.

In "When You're Good to Dubya," the Kinseys' parody of "When You're

Good to Mama," from the musical *Chicago*, the musical arrangement is as close to a reproduction as they could manage within the confines of their ensemble. Technically, the base song here is probably Mary McCarty's 1975 performance on the original Broadway cast recording because it came first, but even if listeners are more familiar with Marcia Lewis's 1996 performance on the Broadway revival cast recording, or Queen Latifah's 2002 performance on the film soundtrack, it will not matter. The performances are quite similar, and listeners will have similar expectations for the song regardless of which recording they know best. The Kinseys' vocal arrangement follows the original to a T. In Hutcheon's terms, the music is "unmarked," in keeping with the ethos of parody.

Like the lyrics of "Anal Warts," the lyrics of "When You're Good to Dubya" are the kind of lyrics Schatz likes to write—they diverge as little as possible from the original in order to change the meaning of a song. For example, the only change Schatz makes to the first stanza of the song is to replace the word "Mama" with the word "Dubya." In keeping with the Kinseys' general parody practice, limiting the number of differences actually brings greater attention to what is different, heightening the effect of the parody.

Under Hutcheon's definition, "When You're Good to Dubya" is properly called satire rather than parody, because unlike in the case of "Anal Warts," the target here is not the original song itself but the eponymous "Dubya," President George W. Bush. The lyrics mock him, accusing him of trading political favors for campaign contributions and starting wars both to deflect from domestic problems and to create economic activity that will benefit the very wealthy. They are scornful of him and seek to correct his behavior. In Hutcheon's model, this song is perhaps best thought of as "parodic satire (a *type* of the *genre* satire) which aims at something outside the text, but which employs parody as a vehicle to achieve its satiric or corrective end" (1985, 62).[3]

## *SEND IN THE CLONES*

Whereas "Anal Warts" and "When You're Good to Dubya" are representative of the Kinseys' typical parody practice of minimizing musical difference to maximize parodic effect, "Send in the Clones," the Kinsey parody of "Send in the Clowns" from *A Little Night Music*, is one of the very few

Kinsey parodies in which the musical arrangement rejects the expectations presented in the source material. As this analysis will suggest, the musical changes, while at first potentially disorienting to the listener, encode additional information and work in tandem with the lyrics to underscore the parody and satire the Kinseys intend.

Few, if any, numbers written expressly for Broadway after the golden age have blurred the line between show tune and popular song as successfully as "Send in the Clowns." Recorded by Glynis Johns in 1973 for the original Broadway cast album, it was immediately covered by Frank Sinatra, and became one of his signature songs. Judy Collins's 1975 recording spent multiple weeks on the Billboard Hot 100 in both 1975 and 1977, and received the Grammy for Song of the Year. The song has also become a jazz standard, recorded by Count Basie, Sarah Vaughan, and others. It has been covered over 900 times (Nachman 2016, 263).

As with most Kinsey Broadway parodies, it would be natural to think of the version on the original cast recording as the base song,[4] and that would probably be the end of the story were it not for the fact that the song has had such tremendous success outside the context of the Broadway show. Under Mosser's definition, Judy Collins's version was so successful that it might be the base song even though it came after Johns's rendition. Rather than having to choose between these performances, we can note that Collins's cover is faithful to Sondheim's original, and that they are both quite similar to another performance Kinsey fans are likely to have heard, Barbra Streisand's rendition on *The Broadway Album* (1985). Taken together, these performances inform a conceptual model of the typical performance of "Send in the Clowns," shown in figure 11.1. But these recordings are not the only basis for the model. The expectations of rhythm, melody, harmony, etc., in the model are also memorialized in the piano-vocal score of the musical and in various published sheet-music versions. Accordingly, performances of the song in coffee shops, cabarets, beauty pageants, singing competitions, elevators, and elsewhere are likely to align with this conceptual model. The more listeners hear the song performed in this way, the more likely they are to adopt the figure 11.1 conceptual model.

Listeners can categorize performances of "Send in the Clowns" as more Type-1-like or more Type-2-like based on their similarity to this model. Sarah Vaughan's recording fulfills many of the expectations of the model, and I would put it clearly in the Type-1 category, but the much

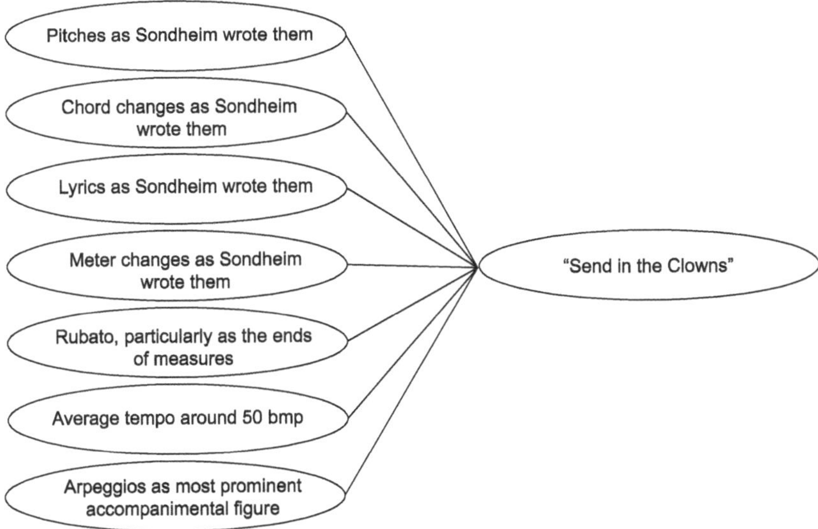


**Figure 11.1.** Conceptual model of "Send in the Clowns."

slower tempo (about 30 bpm) is a noticeable difference. Cleo Lane's version also fulfills many of the model's expectations, but the accompaniment is in simple rather than compound division. Shirley Bassey's version seems a tad quick, eliminates rubato, and turns the $\frac{9}{8}$ measures into $\frac{12}{8}$ measures by extending the second beat. Neither of these versions is as close to a Type-1 version as Vaughan's, but I also don't perceive them as Type-2. Interestingly, although "Send in the Clowns" was a signature song for Frank Sinatra, the orchestration of his 1973 cover is somewhat different from Sondheim's original. His later, live recording with solo piano, which came after Judy Collins's successful cover, hews much closer to a Type-1 expectation of the conceptual model.

There are plenty of Type-2 versions of "Send in the Clowns." Although they mostly preserve Sondheim's melody and lyrics, both Mel Tormé's hard-swinging, big-band version and Grace Jones's disco interpretation retain little of the song's other identifying characteristics. Both versions are faster, in $\frac{4}{4}$, introduce new harmonies, and maintain a consistent tempo throughout. As Zbikowski argues, because of their atypicality, these versions may be in danger of being excluded from the category "Send in the Clowns" by some listeners.

Figure 11.2 provides the lyrics for "Send in the Clones" and some analytical annotations. As the Kinseys begin their performance, they fulfill many of the expectations of the conceptual model in figure 11.1. Though the tempo is a bit brisk (as fast as 68 bpm), the melody and harmony are consistent with the original, the arpeggiated accompaniment is present, and there is a hint of rubato by the lead singer at the end of the $\frac{9}{8}$ measure. The one element of the first verse that clearly does not conform to the model is the lyrics. The lyrics preserve the rhyme scheme of the original, maintain the words "rich" and "on the ground," and treat the opening line as an interrogative, but the textual differences make it quite clear to listeners that this is a parody, not a true performance of the song itself. Nonetheless, listeners—especially listeners familiar with the Kinseys' parody practice—will listen to the first verse and probably match the arrangement to the conceptual model, classifying this as a Type-1 rather than a Type-2 version of the song.

As figure 11.2 shows, in the lead-in to the second verse, the Kinseys sing triplet groupings on nonsense syllables that maintain the speed of the prior groups of three eighth notes, but are altered in dynamics (from piano to forte) and in articulation (from legato to marcato). These changes imbue the triplets with a different character, and as the transcription in example 11.1 shows, by the time the Kinseys sing the lyrics of the second verse, listeners probably perceive that the level of the tactus has changed from ♩. = 68 bpm to ♩ = 136 bpm, and material that took one measure in $\frac{12}{8}$ in the original now takes two measures in $\frac{4}{4}$. The introduction of a new, faster tempo disrupts the confirmation of the Kinseys' typical parody practice by veering away from a Type-1 version of the song toward a Type-2 version.

The Type-2 arrangement changes listener expectations about the genre of this song. This is no longer a ballad. The references in the lyrics to men "dancing to Cher" might create an expectation for the kind of dance-pop heard in Cher songs such as "Believe," which gay men were dancing to in clubs in the late 1990s.[5] "Believe" is in $\frac{4}{4}$, 133 beats per minute, has no perceivable tempo fluctuations, and includes common rhythms and instrumental associations of "four-on-the-floor" dance music. In this style of music, within a measure of $\frac{4}{4}$ listeners are likely to hear bass drum on each beat, hi-hat on each upbeat, and sometimes snare drum or handclaps on beats 2 and 4 (Butler 2006, 82). A conceptual model of the meter, tempo, rhythms, and instrumental associations in Mark Butler's description of "four-on-the-floor" style is shown in figure 11.3.

The new tempo and meter shown in example 11.1 suggest at least

VERSE 1
Don't I look rich dancing to Cher?
Kenneth Cole Shoes on the ground,
Chest shaved and bare.
Send in the clones.

VERSE 2
Give an air kiss.
Have you got ludes?
Let's dance on crystal all night
    till we can't move.
Where are the clones
    with their cellphones?

BRIDGE
Now that I've shopped all the right stores,
Knowing my pecs and my income
    are bigger than yours.
I'll make my gym entrance again with my usual flair.
I'm sure of my wines.
How is my hair?

Type-1 version | Lead-in | Type-2 version (~~Dance Pop?~~ Doo Wop)

♩. = 68    ♩. = 𝅗𝅥    ♩ = 136

$\frac{12}{8}$    $\frac{4}{4}$

VERSE 3
Don't you own land?
Your fault, I fear.
I thought that you earn what I earn.
Pity, my dear.
But where are the clones?
All testosteroned.
Straight acting, not queer.
(Don't act nelly here, dear.)

VERSE 4
Charities pitch.
I go twice a year.
Cause those black tie dinner have cute boys
    and help my career.
There I'll find clones, all coiffed and cologned.
Don't bother – they're here.

Pump-Up Modulation    Type-1 version returns

**Figure 11.2.** Annotated lyrics to "Send in the Clones," used by kind permission of Benjamin Schatz.

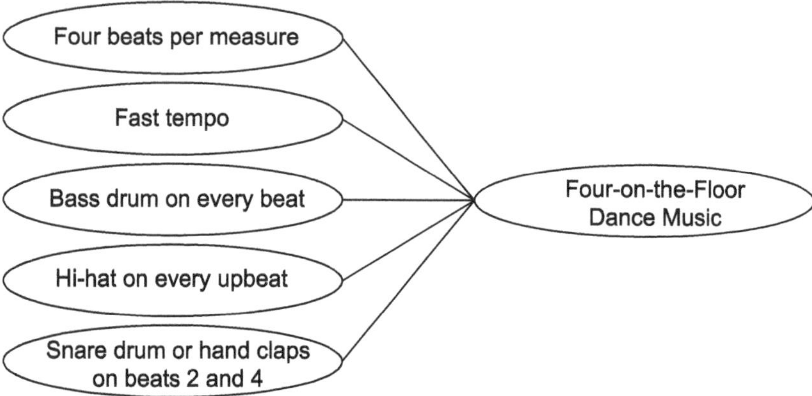


**Figure 11.3.** Conceptual model of four-on-the-floor dance music, after Butler 2006.

the possibility that the Type-2 part of the arrangement will conform to a four-on-the-floor style. As the music continues, however, this conceptual model would not seem to be the best fit for what listeners hear. There is vocal percussion on beats 2 and 4, but since it sounds more like a hi-hat than a snare drum, the rhythmic pattern and timbre do not match. Furthermore, the hi-hat sound is expected to occur on every upbeat, and when it occurs only on beats 2 and 4, it is perceived to be twice as slow as it is "supposed to be." Because of this "dragging" hi-hat, and the "missing" bass drum sound to clearly articulate each beat, the arrangement lacks the drive one expects from dance-pop.

There is a broad conceptual category to which the up-tempo part of the arrangement would belong that might be called "music you can dance to." In other words, this *is* dance music, it's just not the *right kind* of dance music. As listeners ponder the category that fits what they are hearing, they may come to settle on doo-wop. According to Gribin and Schiff, key characteristics of doo-wop include (1) vocal music sung by groups, (2) a vocal range from bass to falsetto, (3) nonsense syllables, (4) a simple beat, and (5) low-key instrumentals (2009, 17). The Kinseys fulfill most if not all of these characteristics in their up-tempo version of "Send in the Clones." Their group-vocal, a capella arrangement features a wide vocal range; the background vocals repeat the syllable "doo" on an eighth-quarter-eighth pattern (see example 11.1); and the instrumentals are so low key, they're nonexistent. All of these factors would finally lead listeners to the more

**Example 11.1.** Rhythmic transcription of "Send in the Clones," opening of verse 2.

specific categorization of doo-wop or perhaps the doo-wop-influenced sound heard in American popular music in the early 1960s. Hearing this version as belonging to doo-wop and related musical genres has important implications for the critique the Kinseys offer in this number.

Unlike in "Anal Warts," the distortion of the expected musical content heard in this Type-2 rendition is not intended to poke fun at Sondheim's most popular song. Rather, the musical arrangement is a vehicle to attack the Kinseys' true target—a group of gay men they call "clones." Thus, this is not merely parody, but parodic satire. As shown in figure 11.2, the lyrics give the listener a clearer picture of who the Kinseys think the clones are. Laden with irony and satire directed at the clones, the lyrics do not flatter. The clones are gay men who are concerned with their physical appearance. They are (or at least aspire to be) upper middle class or upper class, superficial, and have ulterior motives for engaging in philanthropy. They are recreational drug users, and while they are homosexual, they do not want to be viewed as effeminate. Therefore, in certain ways their behavior and performativity reinforce gender stereotypes. The clones clearly see themselves as occupying a position of privilege relative to those who are not as wealthy, not as fit, and not as straight-acting, and they tell them so.

Interpreting the up-tempo music as doo-wop, or at least doo-wop-adjacent, amplifies the lyrics' ironic and satirical tone. The music we actually hear supplants the style of music first suggested by the lyrics—late 1990s dance-pop—with an older, cornier style of music. Since the lyrics are sung from the perspective of the clones, the idea that they might think they are "dancing to Cher," but clearly are not, makes them seem foolish. But the satire goes much deeper than this surface incongruity. Doo-wop and its successors come from a time when gender roles could not be questioned without severe societal consequences. It conjures up images of identically styled singers performing in-sync choreography, with little to no expression of individual identity. By implying a similarity between the gay clones and doo-wop performers, the Kinseys confront the supposition that heteronormative ideals should be replicated in the queer community, what Lisa Duggan (2003) calls "homonormativity." They explicitly call attention to this by accusing the clones of admonishing others for acting "nelly," or girly, and placing "straight-acting" in opposition to "queer." Through their parodic lyrics, the Kinseys echo again and again Duggan's diagnosis that the urge to gain acceptance, by reinscribing the norms of a predominately heterosexual society, is grounded in the neoliberal impulses of the dominant culture ("shopped all the right stores," "don't you own land?," and "black-tie dinners . . . help my career"). In so doing, the Kinseys cleverly question the very idea that there is only one acceptable way to be a gay man in America. In the Kinseys' eyes, the fact that the clones believe their way is the only way, or at least the preferred way, make them, quite literally, out of step.

Certain musical factors align with the satirical interpretation. In the original version in $\frac{12}{8}$, groups of three eighth notes fit neatly into a beat. In the up-tempo version, the triplets are spread over two beats, becoming what Krebs (1999) calls a metrical dissonance. As example 11.1 shows, this dissonance against the prevailing rhythmic texture is all the more pronounced because all the performers interrupt the eighth-note-based rhythmic flow to perform the triplets in unison. Consequently, the groove takes a while to be established, and there is something clumsy about the way the melody fits into its new rhythmic context. Additionally, unlike Tormé's and Jones's up-tempo versions, which remain in $\frac{4}{4}$ throughout, the Kinseys render $\frac{9}{8}$ measures at the original tempo as a measure of $\frac{4}{4}$ and an appended measure of $\frac{2}{4}$ in the up-tempo section. Interpolated $\frac{2}{4}$ measures would not be commonplace in dance music, which often maintains $\frac{4}{4}$ time. Furthermore, the loops and cycles of four-measure groups that can be combined to create larger hypermetric structures in much dance music never materialize (Butler 2006, 193). In deciding to maintain Sondheim's meter changes, the Kinseys are able to remain, in one aspect, faithful to the original song—in keeping with their typical parody practice—and yet, since those meter changes are inconsistent with the overall metric context they have chosen for this parody, they have musically recontextualized this material to make it sound awkward and clumsy, making their satire all the more biting.

The relationship between tonality and form solidifies this parody as a send-up. "Send in the Clowns," as it is performed in concert or in most covers, is in **AABAA** form. (In some performances, as in the original musical, there is an instrumental interlude between the final two verses.) The Kinseys kitsch-up their arrangement by marking the beginning of this last verse with a "pump-up" modulation that raises the key a half step. This rise in pitch comes on the text, "don't act nelly here, dear," evoking feminized behavior or mannerisms that are devalued (or worse) by the clones.

## *CONCLUSION*

"Send in the Clones" is one of four Kinsey Broadway parodies that encourage the gay community to reflect on itself in some introspective way. The other three are "You're Scaring Us" ("Aquarius" from *Hair*), "Buy My Pride" ("By My Side" from *Godspell*), and "Ad Nauseum" ("Maria" from *West Side Story*). "Buy My Pride" and "Ad Nauseum" are similar in that they both focus on how corporations try to get gays to buy their products. "Ad Nauseum" refers specifically to a 1994 television ad from IKEA that was the first mainstream American ad to feature a same-sex male couple.[6] Though unremarkable today, the ad was quite progressive for its time. "Buy My Pride" begins with banter about corporate sponsorships of the Gay Games and Gay Pride events. Like "Send in the Clones," these parodic satires raise consciousness about the trappings of neoliberalism and highlight the tensions between greater acceptance by the mainstream culture and the desire to continue to be "queer" (in the broadest sense of the word). Unlike "Send in the Clones," however, these satires appear to be directed at corporations for their encroachment, not at the gay community or some subset of it. "You're Scaring Us" takes on ageism in the gay community, but not head on. It is written from the perspective of an older gay man unsuccessfully cruising younger men. Rather than taking the gay community to task for its ageism, the satire, which uses the Fifth Dimension's medley of "Aquarius" and "Let the Sunshine In" as the base song, is directed at the older man and what he can do to remedy his situation. The lyrics reminds listeners that "sunshine ages skin" and soon "plastic surgery begins on all your chins" (Kinsey Sicks 2002, track 1).

"Send in the Clones" is the one parody in this group in which the Kinseys' biting satire, often reserved for conservative politicians, is directed squarely at a segment of the gay community itself. Notably, it is one of very few Kinsey parodies that eschews Type-1 classification. In fact, the only other recorded Kinsey parody I could find that unequivocally avoids a Type-1 classification is "Gentle Loving People" from the album *Dragapella!*. The song is a parody of "Singing for Our Lives," which Holly Near wrote in response to the assassination of Harvey Milk in San Francisco in 1978, and which many consider an anthem for the queer community. The Kinseys begin their parody in chorale-style harmony, very much in keeping with the fact that the song has been included as no. 170 in the hymnal of the Unitarian Universalist Church as "We Are a Gentle, Angry People." Much like in "Send in the Clones," however, after the first verse of "Gentle Loving People," the Kinseys' arrangement gives way to an up-tempo version, this time producing something less appropriate for church and more appropriate for a kick line. They use this Type-2 version of "Singing for Our Lives" to describe gay people as "vicious," "catty," "sexually compulsive," "materialistic," "vapid," and "shallow" (Kinsey Sicks 1997, track 2). The Type-2 versions of source material heard in "Gentle Loving People" and "Send in the Clones" suggest that when the Kinseys want to pillory their own audience, they may choose to make considerable changes to the musical material of the original song.

Returning to "Send in the Clowns" specifically, the Kinseys also have the advantage that many people do not seem to understand what Sondheim's original lyrics actually mean. In fact, for her recording Streisand even convinced Sondheim to write new lyrics for an additional B section in an attempt to clarify the song's meaning. As Sondheim has explained, he was referencing an old theater saying, "send in the clowns," which means, when the show isn't going well, do some jokes to try to get the audience engaged. Sondheim said, "As I think of it now, the song could have been called 'Send in the Fools'" (Gussow 2003).

As the last verse of the Kinseys' "Send in the Clones" comes to its final line, the group reverts to a Type-1 version of "Send in the Clowns," complete with slower tempo and arpeggiated outro, somewhat softening the blow. Rather than the line Sondheim originally wrote, "well, maybe next year," the Kinseys, following Streisand, borrow their final line of the original third verse, "Don't bother, they're here," which, according to Sondheim, means "*we* are the fools." With this final line, delivered while looking their own audience square in the face, the Kinseys ask their fans to reflect on their own behavior. They might be apt to say, "But, isn't it *queer*?"

## NOTES

1. I wish to thank the staff at the GLBT Historical Society in San Francisco, where I accessed their Kinsey Sicks collection; the University of South Carolina School of Music for providing financial support for my research trips; and Bruno Alcalde, Nathan Beary Blustein, Clifton Boyd, and the editors for their helpful feedback on earlier drafts of this chapter. The name Kinsey Sicks is a pun on "Kinsey six," a colloquialism for someone who identifies as gay. The term refers to the Kinsey scale, developed by Alfred Kinsey, which postulates that people fall on a continuum between "0," exclusively heterosexual, and "6," exclusively homosexual.

2. The show closed prematurely on December 16, 2001, but not before the Kinseys got to perform alongside the casts of *Aida*, *Chicago*, *Cabaret*, and other Broadway shows as part of that year's "Gypsy of the Year," an annual fundraiser that supports Broadway Cares/Equity Fights AIDS. The show was nominated for a Lucille Lortel Award for Best Musical, and Schatz received a Drama Desk Award nomination for Best Lyrics, alongside the likes of Jason Robert Brown and Jonathan Larson.

3. Noriko Manabe (2022) shows how Kuwata Keisuke cleverly parodies Beatles songs by retaining as much content at the phonemic level of the English-language lyrics as possible while rendering them in Japanese at the syntactic and semantic level. Since the target of these parodies was prime minister Shinzo Abe rather than the Beatles songs themselves, this would also be parodic satire under Hutcheon's definition.

4. In regard to distinctions between original Broadway-cast-album and film-soundtrack performances of a song and how this might determine the base song, in some cases, as with "When You're Good to Mama," the performances are so similar that for many listeners they meld together. When the film is very successful, as in the case of "Edelweiss," it all but erases the original Broadway recording from consideration as the base song. In this particular case, Elizabeth Taylor's performance in the film is, at best, forgettable, and at worst, a subject of ridicule, and it would probably not occur to most listeners that it could be the base song.

5. Although "Send in the Clones" was not released until 2008, very similar lyrics for the song, copyrighted 2000, are included in the Kinsey Sicks collection at the GLBT Historical Society in San Francisco, and so the reference to music from the late 1990s is apt. The suggestion that "cell phones" would be something that marks the clones as distinct would certainly predate 2008, and would have been truer in the late 1990s than at the time the song was recorded.

6. The punny title, "Ad Nauseum," conceals how the Kinseys use "IKEA" in place of "Maria" in their parody.

## WORKS CITED

*Boyz: The Gay Scene Magazine*. 2013 "Life in the Drag Lane." (May 16): 12.

Butler, Mark. 2006. *Unlocking the Groove*. Bloomington: Indiana University Press.

Crouch, Ian. 2014. "Weird Al Endures." *New Yorker* (July 16). https://www.newyorker.com/culture/culture-desk/weird-al-endures (accessed June 26, 2020).

Duggan, Lisa. 2003. *The Twilight of Equality? Neoliberalism, Cultural Politics, and the Attack on Democracy*. Boston: Beacon Press.

Fertig, Jack. 1997. "Drag It Home!" *San Francisco Bay Times* 19 (3) (October 30): 23.

Graff, Gary. 2014. "'Weird Al' Yankovic on Getting Pharrell's Permission: 'He Could Not Have Been Nicer.'" https://www.billboard.com/articles/news/6157636/weird-al-yankovic-interview-pharrell-mandatory-fun (accessed June 26, 2020).

Gribin, Anthony J., and Matthew M. Schiff. 2009. *The Complete Book of Doo-Wop*. Narberth, PA: Collectables.

Gussow, Mel. 2003 "Send in the Sondheim; City Opera Revives 'Night Music,' as Composer Dotes." *New York Times* (March 11).

Hutcheon, Linda. 1985. *A Theory of Parody: The Teachings of Twentieth-Century Art Forms*. New York: Methuen.

Krebs, Harald. 1999. *Fantasy-Pieces: Metrical Dissonance in the Music of Robert Schumann*. New York: Oxford University Press.

Lamble, David. 2007. "At the Top of Kinsey Scale: Kinsey Sicks' *I Wanna Be a Republican* Opens at the Roxie." *Bay Area Reporter* 37 (4) (January 25): 33.

Manabe, Noriko. 2022. "Abe Road: Kuwata Keisuke's Beatles Parody." *SMT-V: The Society for Music Theory Videocast Journal* 8 (1). http://doi.org/10.30535/smtv.8.1

Mosser, Kurt. 2008. "'Cover Songs': Ambiguity, Multivalence, Polysemy." *Popular Musicology Online* 2. http://www.popular-musicology-online.com/issues/02/mosser.html (accessed on June 28, 2020).

Nachman, Gerald. 2016. *Showstoppers!: The Surprising Backstage Stories of Broadway's Most Remarkable Songs*. Chicago: Chicago River Press.

Shapiro, Gregg. 2003. "Laughing Until It Hurts." *Windy City Times* 18 (31) (April 16): 24.

Woods, Wes, II. 2003. "Drag Queen Group Stresses Self-Expression," *The D* (November 1): 28.

Zbikowski, Lawrence M. 2002. *Conceptualizing Music: Cognitive Structure, Theory, and Analysis*. New York: Oxford University Press.

## DISCOGRAPHY

The Kinsey Sicks. 2020. *Quarantunes*. Compact disc.

The Kinsey Sicks. 2018. *GreatesTits*. Digital download. https://kinseysicks.com/greatestits-the-25th-anniversary-collection

The Kinsey Sicks. 2016. *Eight Is Enough: The 9th Album*. Compact disc.

The Kinsey Sicks. 2012. *Electile Dysfunction*. Compact disc.

The Kinsey Sicks. 2010. *Each Hit & I*. Compact disc.

The Kinsey Sicks. 2008. *Sicks! Sicks! Sicks!*. Compact disc.

The Kinsey Sicks. 2005. *Oy Vey in a Manger: Christmas Carols and Other Jewish Music*. Compact disc.

The Kinsey Sicks. 2004. *I Wanna Be a Republican*. Compact disc.

The Kinsey Sicks. 2002. *Sicks in the City*. Compact disc.

The Kinsey Sicks. 1999. *Boyz2Girlz*. Compact disc.

The Kinsey Sicks. 1997. *Dragapella!* Compact disc.

# Contributors

**Nathan Beary Blustein** is a professorial lecturer in the Theatre/Musical Theatre program at American University. His research focuses on the drama of Broadway song form, particularly in the musicals of Stephen Sondheim. He has published in *Studies of Musical Theatre* and the *Journal of Music Theory Pedagogy*. He is a practicing theatre pianist, music director, dance/vocal arranger, and orchestrator.

**Nicole Biamonte** is associate professor of music theory at McGill University. She has published research on the theory and analysis of popular music, nineteenth-century musical historicism, and music theory pedagogy, including her edited collection *Pop-Culture Pedagogy in the Music Classroom*. She is a past editor of the journal *Music Theory Online*.

**Michael Buchler** is professor of music theory at the Florida State University College of Music. He is currently president of the Society for Music Theory. His work appears in *Music Theory Spectrum*, *Perspectives of New Music*, *Journal of Music Theory*, *Music Theory Online*, *Journal of Music Theory Pedagogy*, *Journal of the Society for American Music*, and other journals and edited collections.

**Gregory J. Decker** is associate professor of music theory and assistant dean for graduate studies at the Bowling Green State University College of Musical Arts in Ohio. His publications can be found in *Music Theory Online*, *The Opera Journal*, *Intégral*, *A Cole Porter Companion* (University of Illinois Press

2016), and *Singing in Signs: New Semiotic Explorations of Opera* (Oxford University Press 2020), a volume of essays that he coedited with Matthew Shaftel, which won the Society for Music Theory's Citation of Special Merit Publication Award.

**Jonathan De Souza** is associate professor in the Don Wright Faculty of Music at the University of Western Ontario. His research combines music theory, cognitive science, and philosophy. He is the author of *Music at Hand: Instruments, Bodies, and Cognition* (Oxford University Press 2017) and coeditor, with Benjamin Steege and Jessica Wiskus, of the forthcoming *Oxford Handbook of the Phenomenology of Music*.

**J. Daniel Jenkins** is associate professor of music theory at the University of South Carolina and is a past program committee chair for the Society for Music Theory. His articles appear in *Music Theory Online*, *Intégral*, *Theory and Practice*, and elsewhere. He is editor of *Schoenberg's Program Notes and Musical Analyses* (Oxford University Press 2016), and the forthcoming *Oxford Handbook of Public Music Theory*.

**Robert Komaniecki** is an instructor of music theory and musicology at the University of British Columbia. His research focuses on hip-hop, rap, popular music, and music theory pedagogy; his article "Analyzing Collaborative Flow in Rap Music" appears in *Music Theory Online*.

**Rachel Lumsden** is associate professor of music theory at Florida State University. She is coeditor of *The Norton Guide to Teaching Music Theory* (W. W. Norton 2018). Her peer-reviewed articles have been published in *American Music*, *Black Music Research Journal*, *Feminist Studies*, *Music Theory Online*, and *Studies in American Humor*, among others.

**Drew Nobile** is associate professor of music theory at the University of Oregon, where he specializes in the theory and analysis of popular music. His book *Form as Harmony in Rock Music* (Oxford University Press 2020) received the Emerging Scholar Book Award from the Society for Music Theory.

**Richard Plotkin** is a music theorist (PhD, University of Chicago), musical theater composer, and computer scientist. He has published in *Music Theory Online* and the *Journal of Mathematics and Music*, and served on the theory faculty at SUNY Buffalo for nine years. He is currently a writer in the BMI Lehman Engel Musical Theatre Workshop in New York City and a software architect for United Healthcare.

**Rachel Short** is associate professor of music theory at Shenandoah Conservatory. Her research specialties are choreomusical analysis, rhythm and meter, American musical theater, and theory pedagogy. She is co-authoring a chapter for the forthcoming edited collection *Routledge Companion to Choreomusicology* and has a forthcoming article "Interactions between Music and Dance in Two Musical Theatre Tap Breaks" in *SMT-V*.

# Index

Songs from musicals are indexed under the musical they appear in. Page references in italics refer to illustrative material.